CBS
12497 -4

AF652728

Industrialization and Displacement

About the Author

Dr. Sikta Pati has a brilliant academic career to her credit. She has a masters degree in Economics from Utkal University and secured second position and a PGDM from Xavier Institute of Management, Bhubaneswar where she was one of the toppers. After working with the corporate sector for 17 years, she decided to shift to academics and for the last five years, she is employed with KIIT University. Currently she holds the position of Professor and teaches various papers of Marketing and General Management. Corporate Social Responsibility (CSR) is one of her areas of interest for research and consulting. She can be contacted at siktapati@ksom.ac.in.

Industrialization and Displacement

An Economic Impact

SIKTA PATI

CONCEPT PUBLISHING COMPANY PVT. LTD.
NEW DELHI-110059

© Sikta Pati

All rights reserved. No part of this work may be reproduced, stored, adapted, or transmitted in any form or by any means, electronic, mechanical, photocopying, micro-filming recording or otherwise, or translated in any language, without the prior written permission of the copyright owner and the publisher. The book is sold subject to the condition that it shall not, by way of trade or otherwise, be lent, resold, hired out, or otherwise circulated without the prior publisher's written consent in any form of binding or cover other than that in which it is published.

The views and opinions expressed in this book are author(s) own and the facts reported by him/her have been verified to the extent possible, and the publishers are not in any way liable for the same.

ISBN-13 : 978-81-8069-867-5

First Published 2012

Published and Printed by

Since 1974

Concept Publishing Company Pvt. Ltd.
A/15-16, Commercial Block, Mohan Garden
New Delhi-110059 (India)
T: 25351460, 25351794, *F*: 091-11-25357109
E: publishing@conceptpub.com, W: www.conceptpub.com
Editorial Office: H-13, Bali Nagar, New Delhi-110 015, India.

Cataloging in Publication Data--*Courtesy:* D.K. Agencies (P) Ltd. <docinfo@dkagencies.com>

Pati, Sikta.
Industrialization and displacement : an economic impact / Sikta Pati.
p. cm.
Includes bibliographical references (p.) and index.
ISBN 9788180698675

1. Economic zoning—India—Orissa. 2. Industrialization—India—Orissa. 3. Forced migration—India—Ganjam (District) 4. Rehabilitation—Government policy—India—Ganjam (District) 5. Tata Iron and Steel Company. I. Title.

DDC 338.954133 23

Foreword

Years ago people in Orissa including politicians and economists lamented the absence of industries in the state. They attributed its underdevelopment to the failure of the state to attract investments for developing industries, particularly mineral based industries and for developing infrastructure, like roads, ports and power plants. This would have created conditions favourable for the state's development. This remained a long time concern of the political parties and personalities of the state until, following the macro economic reforms in the nineties and thereafter, the state government introduced and implemented a series of industry related measures to improve the climate of investment and make the state a favourable destination for national and multinational companies. Development of industries assumed priority in the state's approach to growth and diversification of its economy. The state began its most momentous journey towards industrial growth, until thousands and thousands of people raised a hue and cry and launched agitations and protest marches opposing acquisition of agricultural land and homestead land required for setting up of industries and the consequent displacement of families from their ancestral homes.

It was really difficult for the concerned households to reconcile to the loss of their agricultural land which was a source of employment, income, livelihood, and social security for generations. They felt threatened when they were asked, where necessary, to leave their homes and surrender their homestead land along with their paddy fields, betel vines, ponds and orchards for industries which were to be located in those areas. A sense of fear and risk for their future and a feeling of nervousness and helplessness gripped the minds of these people. Once displaced from their own land and villages, they would feel a sense of alienation and the loss of social life. It was agonizing for them to think that industries' development should lead to their homelessness and economic disempowerment. Promise of cash compensation, jobs, housing, education for children and provision of health facilities for these families failed to assuage the fears. Many of these affected households belonged to the disadvantaged sections of the society comprising the SCs, STs and other vulnerable groups. Following the outbursts of anger and discontent in different parts of the state against land acquisition and displacement, many of the social activists and political personalities who earlier used to comment on widespread poverty in a mineral resource rich state, joined the protesters and this helped to intensify the stirs in some places.

Dr. Sikta Pati's study of the problem of development induced displacement and the economic impact of such displacement, particularly in the context of the proposed Tata Steel Plant at Gopalpur in the Ganjam district of Orissa where the state acquired land including homestead land for the location of the steel plant provides an important and interesting and in some ways a very fascinating study of the socio-economic problems that were experienced by the affected households. The project at the time of its announcement by the state was hailed by the people who felt it would have a favourable impact on regional growth and economic development of the local people. The name Tata which in India is respected as a corporate house for its outstanding contributions to society in different fields evoked hopes that there would be enduring improvements in the life of the project affected people and that they would be well looked after.

It is in the fitness of things that Dr. Pati, the author has undertaken the challenging task to assess the impact of the steel project on 200 affected households comprising (i) 45 sample households, that is, 25.7 per cent of the households out of 175 families who lost agricultural land only, (ii) 46 sample households, that is 25.8 per cent of the households out of 178 households who lost homes/ homestead land only, and (iii) 109 sample households, that is 25.7 per cent of the households out of 424 households who lost both agricultural and homestead land. The total sample size constituted, on an average, 25.7 per cent of the total 777 affected families belonging to underdeveloped communities in the project area. The author conducted interviews and interacted with the affected households to assess the impact of the project on their income and employment, health, education of their children, social life, sanitation, living conditions and livelihood following their loss of land and displacement. In view of the nationwide protests against land acquisition and displacement, Dr. Pati's study of the problem of displacement in Orissa serves a bigger purpose of understanding the conflict of interests and the nature of transactions involving the state, the company and the affected people.

Both the governments—the State and the Union—are conscious of the multiple problems faced by the people since long and recognize the need to tackle it by incorporating safeguards for the people and persuading the private companies to accept, adapt and implement the Relief and Rehabilitation Policies framed by the respective States and the Centre. National Rehabilitation and Resettlement Policy, 2007, Orissa Resettlement and Rehabilitation Policy, 2006 and the Tata Steel's Rehabilitation and Resettlement Policies have been critically reviewed by the author to find out their relevance and responsiveness to the complex issues emerging in the context of land acquisition and displacement. She has been rightly critical about the differences in the eligibility criteria used for the payment of compensation, arbitrary fixation of cut-off percentages, filing of affidavits by women divorcees for establishing their identities and subsequent claims for rehabilitation assistance, discriminating attitude on the part of industries including the Tata Steel in extending rehabilitation assistance to certain members of the project-displaced families and lack of a clear cut policy on employment and failure of project authorities to ensure primary education for the children of the project affected families. The author touches a very sensitive issue when she says that following displacement there has been a significant decline in the average income of the households from Rs. 37,692 in the pre-displacement period to Rs. 21,528 (after adjusting as per GSDP deflator) in the post-displacement years. Her survey brings to light that as high as 44 per cent of the people ousted live below the poverty line and have got into indebtedness.

The author has been forthright in her assessment of the diverse issues relating to land acquisition and displacement of households following the decision of the Tata Steel to set up the steel project at

Gopalpur. Nowhere does she make any understatement of the problems. She has raised where necessary legitimate doubts through her discussion about the durability of the different benefits given to the displaced households. She has taken all the pains herself to see how things have been working in the project area and in the newly built villages where the displaced households have been rehabilitated and resettled. All this notwithstanding, she points to the improvement in the living conditions in terms of housing, sanitation, availability of drinking water, use of electricity, and use of fuel for cooking.

The author deserves our appreciation for all her courage for undertaking an in-depth study of a sensitive problem and bringing to light certain painful socio-economic realities that the displaced families have been exposed to. What is important in the light of this study is that when a new project is taken up tomorrow, care should be taken to see that the burden of development is made lighter on the people who are asked to sacrifice the only assets like land and homes they have. The compensation package offered to them should create lasting benefits. It may take some time for them to recover from the shocks of losses but care should be taken to ensure that they become better off than they were.

Prof. Sudhakar Panda
Former Chairman
Orissa State Finance Commission
Professor & Head of Deptt.
of Analytical & Applied Economics
Utkal University, Bhubaneswar

Preface

While employed by TCS and working as a consultant to Tata Steel in 1996-97 at their proposed steel plant at Gopalpur, I had the opportunity to closely observe the process of agitation, displacement and subsequent rehabilitation and the associated trauma of the people. Though the financial compensation were in keeping with the market trends, it was not very instrumental in restoring the livelihood of the people. Rather conspicuous consumption and distortion of professional structure after displacement seemed to be the common pattern. Earstwhile farmers setting up grocery shops and beetle nut shops, constructing houses for giving out on rent and failing to adjust and absorb the new tidings and ultimately going in for non-farm labour to the nearby towns which made them lose their sense of dignity seemed to be the common scenario. The goings on were not only traumatic for the oustees but also for me as an active observer. I call myself active because I was also involved in their rehabilitation process, which made me feel all the more helpless inspite of the enormous steps being taken in implementing various schemes which were lauded by many quarters. We were not dealing with machines but with living beings with thought patterns and preferences and emotions. I asked myself what I would do if I was asked to change my profession and asked to work on the shop floor of a factory and here were people not only uprooted from the land held by their forefathers but also professions inherited from generation to generation. It was as if they knew nothing else and could learn little. The sudden influx of compensation money and the leisure or rather absence of the regular livelihood also created an atmosphere of celebration in many households and marriages long due were suddenly solemnized. Though the people had mud houses earlier, they had number of rooms and necessary privacy. The concrete houses provided at the rehabilitation site were too small to accommodate the people and cattle so compensation money was also spent on constructing additional rooms, cattle sheds, wells etc.

It was all being done for the greater good of the country and the oustees had been promised one job per family in the proposed steel plant. Even at that time there were speculations about the actual setting up of the steel plant. The water sources were in controversy and so also the other infrastructure facilities, like railways, power etc. When all these had not been available, it was perplexing to know why people were displaced in such a hurry.

Fifteen years have passed since the land was acquired and there is still no sight of the steel plant. There are rumours that a SEZ is supposed to be set up by Tata Steel on that land and boundary wall is recently being built but officially nothing is certain as yet. The future of the people hangs in balance.

While working at the site I had realized that this would turn out to be a unique case in India, where people were displaced whereas the proposed steel plant could not be set up. In every project there is the scope to study the pre- and post-situation after the project is set up so that the impact on the people could be assessed. But this was a very controversial project and probably the only one in India where the people were victimized for no fault of their own and the greater good of the people of India, the grounds under which land is acquired in the public domain under various land acquisition acts. Till date, it is not known about whose good has been achieved and how the country has benefited.

I had always wanted to go back to Gopalpur to know what happened to the displaced. Were they really resettled and rehabilitated as is claimed and that too in the absence of the project. Common-sense would reveal that they would be worse off than before. But I wanted to make an empirical study and bring out the facts to light about the severity of the situation and why such mistakes, or should I say experiments should not be repeated at least in India which is struggling with poverty at many levels. While planning for my Ph.D., I got this opportunity to realize my dream and conduct an intensive study of the situation and provide a clear cut comparison of the pre-

and post-situation prevailing over a period of 11 years. One of the issues which I have written about in the 'need for the study' is the necessity of economists to study displacement projects and look at it from the economic angle. Till now study of displacement issues has been the forte of sociologists and anthropologists with Michael Cernea regarded as the one of the top experts in the world. I believe that if the most important factor is income and unless this improves and that too substantially, no other indicators can compensate for the happiness quotient. And the project authorities need to forecast the impact of their actions and also factor in uncertainties before deciding to go ahead. One of the most important indicators; per capita family income showed that people were worse off than before with a substantial percentage belonging to the BPL (below poverty line) and ultra poor category.

I would like to claim that this is the only comprehensive and elaborate work of this kind on the Tata Steel project, Gopalpur based on a wide database. I expect that many corporate houses and scholars will be benefited in terms of assessing feasibility of proposed projects and the severity of the outcome thereof, formulating R & R and CSR strategies and taking the mantle forward and getting further work done.

I would also take this opportunity to appeal to whoever is responsible, be it the Tatas, government, people's leaders, NGOs, academicians to take up the cause of the oustees and ensure that the SEZ comes up and the affected people become equal partners in development so that the deprivation process gets reversed.

Acknowledgements

My efforts are dedicated to the millions of displaced and affected people all over the world who have sacrificed their livelihoods, homes and hearths for the sake of development and the greater good. More than contributing to the area of knowledge, the true worth of my work will be realized only if it can bring about any improvement in the lives of such people.

I am highly grateful to my supervisor late Dr. Sakti P. Padhi, Professor, Nabakrushna Chowdhury Centre for Development Studies for his intellectual inputs and unstinting overall guidance without which this work would have been impossible.

I would also like to express my gratitude to Dr. Kishor C. Samal for sharing his valuable experiences and material on displacement related projects. Acknowledgement is also due to my teacher Dr. Sudhakar Panda, ex-Chairman, State Finance Commission, who stood by me as a pillar of support in undertaking this challenging task. In spite of his busy schedule, he always provided me with his perspectives and guided me in writing articles and papers related to the topic. Dr. L. N. Mishra, Ex-VC, Utkal University has also encouraged me in taking up this work for which I am obliged to him.

I worked with NCDS as my Research Centre where I received tremendous support from all the staff right from the Chairman down to the Class IV employees for which I am grateful. KIIT School of Management (KSOM), where I am currently employed allowed me to take study leave whenever required, without which I would not have been able to devote so much time to my research work. I would like to express my gratitude to KSOM for this.

Any empirical research is not possible without the support of field investigators and respondents. Displaced people live in a volatile environment where it is a challenge to undertake data collection. I acknowledge and thank the efforts of my field staff who worked at the peak of summer and the respondents who cooperated sincerely and selflessly.

Last but not the least, I would like to thank my family members, especially my father who inspired me to take up this subject as he had administered one of the largest displacement projects in Asia and has tremendous empathy for the affected people. Because of him I could adopt a holistic and humanistic approach to the study.

Contents

List of Tables

I

Introduction

This chapter is divided into twelve sections and aims at providing an overview of development and displacement related issues in the context of planned development in India. The methodology and framework of the thesis are also presented here. Section 1 deals with the development strategy followed since Independence, including planned development of the core sector, and its ramifications for the issue of displacement. The next section spells out the contradictory objectives of economic growth and development *vs*. displacement in the planning era and especially their intensification of the same during the liberalization regime. An account is provided of the development dilemma, namely whether development projects should be taken up at all or not, Section 3, Section 4 and Section 5 describe the major protest movements, their causes and the effects of displacement on the marginalized sections of society. The raging debate amongst positivists and negativists as to whether projects for development are beneficial to society and the final rationalization of the views is presented in Sections 6 and 7 which basically concludes that large projects should be implemented but efforts should be made to minimize displacement. Finally, the need for studying the problem of displacement from an economic angle while the issues of resettlement and rehabilitation (R&R) have become the almost exclusive concern of anthropologists and sociologists, is discussed in Section 9. The methodology, limitations of the study and chapter plan are given in Sections 10, 11 and 12 respectively.

Soon after independence, the logic of planned development in India was to create heavy industries to achieve rapid economic growth which could create conditions to improve the living conditions of the common man and for reducing development disparities between people and regions. Thus, soon after Independence, the different Governments in Independent India, both at the centre and states launched many large development projects based on the five-year plans, as the philosophy of development strategy rested on lumpy public investments so that the state would control the commanding heights of the economy. This would then provide the foundation for the private sector's growth.

To this end some of the major areas of intervention have been development of infrastructure by way of power (mostly hydro-electric and thermal power), transport and communication, large scale mining operations and multipurpose river valley projects. Such an induced development inevitably ran the risk of causing social disruption due to massive human relocation while attempting to bring benefits to the people (Ravindran, 1998). The problems of relocation could be simply assumed away or brushed aside at that time.

Thus, at the behest of the nationalist leaders and the country's first Prime Minister, Pandit Jawaharlal Nehru, a large populace was motivated to sacrifice their homes and hearths for the cause of modernization and economic development of India, especially the core sector. In the words of the country's first Prime Minister, such development projects were to be seen as the temples of modern India. Wherever the oustee populations resisted sacrificing their lands, they were silenced by the proponents of modernization and morally pressurized to sacrifice for the economic development of the new nation and for the greater good and in public interest.

Since the days of the Industrial Revolution in the medieval period mankind has never looked back. It has continuously progressed on the path of economic progress and affluence. Increase of wealth of the nations and economic development of human society has become the primary goals of the human race. The Industrial Revolution coupled with the technological revolution of the twentieth century have created the ideas that modern science and technology is endowed with unlimited power to tap the natural resources and bring about rapid socio-economic transformations in terms of progressive increase in Gross National Product (GNP) and material wealth all over the world. Imbued with a materialistic ideology, human society in every part of the earth has tried to achieve its goals of economic growth and development without looking deep into its unintended consequences and negative effects among different strata of human population, other bio-ecological and social systems (Sahu, 2000).

In the present day world, development paradigm is understood as uninterrupted growth of GNP by the application of modern science and technology for the construction of hydro power dams, irrigation and drinking water systems, extension of transportation and highway networks, excavation of mines, exploration of minerals and the like. However, this type of development has no unmixed blessings for mankind when looked at from the point of view of the distribution of benefits and costs.

It tends to create increasing prosperity for a privileged few while causing impoverishment among large sections of the people. While the nation at the macro level enjoys the benefits of 'spread effects' which are limited to a privileged few, the locals of the project area acutely suffer from the negative impact due to displacement. Application of traditional cost-benefit analysis to such issues to justify investment is a relatively recent phenomenon, but has been a powerful tool. Many such cost-benefit analyses while making an estimation and appraisal of the scheme from the point of view of economic loss and gain altogether ignore the social angle. Ignoring the social cost-benefit aspects of the projects often brings untold miseries and hardships for the locals and leads to ecological imbalances and economic un-sustainability in the long run. Social costs of projects have rather conveniently escaped the attention of the planners and policy makers, mostly because measuring them is often not possible through conventional approaches.

1.1 Development Strategy in Independent India

To come back to the Indian context, on the eve of independence the country's economy was almost in a shattered condition, due to long years of colonial rule and subsequent partition. Soviet economy then was at its heights of success and with centralized planning under the socialist regime providing an alternative paradigm to the entire world. India, being a democracy, it was not possible to follow the Soviet model completely. At the same time, without government initiative it would not have been possible to save the economy and bring about economic growth and development. The private sector was almost conspicuous by its absence. The Government of India adopted a middle path and adopted the tenets of a mixed economy with State-centred planning to set up and accelerate the pace of economic development in the country.

The country's First Five Year Plan of the 1950's was focused on restoration and reconstruction, while the Second Five-Year Plan emphasized on development of the core areas and key infrastructure such as shipping, air and rail transport and core industries like iron and steel, heavy engineering, heavy electricals, machinery and machine tools, etc. to provide the fillip and the foundation for a self-sustaining economy under the leadership of public sector. Since then the country has been making continuous efforts to build-up the key infrastructure like power and irrigation in all parts of the country for the development of agriculture and industry. Concomitant to this development strategy, the Government has put a lot of emphasis on construction of multi-purpose river-dam projects on India's major rivers to generate hydro-electricity at a cheaper cost and provide irrigation to agriculture.

It is needless to emphasize that inanimate sources of energy are the life blood of modern industry. Modern large scale systems of canal irrigation were regarded as highly essential system to stabilize and increase agricultural yield and cropping intensity protected from the various monsoon and weather related uncertainties. Thus the construction of many multi-purpose river dam projects in different parts of the country was a necessity for successful adoption of the new 'green revolution' technology which was responsible for a three-fold increase in foodgrain production and achievement of self-sufficiency in foodgrains. In contrast to the status of a food deficient country in the 1950s and 1960s, India has earned the status of a net food exporting country with a high level of buffer of food stock of more than 20 million tonnes to meet any type of food shortage and drought eventuality in any part of the country. Being happy and enamoured with the commissioning of the independent India's first multi-purpose river dam project, Bhakra-Nangal on river Sutlej, Pandit Jawaharlal Nehru, the first Prime Minister of the nation unhesitatingly designated such monuments as the "temples of modern India". He hoped that building of many large multi-purpose river dam projects in different parts of the country would not only enable the country to accelerate the pace of agricultural growth by controlling nature's fury such as recurring floods and droughts, but would also lay the foundation of a strong energy base in the form of hydro-electricity at a cheaper cost accessible to the common people (Sahu, 1998).

However, over time it is being realized that such massive projects are never an unmixed blessing to mankind. Commissioning of large dams results in massive involuntary displacement of population, destruction and loss of prime forests and agricultural lands. Ecological imbalances and degradation of the natural environment are a by-product of such development. In many cases the official cost benefit analysis of the project made under the traditional method does not truly reflect the actual social losses and gains. Moreover, the actual life span of such dams gets reduced at a faster rate due to increasing siltation, reducing their storage capacity. While such projects add to nation's prosperity at the aggregate level, the nature of socio-economic gains emanating from them are shared in such a manner that it favours a privileged few at the cost of pauperization and deprivation of the underprivileged sections. Thus, different strata of population and especially rural households get affected and impoverished by such development in different ways and to different degrees.

1.2 Development and Displacement

Development related displacement is a common phenomenon in developing countries. In a country like ours where poverty is rampant and unemployment is widespread, establishment of large scale developmental projects in infrastructure sectors, viz. irrigation, hydel and thermal power and industries, mining and ports etc. has been one of the thrust areas in the planning process. In the post-liberalized economy the number of such projects is going to grow. Construction of such large projects entails large scale land acquisition and result in forced displacement. Importantly most of such projects come up in backward areas inhabited mostly by tribals (Jena, 1998).

One type of profound social disruption that occurs is the forced/ involuntary displacement of populations. The most visible negative externalities of development are the acquisition of land and other immovable properties and displacement of people by uprooting them from their original places of habitats. While the activists are against the principle of "Rob Peter to pay Paul", those in-charge of implementing such projects defend that "sometimes few have to make sacrifices in the interest of the larger populations" and the debate continues. However, there is little disagreement about the fact that displacement is a sacrifice the displaced have to undergo (Ravindran, 1998).

The present pattern of development based on the measurement of GNP oriented growth does not reflect the level of disparities generated in the economy and it does not reveal the type of injustice that is done to a section of population in the name of development. The oustees who belong to weaker sections, with no ability for self-articulation continue to remain powerless and they get evicted without any participation or share in the benefits of the development projects that displace them. The rehabilitation measures adopted by the Government have so far remained only nominal and various studies have pointed out that fewer than 25 per cent of those displaced during the last three decades between 1950s and 1970s have been rehabilitated properly (Hansda, 1983:23). Between 1950s and 1980s the number of people in India, those who have been displaced and not rehabilitated properly is over 11.5 million or roughly 1.45 per cent of the country's population. Unlike the developed countries of the West, the styles of living and settlement patterns of the people in a pluralistic and multi-ethnic country like India are quite different and heterogeneous in nature with a unique ecological niche. Even the remote hills and forests are widely inhabited and these are a source of subsistence for the tribal and poor people.

It may be mentioned here that even before independence, the country has witnessed many types and large numbers of involuntary human displacement initiated as a part of the modernization process of economy and society under the British colonial rule. However, such involuntary displacements of human population during the colonial rule remained rather limited because the colonial masters were not interested in value addition inside the country. They were more interested in the exports of precious raw materials and intermediate goods to the European countries via the primitive port cities of Bombay, Calcutta and Madras for industrialization of the colonial metropoles. So, they did not encourage development of road and transport infrastructure except in the hinterland and periphery of a few important urban centres. The need for a higher level of consumption of inanimate source of energy to run the wheels of industry or to increase agricultural productivity, was not felt. The colonial government was mainly interested in the exploitation of precious and scarce mineral resources, proliferation of plantations and cash crops such as tea, coffee, jute, cotton opium etc. As a result, the development induced displacement on account of laying of national and state highways, railway lines, exploitation of forests and mines, construction of water reservoirs and dams for irrigation and electricity generation and the like, took place to a very limited extent (Sahu, 1998).

Though millions of people have been displaced by various planned developmental projects since independence, the state has not taken the issue seriously and till date it has not promulgated a National Policy on Resettlement and Rehabilitation for those who have been displaced in the name of nation's prosperity. In the absence of a National Policy, the whole process of dealing with the issues of displacement and rehabilitation remains *ad hoc* and piecemeal. It is only recently that a Draft National Policy has been prepared. Most states have come up with their own policies and acts based on the land acquisition acts. Adding to this lack of uniformity and consistency, most projects causing displacement have drawn up separate policies based on the state policy and project specific needs. Between projects there is no uniformity on the compensations paid as this is mostly based on the bargaining power of the people and local leaders. It can be imagined how the marginalized and weaker sections with limited ability for self-articulation can bargain with the representatives and get their due. The World Bank and other UN agencies like UNDP are playing an active role to ensure that the interests of the stakeholders are properly represented and people get their due by facilitating creation and implementation of policies and acts matching global standards.

Various case studies conducted by scholars show that as many as 75 per cent of the displaced people have not been rehabilitated suitably and their income sources and livelihoods have not been restored properly (Fernandes, 1991, Fernandes *et al.*, 1989). The displaced people who generally belong to the most underprivileged and disadvantaged communities of Indian society, in the absence of proper resettlement and rehabilitation pushed themselves into impoverishment, marginalization and more backwardness.

This is nothing but brutal violation of both Fundamental Rights (the rights to settle and reside anywhere in the county, Article 19(1)(e) and right to life and livelihood Article 21 and Human Rights (Jai Sen, 1995:241). This also implies *de facto* lack of social justice and inequality in involuntary resettlement process. In an avowedly welfare state like ours, it is an irony that the benefits of development have not been shared by all sections of society. In the developmental process, it is the displaced people who share only pains of development while a minority enjoy the gains. It is, in fact, profoundly contrary to the very goals of development.

1.2.1 The Planning Era

Over the years this process of displacement has acquired a massive scale with the commencement of the planned development process since early 1950s. The Second Five Year Plan emphasized on development of large and heavy industries to accelerate the process of economic development. The plan strategy was mainly based on Harrod-Dommar growth model, Lewis's two sector model consisting of (i) the 'traditional' rural subsistence sector and (ii) a highly productive modern urban industrial sector into which labour from the subsistence sector is gradually transferred. This necessitated the development of key infrastructure projects such as big dams for water electricity, large scale exploitation of forests and mines, setting up of large many basic and capital goods industries in mineral rich tribal and hilly areas. When the setting up of so many large key industries and infrastructure projects in different parts of the country became the order and ideology of the day to accelerate economic development, the unintended consequences of such efforts were reflected in the form of massive displacements of human population from their homes and hearths, deforestation and ecological degradation (Sahu, 1998). The unique nature of life, living and their underlying philosophy in the case of 'little traditions' was looked upon through a narrowly defined notion of rationality, and as 'the other'.

1.2.2 Liberalization Era

The liberalization and privatization era of the early nineties witnessed the growth of industries and infrastructure at the same time creating large scale displacements of population and consequent impoverishment. With the opening up of the core areas to the private sector, proliferation of mega projects took place especially in the area of steel and allied sectors, transportation, power generation, telecommunication etc. Allowing Foreign Direct Investment (FDI) and the stake of foreign companies to be increased opened up the economy thus facilitating more projects and massive displacements. While the new projects generated income and employment, at the same time they caused large groups of people to lose their homes and hearths, especially the marginalized sections with little hope for rehabilitation. Power sector, steel and mines, SEZs are some of the areas which were mostly responsible. It is not that attempts are not being made to rehabilitate the people and provide them with employment or their other means of livelihood. It has not been possible because of two main reasons. The first, given the scarcity of cultivable land, can provide the basis for alternative rehabilitation. The other reason is the lack of skills of the oustees which prevents them from getting jobs with the projects which displace them. Thus the basic source of livelihood, i.e. land has not been replaced and neither are the affected and displaced people eligible for being absorbed in the units. Low skill and education levels also bar the oustees from taking up other occupations. In fact there is a process of destruction of traditional skills which become redundant in a new setting. It is other people and sometimes people from other states who stand to gain by getting employment and income as has been alleged in the case of Rourkela Steel plant where the beneficiaries belonged mostly to the adjoining state of West Bengal and erstwhile Bihar.

In many projects like in NALCO, Angul, the oustee population has been given jobs by the company on the basis of one job per family and also they have been employed by the contractors during the construction phase. Due to their lack of education and technical skills they have been absorbed into the lowest grades of employment while the other categories of employment have absorbed the non-oustee population and also professionals from other states.

Along with economic reforms since 1991, the focus changed to upgradation of technology or importing technology from overseas so as to increase production efficiency and make the products acceptable by international standards and markets. This entailed setting up of highly capital intensive units which have place for very skilled professionals only. It became increasingly difficult for the oustees with certain unique skills to be absorbed into such projects. Steel companies of the size of Rourkela or Bhilai set up in the Nehruvian era could create employment for around 50,000 people while now a steel plant of the same capacity would employ one-tenth of the same. It would mean that improvement in efficiency and lower costs would increase the capacity to compete in the global markets, but the question arises, how this helps the affected population who sacrificed their source of livelihoods and fell into the trap of poverty and mental trauma.

The issue is not only about creating disparities between population groups but also between states at various levels of development. It is not only from employment that other states have been benefiting. There is a contention (Samal, 2009) that with liberalization and privatization the rich states are becoming richer and the poor becoming poorer. Since the value addition takes place outside the mineral rich states like Orissa, with the advent of new industries and infrastructure such states do not benefit in terms of growth in overall employment and income.

For example, the focus of the steel sector in economically poor states like Orissa, Bihar, Jharkhand and Chhattisgarh which are the richest in minerals, are to take possession of the mines as early as possible and take the minerals to other states and set up the plants there. The excuse being given is that such states do not have adequate infrastructure. It is only natural that the employment and income will be generated in other states and the people there will stand to benefit. Tata Steel, Gopalpur is an example where land was acquired in 1996-97 but no unit was set up. The planned expansion by TISCO in Orissa was finally carried out in Jamshedpur and only a handful of the oustee population from Orissa have been given employment.

The governments of the poor states have to be vigilant and ensure that the people and the states benefit from new mega projects and not become victims of development leading to further disparity. The maximum possible value addition must take place inside the state. For that the infrastructure and the government machinery have to be strengthened. When land is acquired in the public domain and in the public interest, it becomes the responsibility of the government to see that such greater good is actually achieved.

1.3 Development Dilemma

Researchers by independent groups have established that rehabilitation and resettlement of project affected population is mostly neglected throughout the world. Everywhere the affected population is under-estimated, sometimes due to lack of database but more often deliberately, due to political and bureaucratic reasons. The governments do not show adequate concern for the oustees which can be evident from lack of a well articulated policy, lackadaisical planning and the irresponsible manner in which R&R activities are implemented. Experience has proved that R&R is always second in priority following the construction of the project (Jena, 1998).

Research has shown that compulsory dislocation causes special cultural, economic and technical problems that are not only largely different from, but usually more severe than, those entailed by voluntary migration and relocation. A feeling of alienation, helplessness and powerlessness is instilled in those uprooted, social cohesion is weakened, and increased psychological and sociological stress diminish the initiative and capacity for collective action of those affected (Ravindran, 1998).

Since investments in infrastructure and development projects are supposedly in public interest, private lands are acquired under the provisions of Land Acquisition Act, 1894 as amended in 1984 which defines what is 'Public Purpose'. Unfortunately, the definition continues to suffer from a class bias introduced originally by the colonial masters. The act proceeds for cash compensation only and further in the case of only those with right, title and interest in the land under acquisition are entitled to it. Since Indian society is highly stratified and one with skewed land ownership patterns (adoption of Land Reforms Acts notwithstanding), a significant section of the displaced society gets left out automatically. The most visible victim of this Act is the tribal society wherein historically land has been held as a community asset and used customary rights decided by the local society, and the idea of individual ownership and title to land are as alien to such communities as will be seen later in this chapter, as a class it is the tribal society that has faced maximum displacement including multiple displacements. This is the irony (Dalwai, 1998).

1.4 Development Induced Displacement-Protest Movements

Singur is one of the latest examples of peoples' resistance to land acquisition and displacement. Involuntary displacement of human population caused by to building of large dams and other mega projects have become a burning issue of the day and the country has witnessed several protest movements of displaced people with moral support from environmentalists and social activists raising their voice against many development projects that lead to massive displacement of human population, submergence of forests and fertile agricultural lands. The ongoing movements of people against the Narmada Valley Project in Madhya Pradesh, Tehri Dam Projects in Uttar Pradesh, BALCO (Bharat Aluminium Company), Mining Projects and Baliapal Rocket Launching Projects in Orissa and Koel-Kero Hydro-electric Project in Bihar are quite well-known. Even in the past the oustees of Hirakud Dam, Rourkela Steel Plant, NALCO (National Aluminium Company), HAL (Hindustan Aeronautics Limited), Rengali Dam Project, Upper Indravati Project and the displaced people in various mines and industrial areas of Orissa had fought against the location of these projects in their respective regions. The main reasons for such protests were apprehension of (i) loss of livelihood, (ii) destruction of social fabric and loss of existing community life, (iii) inadequate compensation measures, (iv) occupational shift and displacement, and (v) improper rehabilitation measures by the Government and the like (Sahu, 2000).

1.5 Displacement Effects

Involuntary displacement means displacement of indigenous people from their land to a place unknown to them. Their land and houses are acquired and they are relocated to an alien socio-cultural environment. Operational directive 4.30 of the World Bank summarizes, "all involuntary displacement destroys a previous way of life. Production system is dismantled; Community structure and social network are weakened; traditional authority and the individual social contacts and economic interdependence among families and kinship groups are ruptured." Everyone is affected, though to a varying degree and no one is in a position to help anyone. The displaced community is subjected to change from a native self-sustaining system, mostly barter economy to a market oriented monetized economy. The surplus economic regime suddenly faces a deficit family economy. Besides, the affected population is put to severe psychological stress. Michael Cernea describes how such a process of displacement causes 'socio-economic impoverisation' of Project affected population largely due to (i) landlessness, (ii) joblessness, (iii) homelessness, (iv) marginalization, (v) food insecurity, (vi) increased morbidity and mortality, (vii) social disruption, and (viii) loss of access to common property resources (Jena, 1998).

Displacement particularly, 'development induced displacement' imposes significant eco-psycho-socio-cultural and environmental stress on DPs (Displaced Persons). Their normal flow of life is dismantled. Valuable assets and productive means are lost. Deep rooted community link and cultural bond are disintegrated. The emotional inclination to the land of origin is thoroughly ruptured. Displacement becomes a problem because of the dispossession that results from it.' Besides DPs, the PAPs (Projects Affected Persons) face similar problems being deprived of their livelihood due to taking over of their income bowl and Common Property Resources (CPR) though they are not physically displaced (Jena, 1998).

A large number of studies relating to displacement aspect of development projects in India and other foreign countries, focus on human problems associated with involuntary displacement such as the complex social and cultural problems inherent in the resettlement process, poorly managed resettlement resulting in increased poverty, the labyrinth of broken communities, broken families, loss of social ties, destruction of life supporting system, ecological disorder and the like.

1.6 Development-Displacement Debate

In this era of liberalization and privatization leading to imperialistic globalization, the scale of involuntary displacement due to industrial and infrastructural projects has increased, and, as a consequence, has caused serious concern in the developing countries, as the victims often are found to be depressed and marginalized sections of society. People in the developing countries are involuntarily evicted and displaced from their native places in large numbers in order to make way for the location of development projects in their traditional homeland. They get deprived of their subsistence and self-sustenance form of livelihood. The displaced persons are pushed into an open-market situation as they compete for their survival in a hostile new environment. A majority of them, as a consequence, are losers. The situation is further worsened by induced urbanization of the fringe areas of growing cities (Sharma, 2003). The role of international funding organizations including the World Bank, has come under severe criticism, for facilitating such anti-people development. In response, the World Bank puts pressure on the concerned government for comprehensive R & R policy (*Ibid.*).

One section, denies in principle, the acceptability of any involuntary resettlement and it questions such development and legitimacy of projects which leads to massive displacement of human population and submergence or loss of forests and agricultural lands. At the other end of the spectrum, the alternative viewpoint is not totally averse to the commissioning of large development projects causing massive involuntary displacement, but it criticizes the quality of specific resettlement operations (Cernea, 1994).

1.6.1 The Negativists

There are two arguments advanced in this debate (World Bank, 1994). First, development project involving involuntary displacement and resettlement is rejected outright. This view argues that the development project which causes massive involuntary displacement, often fails to restore the earlier socio-economic status of the oustees population notwithstanding several policy measures for proper rehabilitation. Besides, such projects affect the regional ecosystem adversely due to conversion of forest and agricultural lands for industrial and unsustainable use. Very often, the social costs of such projects are often underestimated or are simply not quantifiable and the benefits are overestimated (Samal, 2008), because of the market-based valuation system adopted.

The negativists in principle are opposed to all projects which cause displacement. Knowing fully well that such projects are necessary for the growth and development of the economy, they do not support as they feel that it leads to a skewed pattern of development which is in favour of a few people. All the issues of public domain and public interest do not hold good in their eyes because they analyze in terms of numbers and the standard of living of the people affected and have come to the conclusion that a huge section of already marginalized population suffers at the cost of a few beneficiaries of the project.

1.6.2 The Positivists

The second view criticizes the quality of specific resettlement operation, and suggests improvement on it, but is not against development project involving involuntary displacement. Some scholars (e.g., Chakravarty, 1987) state that the opposition to development projects on the ground of massive involuntary displacement and ecological disorder is the creation of feudal and orthodox elements of society who are afraid of rapid socio-economic transformation and uplift of the downtrodden. According to this view, these feudal and parasitic groups create many types of coward and baseless phobia among the poor in the name of involuntary displacement, loss of livelihood, socio-cultural ties, and that they incite the poor to oppose such development projects in every possible manner. As building of multi-purpose dams and large irrigation projects challenge the supremacy of existing feudal agrarian structure by ensuring regular wage paid employment for the rural landless and increase in earning of small and marginal farmers, many such projects have witnessed anti-dam movements under the leadership of big landlords, religious institutions and other feudal elements (Samal, 2009).

The second view argues that the single most damaging factor to the quality and outcomes of resettlement is the absence of policy and legal framework in many countries that define the rights and entitlements of people affected by development-related, state-imposed displacements. They mainly emphasize on the issue of protection of interests of the affected people by devising suitable policy measures (Samal, 2008), and putting in place an effective agency for acting in the larger interest of affected people.

1.7 Rationalization of Present Development Strategy

The economic development strategy of many developing as well as the developed countries in the contemporary world is mainly based on setting up of large key sector industries and infrastructure projects. More so, such projects are highly essential to feed the teeming millions and to maintain the present standard of living of the various categories of population in future. Under these circumstances, unless there is a serious and immediate threat to survival, many types of proposed development projects or the new ones cannot be stopped or discouraged on the ground of either ecological disorder or massive displacement and dislocation of the human population. If the development strategy in the case of such big infrastructure projects aims at minimization of the cost of displacement and dislocation of human population and preservation of the ecological balance, then there is little possibility of conflict between national interests and interests of the projects affected people (Sahu, 1998). But this remains a possibility, rather than a practicality.

1.8 Need for the Study

Till recently resettlement and rehabilitation has been a forte of the anthropologists and sociologists and most studies have focused on the socio-cultural aspects of displacement. The World Bank and other international development agencies have also been emphasizing on the same. This aspect is definitely necessary but perhaps the most important issue is the economic aspect because of which huge protest movements are taking place. When the affected people's standard of living takes a beating because of displacement, no degree of reconstruction of socio-cultural factors can make up for the economic impoverishment. It is increasingly being realized that the economic feasibility of such massive displacements including sustainable resettlement should be assessed.

While it is very difficult to estimate the costs and benefits of such displacements, it is imperative to study the situation before and in the aftermath of resettlement projects to find out whether the standard of living and other economic conditions of the oustees and affected people has changed and if so in what direction.

Protest movements and stalling of projects is not the only basis for studying this issue. Over the last two decades the number of projects involving displacement has increased by leaps and bounds. New concepts like SEZs are also being implemented. In the light of this if it cannot be justified that displacements would either restore or improve the socio-economic condition of the oustees and affected population, it would become difficult to justify and move the main project forward.

Even after 50 years of independence in India, we are struggling for execution of development projects. The struggle is for implementation of quality R & R (Resettlement and Rehabilitation) activities for the people displaced due to execution of these projects with the overall objective of improving the socio-economic conditions of the oustees so that they become equal partners in development process as the beneficiaries of the main project. That continues to remain a challenge.

1.9 Objectives of the Study

Keeping the aforementioned scenario in view, an empirical study has been taken up with the specific objectives as follows:

I. Critical review of selected major issues and evidences relating to resettlement and rehabilitation;
II. Examine the magnitude of loss of homes and homestead land;
III. Examine the extent of loss of agricultural land holdings;
IV. Examine the extent of change in and nature of non-land asset holdings;
V. Examine the loss of other income earning activities like business, trade and commerce;
VI. Examine the extent of change in current income;
VII. Examine the loss of social services; and
VIII. Examine the extent of deprivation of socio-cultural transactions among the affected households.

1.10 Methodology

The methodology of the study is rooted in a comparison of selected values of indicators before and after displacement through a process of reconstruction. Thus the database is essentially in the nature of panel data where the same set of households are tracked over a period of time, basically at two time points separated by eleven years. Reconstruction has been done through primary survey and cross-checking with secondary data. Because panel data are used, inferences drawn from them have not been subjected to statistical tests of significance, and only direction of change, has been looked at. This is akin to mobility studies where panel data are typically used.

1.10.1 Sources of Data

This study is based on both primary data and secondary published data available with the Government of Orissa, TATA Steel and District Administration. Relevant research publications and data published therein are also made use of.

1.10.2 Tools and Techniques

For this study, the researcher has used the following tools and techniques:

I. Village/Colony Schedule
II. Interview Schedule
III. Case Study
IV. Focus Group Discussion
V. Participatory Rural Appraisal.

1.10.3 Sample Design

Stratified proportionate random sampling method has been adopted for the sample design.

At the onset of the project, a total of 2083 families (Tata Steel, 2006) were proposed to be displaced. Due to people's resistance there was a difference between the actual and proposed numbers and villages to be displaced. The actual numbers were obtained from field level data and corroborated by information from Tata Steel and district administration. It was also found that 4 villages, which were affected and lost agricultural land only, still continue to cultivate the lands stealthily after receiving compensation. The villages that have been purposively excluded from the study universe on this ground are Chamakhandi, Basanaputti, Jagannathpur and Laxmipur.

Table 1.1: Sample Selection by Three Strata of Households

Sl. No.	*Strata*	*Total Households (Universe)*	*Sample Households (Sample)*	*Sample as %tage of Universe*
1.	Affected Households (Lost only Agri Land)	175	45	25.7
2.	Displaced Households (Lost only Homes/ Homestead Land)	178	46	25.8
3.	Displaced Households (Lost Agri and Homestead Land)	424	109	25.7
	Total	**777**	**200**	**25.7**

The universe and sample are given in Table 1.1. As against 2083 families, it was found that 777 families were actually affected/ displaced. They belonged to 3 strata according to their loss of homes and agricultural land or both, as given in Table 1.1. Total sample size was fixed at 200 families. This was drawn from the three strata on a proportionate basis and works out to a high sampling fraction of 25 per cent. In order to generate a representative sample, households across villages were chosen on a proportionate basis and within villages on a random basis.

The villages which were affected and covered by the survey are Madua, Sitlapalli, Bada Kusasthali, Sana Kusasthali, and Narendrapur. Displaced villages whose people are currently residing in Tata Colony also known as Rehabilitation Colony and included in the survey are Badapur, Patrapur and Sindhigaon.

1.11 Limitations of the Study

Before going on to elucidate the limitations of the study it would be pertinent to spell out some of the rather unique features and potential contributions of the same.

The entire thesis is a contribution as no comprehensive research work has been carried out on the Tata Steel, Gopalpur's displacement issue till date. The main project did not take off but the process of resettlement and rehabilitation was completed unlike in the case of BALCO, Baliapal and Chilika Aquatics where even R&R was not complete. Previous studies have remained in the domain of Anthropology and Sociology with few studies attempting to assess the economic impact which is most crucial. Effort has been made to quantify certain parameters like income and asset holding, indicating economic changes and deprivation over a period of time using panel data.

The study however has certain limitations. Methodology of the study is rooted in comparison of selected values of indicators before and after displacement through a process of reconstruction. Primary data has been cross-checked with secondary data. Therefore only those indicators have been taken into account where the recall lapse was minimal. The thesis confines itself to making comparisons between two time points only for certain indicators and leaves out certain indicators for which either data were not available for the earlier time point or where there could be serious recall lapse. Statistical testing has not been done because the study essentially deals with changes using panel data over a period of time and therefore does not go into statistical analysis of significance of such changes, as earlier mentioned.

1.12 Chapter Plan

The Chapter Plan is as follows. Following the present Chapter I, Chapter II provides a review of issues and evidences pertaining to what transpires in the aftermath of displacement—the processes of resettlement and rehabilitation which in a way constitute the crux of the problem. Chapter III gives a detailed description of the socio-economic profile of the district, the affected areas and the households.

Implementation of Resettlement and Rehabilitation (R&R) programmes by Tata Steel is dealt with in the next chapter, i.e. Chapter IV. In the succeeding Chapter V, the R&R policies of Tata Steel are evaluated against those of the Government of Orissa. Chapter VI makes an assessment of the economic impact of displacement for the Tata Steel project, on the affected population and provides a before-after scenario separated by a period of eleven years. The assessment is based on an intensive analysis of primary data. In addition, a dominant model of 'impoverishment risk' caused by displacement has been used in order to provide deeper insights into and further elucidation of the empirical findings. Finally, the summary and conclusions of the study based on both secondary and primary data comprise in Chapter VII.

II

Resettlement and Rehabilitation: Issues and Evidences

This chapter addresses the issues and evidences at the local and global level through review of literature. Adoption of the capital intensive Western model of development in India after independence and its implications for displacement have been discussed in Section 1 along with global estimates. Section 2 outlines the magnitudes of displacement in India which have been caused by various development projects. A brief history of types of projects in Orissa which have caused displacement and their detailed impact has been examined in Section 3. They range from thermal power, industrial, mining and irrigation and also include other projects like wildlife sanctuaries and urban projects. Section 4 describes Michael Cernea's risk model and makes an attempt to identify the symptoms of displacement which lead to ultimate impoverishment and marginalization of the weaker sections. How this marginalization is further intensified through repeated displacement of the same group over time in cases like the Rihand dam and Hirakud dam is termed as 'multiple displacement' and discussed in Section 5. The compensation issue and how it fails to ensure restoration of livelihood is dealt with in Section 6.

Resettlement and rehabilitation are two distinct processes. Resettlement is a one time event of physical relocation. Only the Displaced Persons (DPs) go through it after displacement. Rehabilitation is a long term process that involves rebuilding people's physical and economic livelihood, their assets, their cultural and social links and psychological acceptance of the changed situation.

The paradox that afflicts numerous development projects aimed at alleviating poverty is that during implementation, many such projects are causing, instead of reducing, impoverishment by forcibly displacing large number of people. Vast cohorts of people are displaced by administrative fiat and not viably re-established. Both critics and supporters of development projects, and often government projects as well, agree on this key point; that imposed displacement and resettlement produce significant and stubborn poverty. It is also increasingly recognized that the risks of impoverishment are embedded in the nature of displacement and must be counteracted and reversed. The first solution is to give up displacement but then that would mean giving up projects in energy generation, irrigation, urbanization, drinking water supply, industry building, employment creation, transportation and other services (Cernea, 2008).

The emergence of Third World as a force in the second half of the twentieth century has thrown open many questions and challenges. The foremost among them is the path of development in the Third World countries. The task of improving the conditions of the impoverished masses living in the underdeveloped Third World countries has been the biggest question before the statesmen and policy makers. To improve the conditions of the people and for rapid economic growth, planners in India like other Third World countries perceived development in terms of economic growth measured by the growth of GNP or increase of per capita income. To achieve this target growth they emphasized on 'big push model' and focused on heavy industrialization, modernization and urbanization. Though some progress was achieved in agricultural, economic and industrial front, development on the other side has pushed indigenous people and weaker sections of society into poverty and backwardness.

The level of economic development and distribution of population of any region depends on the relationship between man and the environment around him, different elements of which are used for different requirements. Man's knowledge of various characteristics of the ecology helped him to search food and other useful products in different habitats and seasons leading to the exploitation of the natural resources. The rapid growth of population in recent times has led to the overexploitation of natural resources. In the process it was forgotten that there has to be an equilibrium between the depletion of natural resources and their replenishment; between the transformation of natural habitat and the presentation of those elements in it which are needed for man's well-being. This has led to a conflicting situation between man's interest and preservation of nature. This conflict of interest comes into sharp focus when it is found that overexploitation of natural resources has wrought irreparable damages to the environment.

Thus, to bring economic prosperity, to overcome the handicap of its colonial past and to catch up with the west, a Eurocentric model of development was adopted by planners. Development was exclusively defined in terms of growth of GNP, increase in real national income. The objectives and processes were viewed in economic terms and great reliance was placed on economic factors and centralized decision-making to achieve the result. So far as the problems of poverty, unemployment and income distributions were concerned, these were given secondary importance. It was believed that rapid economic growth could take place and the cumulative gains from the growth of GNP would automatically 'trickle down' to the poor in the form of increased employment and income opportunities.

In a developing country like India where an overwhelming majority of the population lives in rural areas and is oppressed by chronic poverty, widespread unemployment, subsistence production, and poor basic facilities, the execution of large development projects plays a vital role. The process of socio-economic development initiated under the successive Five Year Plans had given an opportunity for implementing various development projects related to irrigation, power generation, mining, defence, communications as well as industrial production such as steel, aluminium, cement, fertilizers, heavy engineering etc.

2.1 Displacement and the Pattern of Development

The first point that emerges out of this discussion as well as the main debate that is taking place in the country is that displacement is an offshoot of the present pattern of development, when after a century of colonial occupation of Third World Countries attained political independence, their Governments assumed responsibility for economic progress. In this aspiration for a better tomorrow, most of them took for granted that the Western model was the only one available to them. Like most other newly independent countries, India too took for granted that the growth of the GNP was the real criterion of national development. Concentration, therefore, was on sophisticated technology and on heavy capital investment. The assumption was that technological progress was the cause of development in the West and that transfer of those techniques to an underdeveloped country would create conditions favourable to social and economic progress. It was the offshoot of the Industrial Revolution with its background of the exploitation of the colonies abroad and of the workers at home. Profit was the main criterion of progress in this model.

It is this pattern of development and technology that was transferred to India and other Third World Countries in the name of development. What the Third World required was not a capital intensive, but a labour-intensive economy that would safeguard the weaker sections that had been further marginalized in the colonial era. But given their Western orientation, the new rulers of the country could not think of alternate models suited to the Indian situation. Technology transfer was their answer and further marginalization of the already weak, the consequence (Fernandes, 1985: 3-4). Briefly, the introduction of sophisticated technology without changing the power structures and land ownership pattern, only strengthened those who already own productive assets since they took control of the new power structures and technical inputs. The results of this development evaluated in per capita and GNP-based statistics hide the fact that a few have the power to convert all increase in production into benefits to themselves and hide inequalities.

Involuntary displacement and resettlement has been a companion of the present development process all over the world. People in both the developed and developing countries are observed to be equal victims of the present development model. However, it has caused serious concern in the developing countries as the victims often are found to be depressed and marginalized sections of society. Construction of major hydel dams, irrigation, drinking water systems or the extension of highways have led to displacement of people from their original habitat in all parts of the world. The beautiful master-plan of Paris today was made possible by the painful relocation of people and their settlement in the nineteenth century under the firm hand of Baron Haussman.

Similarly, the impressive Cross Bronx Expressway at New York led to the slashing of many neighbourhood and the huge hydro-electronic complexes in Canada uprooted many indigenous groups (World Bank, 1994a). It is observed that, in recent years due to the influence of Western developmental model emphasizing on large project based economic growth; people in the developing countries are involuntarily evicted and displaced from their native places in large number in order to make way for the location of development projects in their traditional homeland (Sahu, 1998).

It is needless to mention that under the present development strategy, involuntary displacement and resettlement of human population have become a global issue of serious nature. Many big development projects aiming at increasing economic growth at the national level generate adverse effects in the form of massive displacement of human population especially, the marginalized ones from their hearths and homes. They get deprived of their subsistence and self-sustenance form of livelihood. Although there is hardly any statistics existing at the global level to focus on the magnitude and size of involuntary displacement, estimates of national level resettlement caused by development projects in some of the large and important developing countries of the world by Guggenheim and Cernea (1993) clearly reveals that human displacement of development projects has now taken a serious and critical shape. During the period 1950-1990, nearly 4 crore people have been displaced and resettled due to different development projects in different countries (Table 2.1). This means annually on an average around 5 lakh people have been displaced by such development projects in each of the two countries. In other less populated countries, in terms of land-man ratio although the problem is not so acute, nonetheless this is found to be quite substantial and much higher (Sahu, 1998).

In recent decades, the scale of development related population displacement has registered marked increase in developing countries particularly in Asia. World Bank (1994a) estimate states that this type of development related displacement affects at least 10 million people on an average are displaced by around 300 large dams and another 6 million due to urban development and transport programmes. Over the past decades, it is estimated that around 80-90 million people have been forcibly resettled by such investments (Cernea, 1994). In order to cater to the needs of basic services and infrastructure for

Table 2.1: Estimates of National Resettlement Caused by Development Projects

Countries	*Time period*	*Number of People*
China	1950-1990	20,000,000
India	1950-1990	18,500,000
Thailand	1960-1977	1,30,000
Brazil	1980-1990	4,00,000
Turkey	1980-1990	3,00,000

Source: Roli Asthana (1996) 'Involuntary Resettlement: Survey of International Experience', *Economic and Political Weekly*, Vol. 31, No. 24, June 15, p. 1469.

growing population density, developing countries used to invest around $200 billion per year in new infrastructure such as multi-purpose dam construction, urban development and transport development programmes.

According to Michael M. Cernea (2008) over a twenty-year period up to 1994 and counting only three economic sectors World Bank estimated that up to 190-200 million people were displaced by public sector projects alone at an average of 10 million people annually. Taking all sectors into account, the conservative estimate of development displacement rises to about 280-300 million over 20 years or about 15 million people annually. In China 70 million people were displaced during 1950 to 2005 (Guoquing, Zhou and Chen, 2006) whereas in India over 60 million people were displaced during the same period. This may seem a small percentage of the total population but it has significantly contributed to the country's impoverishment.

"Empirical research has documented this aggravated pauperization" (Cernea, 2008). "Out of the 60 million people displaced in India, as mentioned above an unbelievable proportion—75 per cent, have ended up poorer than they were before displacement; no demographic segment of oustees in India is reported to be better off (Fernandes, this volume). In China along the last half century alone, out of one-third of China's displaced, about 33 per cent were 'resettled well'. The majority 66 per cent of the total is estimated by Guoquing, Su and Yuan (2002) as resettled either not well (one-third) or just so-so (another third)".

"The severity of impoverishment effect however is not the same in all displacement processes. The most severe effects occur in the sector, which requires massive displacements such as hydropower dams, reservoir and mining projects (Scudder, 2005, Downing, 2002; Mathur, 2006; this volume). In other sectors for example in linear displacements along transport corridors, residents may lose only part of their land while in reservoir situations entire communities have to be uprooted and often dispersed, losing virtually everything. This also makes the compensation issues vary from sector to sector (Cernea, 2008)."

2.2 Development Projects and Displacement in India

Displacement, resettlement and rehabilitation have been serious concern for all developing countries including India. A large number of development projects such as dams, factories, mines etc. have been initiated and established in the last five and half decades resulting in eviction of 40 to 50 million people approximately, mostly tribal/rural. Only about 25 per cent have had some sort of rehabilitation, the quality of which is far from satisfactory. Projects have been poorly formulated and inefficiently implemented resulting in an undesirable impact on environment leading to deterioration in the quality of lives. Disruption in the established pattern of life of displaced people is traumatic and results in a spiral of impoverishment; economically, socially, culturally and politically. It resulted in landlessness, marginalization, poor food security, increased morbidity, loss of access to Common Property Resources (CPR) and social disarticulation. Most displaced and project affected people belong to the marginalized and powerless classes: assetless poor such as landless labourers and small and marginal farmers (Somayaji, 2008).

Around 35-55 million people in the country have been displaced due to urban development projects alone (Sen, 1995). The number of displaced persons in India was between 2 to 20 million in the early 1980s (Mankodi, 1989). Fernandes, Das and Rao (1989) in their study report have said that displacement has now become a serious human issue of the day and according to their estimate the number of people displaced due to development projects of the country was around 15.5 million in the mid-eighties.

From the estimates made on involuntary displacement caused due to development projects in India at different points of time by the various researchers, it is felt that the country has failed to keep proper accounts of displacement and rehabilitation at the national level. Of late, Fernandes (1994) has made an attempt to provide a conservative estimate of displacement and rehabilitation of people in different parts of the country caused due to various development projects. Altogether 213 lakh people in India have been displaced involuntarily by the various types of development projects such as dams, mines, industries, wildlife sanctuaries and others (Table 2.2). Interestingly, out of this as high as 77 per cent of the displacement is caused due to building of river dams and the percentage share of tribal population among the victims of displacement is found to be as high as 40. Further, when we look at the resettlement figures of these persons, it is found that only 25 per cent at the aggregate level has been resettled by the project authorities or Government.

Table 2.2: Total Number of Persons Displaced by Various Developmental Projects in India during 1951-1990

(in lakhs)

Type of Project	*All DPs*	*% of DPs*	*Resettled*	*% Resettled DPs*	*Back-log*	*% Back-log*
Dams	164.0	77.0	41.00	25.0	123.0	75.0
Mines	25.5	12.0	6.30	24.7	19.20	75.3
Industries	12.5	5.9	3.75	30.0	8.75	70.0
Wildlife Sanctuary	56.0	2.8	1.25	20.8	4.75	79.2
Others	5.0	2.3	1.50	30.0	3.50	70.0
Total	**213.0**	**100.0**	**53.80**	**25.0**	**159.2**	**75.0**

Source: Walter Fernandes (1994). *Development Induced Displacement of Eastern India,* pp. 24, ISI, New Delhi (Mimeo).

According to Fernandes (2008), during 1947 to 2000 the total number of displaced people and others economically deprived of their livelihood are estimated at more than 60 million. Of this magnitude, West Bengal comprised 7 million, Assam 1.9 million and Gujarat 7 million approximately. One-third of the DPs have been resettled in a planned manner. For the other two-thirds there is no evidence of organized resettlement. The percentage of DPs resettled in Orissa, Andhra Pradesh, Goa, and West Bengal are 35.27, 28.22, 33.23 respectively. In Assam people have been resettled in less than ten projects.

2.3 Development and Displacement in Orissa

Ever since Independence, a large number of Development Projects have been taken up in State to usher economic growth and development. Development Projects which have been taken up so far include Dam/Irrigation, Industrial, Mining, Urban Infrastructure Development, Wildlife Sanctuary, Linear Projects like road, railways and so on. Conservative estimate reveals that so far more than 10 lakh people have been displaced and more than 50 lakh people have been affected adversely in varying degrees without getting displaced. Empirical studies reveal that the displaced persons in most of the development projects have failed to regain and restore their pre-project living condition in the post-project period and majority of them have slipped below the threshold of poverty.

Project based development activities in Orissa began in late forties but it gained momentum in the fifties after the implementation of Five Year Plans. The important developmental projects in the fifties were the Rourkela Steel Plant and Hirakud Dam project. In the sixties Hindustan Aeronautics Limited (HAL), Talcher Thermal Power Station (TTPS) and the Balimela Dam were established. During Seventies Rengali, Upper Kolab, Upper Indravati and Subernarekha multi-purpose dams were established in the State. The Ib Thermal Power Station (ITPS), Talcher Super Thermal Power Project (TSTP) and the National Aluminum Company (NALCO) were set-up in the eighties. These projects were established in resource rich highland districts of the State, which are predominantly inhabited by the tribals and other depressed categories of people (Sahu, 1998).

The establishment of these large projects although primarily intended to generate economic development at the national/state level, they could not be made totally free from many types of unintended negative effects at the local level. The adverse consequences of these developmental projects are massive population displacements, which cause socio-cultural and economic problems (Sahu,1998).

The extent of displacement caused due to development projects in Orissa may be divided into *five* categories such as:

(a) Thermal Power Projects;
(b) Industrial Projects;

(c) Mining Projects;
(d) Irrigation Projects; and
(e) Other Projects.

There are large displacements due to various projects in Orissa (Table 2.3). According to official estimates, 81,176 families from 1,466 villages were displaced due to acquisition of 14,82,626 acres of land for development projects in the state of Orissa from 1950 to 1993. In the era of liberalization and privatization, many projects are coming to Orissa mainly in mineral processing industries and power sector, thus marking a shift of development projects from the irrigation sector to the industrial sector. Therefore, displacement at an increasing rate is a reality at present. Of course, the magnitude of involuntary displacement by industrial projects is lower than that by multi-purpose dam projects, and capacity of the former is higher than the latter in providing employment opportunities. However, the resettlement and rehabilitation measures adopted for the displaced persons of the development projects have been unsatisfactory. The marginalized sections that are displaced suffer the most (Samal, 2009).

Though the World Bank, in its report recognized the regional imbalance and rise in regional and social inequality in India since the Reform era, the Government of Orissa is unable to realize the dynamics of liberalization and privatization in the poor state of Orissa and inviting and signing MOUs with more than 35 companies mostly for mineral processing industries (Samal, 2008).

2.3.1 Thermal Power Projects

The large coal deposits in both the Ib valley area of Jharsuguda district (erstwhile Sambalpur) and Talcher area of Angul district (erstwhile Dhenkanal) have led to the establishment of many Thermal Power projects in the State.

The Talcher Super Thermal Power Project (TSTP) is executed by National Thermal Power Corporation (NTPC) and is located at Kaniha near Talcher. In order to establish the project the authority has acquired 1463.16 ha. of land affecting 940 families in 53 villages in and around Talcher (NTPC, 1993). According to another report the number of affected families is 1632 in TSTP at Kaniha (Rout, 1991).

Table 2.3: Mega Projects and Displacement in Orissa

Sl. No.	*Name of the Projects*	*Affected Villages (nos.)*	*Affected Families (nos.)*	*Land acquired (ha)*	*Remarks*
Thermal Power projects:					
1.	Talcher Super Thermal Power Project (TSTP)	53	1632	1463	
2.	Talcher Thermal Power Station (TTPS)	17	157	206	
3.	Ib Thermal Power Station (ITPS)	3	329	486	
Industrial projects:					
1.	Rourkela Steel Plant	30	4251	7918	
2.	NALCO Damanjodi Sector	26	NA	2741	
3.	NALCO Angul Sector	40	3997	3878	
4.	MIG Factory, Sunabeda	10	468	3764	
5.	Ordnance Factory, Saintala	14	1200	NA	
Mining projects:					
1.	Mahanadi Coal Field, Talcher	61	NA	2576	(by 1994)
2.	Mahanadi Coal Field, Ib Valley	17	130	930	(by 1993)
Multi-purpose Hydel dams:					
1.	Hirakud Dam	249	22144	74300	
2.	Balimela	95	1907	17496	(AP,648ha)
3.	Rengali Dam Project	263	11289	423000	
4.	Upper Kolab	49	3189	11350	
5.	Upper Indravati	99	5301	11000	
6.	Rengali Irrigation Project	38	1054	2888	
7.	Salandi	5	589	NA	
8.	Subernarekha Multi-purpose	75	5214	4000	(Bihar,2600h)
9.	Machhkund Dam	NA	2938	NA	
10.	Major Irrigation projects (Kanpur, Lower Indra, Ib, Lower Suktel)	122	9221	30233	
11.	Medium Irrigation projects	210	5889	26583	

Source: Sahu (2000).

The Talcher Thermal Power Station (TTPS) was the first thermal project in Orissa and set up in 1964. This led to the acquisition of 205.67 ha. of land and displaced 157 families affecting 17 villages in and around Talcher town of the erstwhile Dhenkanal district and the present day Angul district of the State.

The Ib Thermal Power Station (ITPS) at Banharpali in Jharsuguda district (erstwhile Sambalpur) was started in the early 1990. The project acquired 486.48 ha. of land from three villages, affecting 329 families. Out of this 169 families were fully displaced and evacuated for the commissioning of the project in its present site.

Thus, altogether commissioning of thermal power projects in the State has led to the displacement of around 1,500 families from their hearths and homes and for the purpose altogether around 2,155 ha. of cultivable and homestead lands have been acquired by the government. According to a recent estimate the number of families displaced and affected by Thermal Power Projects are 2426 and this accounts for 2.60 per cent of total displacement in the State (Ota, 1999).

2.3.2 Industrial Projects

Major industries of Orissa are Rourkela Steel Plant, National Aluminium Company's plants functioning at Angul and Damanjodi, Fertilizer Corporation Plant at Talcher, Paradeep Phosphates at Paradeep, Aluminium Plant at Hirakud, Tata Refractories at Belpahar, Hindustan Aeronautics Limited at Sunabeda, Ordnance Factory at Saintala and the like. Further there are plans to construct five steel plants at Daitari, two at Gopalpur and two Aluminium plants at Kashipur near Rayagada. The establishment of these huge industries has led to large scale acquisition of land and displacement of the marginalized and downtrodden people mostly in the backward but mineral rich highland districts of the State.

The Rourkela Steel Plant in late fifties acquired 7,917.84 ha. of land. The project affected 2,464 families from 30 villages of Sundargarh district in early 1950s (Roy-Burman, 1966). According to the estimate given by Mahapatra, the project affected 2464 families out of which 1231 families (50.37%) were tribals and 733 families (30%) were Scheduled Castes (Mahapatra, 1960). However, the actual estimates are on the higher side, i.e. 4,251 families (Reddy, 1993).

NALCO, Damanjodi sector in the district of Koraput acquired 2741 ha. of land for aluminium plant, mining activities and township etc. The project affected 17,678 population in 26 villages, out of which tribals constitute 52.44 per cent, Scheduled Castes 10.84 per cent and other castes 36.72 per cent (Kar, 1991). NALCO for its smelter plant, captive power plant and township in Angul has acquired 3877.81 ha. of land. This affected 3,997 families in 40 villages. Out of the affected families, 12.76 per cent are reported to be Scheduled Castes and 2.78 per cent are Scheduled Tribes by origin (Fernandes *et al.*, 1992).

The MIG factory at Sunabeda in Koraput district was set up by the Hindustan Aeronautics Limited (HAL) in 1963. The project acquired 3,764 ha. of land and displaced 468 families from 10 villages (Reddy, 1993). The ordnance factory at Saintala in Bolangir district was established in 1984. The factory displaced 1200 families from 14 villages (Pandey, 1998). The total number of families affected by industries in Orissa is 10,704. This accounts for 11.47 per cent of total displacement in the state (Ota, 1999).

Thus, it seems besides dams, industries have played a major role in displacement of people in Orissa. Moreover the number of people displaced by mineral-based industries is comparatively larger than that of other industries.

2.3.3 Mining Project

In mining operations in Orissa coal mining have led to maximum displacement of people. Though mining of iron ores have displaced people in north Orissa, the number of displaced is not fully documented (Mahapatra, 1960). So only the coal mining operations are mentioned here. Orissa's coal deposits are concentrated in two areas such as the Talcher area of present Angul district and the Ib valley area of Jharsuguda district. Coal mining operations in Orissa is carried out by Mahanadi Coalfields Limited (MCL), a subsidiary of Coal India Limited (CIL). By 1994 MCL in Talcher area has acquired 2,576 ha. of land. It is found that MCL operations in Talcher area had affected 23 villages due to four underground mines and another 38 villages due to five open cast mines (MCL, 1994). In the Ib valley area of Jharsuguda district MCL has acquired 929.58 hectare of land by 1993 for five open cast mines. These five open cast mines have affected 17 villages and 130 families from two affected villages have already been displaced (MCL, 1993).

There are around 700 mines all over Orissa, located mostly in the tribal areas of the State. It is needless to mention that exploration of minerals through open cast mines results in displacement of human settlements, felling of forests and acquisition of agricultural lands also. Although the magnitude of displacement caused due to mining projects in the State is not available from the official record, we may estimate that one mine on an average affects the livelihood of around 50 to 100 families in the project area. Thus, operation of 700 mines in the state must have led to the displacement of around 50,000 families belonging to the marginalized sections of society. This is more or less evident from Table 2.3. It is seen from the Table that operation of 79 mining projects in Orissa caused displacement of 3,143 families and acquisition of 2,427.03 hectares of land during 1950-1993 and this accounts for 3.37 per cent of total displacement in Orissa (Ota, 1999).

2.3.4 Irrigation Projects

The irrigation projects that the researcher finds in Orissa before and in the early stages of independent India are Machhkund, Hirakud and Balimela. Rengali, Upper Kolab and Upper Indravati started during 1970s, Machhkund dam on river Dumuma in Koraput district was the first major dam project of Orissa. The project displaced 2,938 families in 1940s. Out of the displaced families 51.00 per cent belonged to Scheduled Tribes and 10.21 per cent were Scheduled Castes (Mahapatra, 1960). The Hirakud multi-purpose dam project was constructed in post-independent era on river Mahanadi in Sambalpur district and was completed in 1957. The project has affected 249 villages of Orissa and 36 villages of Madhya Pradesh (Baboo, 1992). The families affected by the dam are 22,144 consisting of about 1,10,000 people (Government of Orissa, 1968; Patnaik *et al.*, 1987). The project submerged an area of 74,300 ha land, which included 23,988 ha. of forest land and 49,888 ha. of agricultural land (Dalwai, 1991).

The Balimela multi-purpose dam project, which happens to be an inter-state project of Orissa and Andhra Pradesh, constructed in the district of undivided Koraput in Orissa in the year 1962-63 has submerged 17,496 ha. of land in Orissa and 648 ha. in Andhra Pradesh affecting nearly 2000 families, who are mostly tribal by origin. The estimated number of displaced tribal families was 1,507 (79.31%).

The Rengali multi-purpose dam project on River Brahmani in Angul district of Orissa (erstwhile Dhenkanal) was started in 1973 and all other works of the Project were completed by March 1991. The project submerged 4,23,000 ha. of land in the undivided districts of Sambalpur and Dhenkanal and a total of 263 villages from Deogarh, Pallahara and Talcher sub-divisions of the said districts were submerged under water. The total number of families affected by the dam was 10,897, out of which 1,710 (15.69%) belonged to Scheduled Castes and 1,172 (10.75%) were Scheduled Tribes. The rest belonged to general cast Hindu category and many among the latter were from the cultivator caste popularly called *Chasa* in Orissa (Dalwai, 1993).

Upper Kolab multi-purpose dam project on the Kolab river in Koraput district was started in 1976 and was completed in 1991. It submerged 16,258 ha. of land and 3180 families from 53 villages were displaced by the project (Status Report on Upper Kolab Irrigation Project, August 2005). Out of the total displaced families 442 (13.90%) belonged to Scheduled Castes category and 1,421 (44.70%) were Scheduled Tribes by origin (Government of Orissa, 1993).

The Upper Indravati multi-purpose dam project was started in the year 1978-79 and it is proposed to create a composite reservoir by damming four rivers such as Indravati, Padagoda, Muran and Kapur in undivided Koraput and Kalahandi districts of Orissa. The project will submerge a total area of 11,000 ha. of land and 99 villages (Dalwai, 1991). By now 5,301 families have already been displaced from 99 villages; out of which 2,223 families (41.94%) were tribals and 796 families (15.02%) were reported to be Scheduled Castes by origin (Government of Orissa, 1993). The number of people to be affected by the dam is around 20,000 in 105 villages as mentioned in the World Bank Staff Appraisal Report (Mahapatra, 1960).

The Subarnarekha multi-purpose project is an inter-state project of Orissa, Bihar and West Bengal on the river Subernarekha. The project aims at creation of two major dams, namely Chandil and Ichha dam will affect 3,830 families in the 36 villages of Orissa, affecting 3152 S.T. families (82.3%), 116 S.C. families (3.0%) and 562 (14.7%) families belonging to other castes (Government of Orissa, 1990). According to another report both Ichha and Chandil dam will submerge 2,600 ha. of land in Bihar and around 4,000 ha. in Orissa. The number of families to be affected in the areas will be 10,000 in Bihar and 1,000 in Orissa (World Bank, 1982).

Further, the three reservoirs created by these two dams in Orissa, namely Jambhira, Haldia and Baura will displace 2,483 families in Orissa (Government of Orissa, 1990).

2.3.5 Other Projects

People are also displaced and affected due to development of urban infrastructure and wildlife sanctuaries in Orissa. So far a total of 12,000 slum dwellers have been displaced from various parts of Orissa. The two wildlife sanctuaries such as Similipal Tiger Sanctuary and Chandaka wildlife sanctuary have displaced 42 and 100 families respectively (Ota, 1999).

Table 2.4: Magnitude of Displacement due to Various Developmental Projects in Orissa during 1950-1993

Types of Projects	*No. of Villages Displaced/Affected*	*No. of Families Displaced/Affected*	*Total Land Acquired (in ha.)*
Mines	79	3143	2427.03
Industries	113	10704	21963.00
Thermal Power	73	2426	3155.31
Irrigation and Hydel Dams	1181	64903	595918.60
Total	**1446**	**81176**	**622463.94**

Source: Balaji Pandey (1998). Depriving the Underprivileged for Development, ISED, Bhubaneswar, p. 116.

Table 2.4 further reveals that during 1950-1993 all types of development projects in the State such as mining, industries, thermal plants and irrigation and hydel dams have displaced 81,176 families and led to the acquisition of 6.22 lakh hectares of land. In Orissa different developmental projects have displaced more than four hundred thousand people. Further, the major displacement has occurred due to the construction of major and medium dams and these have altogether displaced and affected 65 thousand families and around 6 lakh hectares of land and accounts for about 70 per cent of total displacement in the state.

2.4 Risks and Marginalization

Michael Cernea by going beyond economic factors attempted to study social, psychological, cultural and health parameters (Verma, 2004). He identified eight areas of impoverishment risks after studying displacement cases all over the world. These impoverishment risks are:

(i) Landlessness

Expropriation of land removes the main foundation upon which people's productive systems, commercial activities and livelihood are constructed. This is the principal form of de-capitalization and pauperization of the displaced people, as they lose both physical and man-made capital.

(ii) Joblessness

Loss of wage employment occurs in both urban displacement and in rural areas, and those losing jobs are landless labourers, enterprise or service workers, artisans and small businessmen. But creating new jobs is difficult and requires substantial investments. Resulting unemployment or underemployment among resettlers lingers long after physical relocation.

(iii) Homelessness

Loss of housing or shelter may be only temporary for many displaces, but for some homelessness remains a chronic condition. In a broader cultural sense, homelessness is also placelessness, loss of group cultural space and identity or cultural impoverishment.

(iv) Marginalization

It occurs when families lose economic power and slide on a downward mobility path; middle-income farm households do not become landless, but become small landholders; small shopkeepers and craftsmen are downsized and slip below poverty thresholds. Relative marginalization may often begin long before actual displacement for instance when land are condemned for future flooding and implicitly devalued, new public and private infrastructure investments are prohibited and the expansion of social services is undercut.

(v) Increased Morbidity and Mortality

Serious decrease in health levels result from displacement caused social stress, insecurity and psychological trauma, and outbreak of relocation related diseases. Unsafe water supply and poor sewerage systems heighten vulnerability to epidemics. The weakest of the demographic segment, infants, children and the elderly are affected the most.

(vi) Food Insecurity

Forced uprooting increases the risk that people will fall into chronic undernourishment and food insecurity, defined as calorie protein intake levels below the minimum necessity for normal growth and work.

(vii) Loss of Access to Common Property

Loss of assets belonging to communities that are relocated represents a major form of income and livelihood deterioration. Typically such lost resources remain uncompensated by the government relocation schemes.

(viii) Social Disintegration

It tears apart the social fabric and the existing patterns of social organization. Production systems are dismantled, kinship groups and family systems are often scattered, local labour markets are disrupted, and people's cultural identity is put at risk. Life sustaining informal social network of mutual help among people, local voluntary associations, self-organized service arrangements etc. are dispersed and rendered inactive. This unravelling represents a massive loss of social capital incurred by the uprooted people, yet a loss that remains unquantified and uncompensated. Such elusive disintegration process undermines livelihoods in ways unaccounted for by planners.

Except for social disintegration the remaining seven areas that he mentioned can be placed in the formal and informal economic sphere (Verma, 2004).

2.5 Multiple Displacements

Another major disquieting result of land acquisition for development is multiple displacement, i.e. successive displacement of the same families from one place to another following establishment of projects in those areas (Dutta, 2007).

The story of the oustees of the projects like Rihand Dam, Hirakud Dam and HAL clearly bring out this plight. In the early 1960s, the oustees who are displaced due to Rihand dam had to face displacement from their new settlement for the second time in 1970s because of coal mining projects and again for the third time in the mid-1980s due to the setting up of a number of energy intensive industrial units. With each displacement the villagers were progressively pauperized. Similarly, the oustees of Hirakud Multipurpose Dam Project in the Jharsuguda district of Orissa who were resettled in mid-1950s in the nearby areas of reservoir, faced displacement for the second time in 1980s when the Thermal Power Station came up and again for the third time in 1980s-1990s due to the Valley Coal Mining Projects. Again the oustees of the Hindustan Aeronautics Limited (HAL) who were displaced in the early 1970s were displaced for the second time in 1980s with the establishment of the Upper Kolab Irrigation Project in Koraput district of Orissa and were displaced for the third time with the establishment of the Naval Armament Depot and Agricultural farm that came up in the area.

Multiple displacements do not even attract the attention of the National Policy. The Orissa Policy recognizes the harassment involved to the affected persons who have gone through the experience before and therefore provides for at least additional 50 per cent compensation over and above the normal compensation to mitigate it. The Orissa policy also requires steps to be taken by the rehabilitation and resettlement agency to acclimatize the resettled people in the new habitat including development of a cordial relationship with the host community in the resettlement site (Dutta, 2007).

2.6 Resettlement, Rehabilitation and Restoration of Livelihood

There is no doubt whatsoever that compensation for inflicted losses is economically justified, is legally obligatory and is immediately indispensable. But it is argued that in and by itself, compensation alone cannot provide the financial platform needed for full economic recovery. Those caught in the grips and gaps of development-displacement do not get their prior poverty reduced; on the contrary most become 'worse off', get further impoverished.

Above all, empirical analysis demonstrates contrary to traditional wisdom that the magnitude of the combined material and non-material losses and the impoverishment of those displaced far surpasses the redeeming power of compensation 'solutions'.

Compensation for 'taking of lands and homes has become a routine element in development-caused displacements, but its constant distortions are as routine as the compensation itself. Affected people (AP) fight these distortions anyway they can and researchers and specialists are criticizing them in countless papers. But the very critique of such distortions, and the struggle for obtaining compensation has diverted the attention of researchers and specialists away from even a more fundamental question. This question is whether compensation in itself, as it is defined in India's Land Acquisition Act (LAA) is able, to begin with, to perform the functions that it is estimated it can perform primarily the function of restoring those expropriated to their prior situation. This question has been increasingly raised by resettlement researchers in the last decade (Cernea, 1999: 5-49, 2000: 11-55, and this volume: Kanbur, this volume; Kanbur and Cernea 2002, yet policy makers have not responded to it in any convincing way (Cernea, 2008).

Compensation is the recognition of loss and a substitution for that loss, the appropriateness and adequacy of the substitution aside; substitution is the essence of the principle. Cernea defines compensation as damaged substitution: simply put, compensation only returns to the Displaced People (DP) something that way taken away from them. By definition, it does not provide them with anything more than simple repayment that is worthnoting above what they had before. In real practice the situation is even worse: under current valuation procedures, DP are left with less than what they had before. Cernea argues that DPs must become project beneficiaries and that resettlement be treated as a stand alone investment project, maintaining that while compensation is indispensable, it is wholly inadequate to ensure rehabilitation (Cernea, 2008).

The IR policies of the World Bank (WB) and the Asian Development Bank (ADB) for example require at the minimum that APs be assisted to be 'as well off' as they were before the project, that is to restore their livelihoods at least to their original standard of living. However, the requirement that people affected should be 'well off' is not enough; restoring people to their pre-project standards of living, which in many instances may be well below the poverty line (BPL), only returns them to their previous impoverished conditions. For us it is no problem to restore people to their original standards of living, they were living in remote poor rural areas. Restoring APs to poverty conditions can hardly be justified as good development practice. If resettlement were narrowly defined as merely restoration of standards of living, which ignores differential impacts and limit success to what is measurable, it would be possible to find cases of successful resettlement. But a definition of resettlement that encompasses well being and accounts for people's needs and wishes will probably result in a very different outcome (Cernea, 2008).

By emphasizing on compensation package, Michael M. Cernea says: Sometimes borrowing agencies propose cash compensation only in lieu of resettlement facilities. Experience with the resettlement of large population tends to show that the payment of cash compensation alone is often a very inadequate strategy for dealing with the displaced. In some instances the entire compensation has been used for immediate consumption purpose leaving the displaced with nothing to replace their lost income-generating assets and opportunities.

Savitri Ramiah has also come out with a similar kind of observation in her study of several projects of India. She observes that physical reproducible assets such as quality of housing and household assets were largely dependent upon the income levels of the household. A large number of PAPs have utilized parts of their compensation to construct better quality of houses and to buy household assets such as transistor, radio, tape recorder etc. soon after resettlement. However, the economic prosperity experienced by the PAPs soon after receiving compensation has declined. For example, several households were unable to afford basic maintenance of the house and repairs of electronic goods after a few years of resettlement because of inadequate finances.

Even the policy of giving one job to one family member is not going to solve the problem. NTPC, NCL and other management, which have taken over farmland, promised jobs for one member of each ousted family. But this one job of family has led to social problems. Suppose there are four brothers in a family, when one of them gets a job he wants to keep his salary to himself. He finds rest of the family a burden and takes the first opportunity to start living separately.

It clearly emerges that forced displacement of persons may be allowed in certain circumstances but that these exceptions from against displacement are restricted to cases of an ultimo ratio which shall be resorted to only if there are no alternatives. In this regard the term arbitrary implies that the acts in question contain elements of injustice, unpredictability and unreasonableness.

It is in this context, the present study proposes to make an attempt to undertake an economic evaluation of the impact of the relief and rehabilitation measures offered by the Tata Steel to the displaced families at Gopalpur, Ganjam, Orissa. As many as 2083 families were proposed to be displaced. They lost their land and more than 50 per cent of the affected families lost both land and homes.

The study will examine the magnitude of loss sustained by the families *vis-à-vis* the compensation package offered to them in terms of land, financial compensation, jobs, houses and other social benefits. As we have seen above, there are only a few studies which attempt to assess the effectiveness of the rehabilitation package *vis-à-vis* the conditions obtaining prior to displacement. This would enable us to say something about the dynamic impact of rehabilitation, as well as some inherent limitations of the same. This also may have some implications somewhat similar to rehabilitation policies adopted in a number of other cases of displacement in Orissa.

III

Socio-Economic Profile of the District, the Affected Areas and the Households

In the proceeding chapter, we have discussed the problems and issues of displacement and rehabilitation in general. It was sought to be highlighted that the eastern region which is richly endowed with mineral as well as water resources has been feeling the impact of sequential exhaustion during last two decades. This is true to a great extent in the case of Orissa, where many developmental projects have been built by the state. In order to more concretely understand the position of displacement, in this chapter, the situation in Orissa in general and the study area in particular will be analyzed.

The first two sections give an outline of the socio-economic situation of Orissa with specific emphasis on the displacement scenario. Detailed profile of Ganjam district, in the backdrop of which the study is located, is given in Section 3. Section 4 discusses the genesis of the project in Ganjam district and the reasons why this area was selected. Estimates of population to be displaced and affected as also that of the land area is given in this section. Sections 5 and 6 provide details of the erstwhile villages proposed to be displaced. A brief scenario of the affected area as it exists today is outlined in the last section, i.e. Section 7.

3.1 Situation in Orissa

Famous in mythologies and in ancient history as 'Kalinga' and in medieval history as 'Utkal', modern Orissa took its present form on April 1, 1936 the first state in India to be formed on linguistic basis (Encyclopaedia of India, Vol. V., p. 1). Situated on the east coast of India, Orissa is surrounded by West Bengal in the north-east, Bihar in the north, Chhattisgarh in the west, and Bay of Bengal in the east.

The state of Orissa extends from 17° 49′ to 22° 34′ N latitude from 81-29′ E to 87-29′ E longitude. It covers an area of 1,55,826 sq. kilometres (about 4.7% of the total area of the country) and had a population of 77,38,065 in 2001 (Government of India, Census Report, 2001). It has a coastline of about 480 km. Administratively the state is divided into 30 revenue districts, 30 agricultural districts, 114 Tahsils, 314 blocks, 57 sub-divisions, 3 revenue divisions, 50,854 villages and 124 towns (including 6 cities). A little over 40 per cent of the State's area is under cultivation, 38.8 per cent under forest and the remaining 20 per cent is used for other purposes (Mohanty, 1992).

On the basis of its physical features Orissa is divided into four parts, viz. (a) the Northern plateau consisting about 23.1 per cent of the state's geographical area; (b) the central table land consisting another 23 per cent; (c) the eastern ghat region, consisting 36 per cent of the area; and (d) the coastal plains making up the remaining 18 per cent.

The State's climate is tropical with uneven distribution of rainfall, constant droughts and floods, all of which have an adverse impact on the state's domestic product.

The state is regarded as one of the resource rich states of India. It possesses 17.99 per cent of the total mineral resources of the country. In this chromite accounts for 95.26 per cent, i.e. almost the entire production of chromite in the country and is also a leading producer of manganese. The details of mineral reserves of the state and as a percentage of all India reserves is given in Table 3.1. In the case of forest resources, it does not lag behind other states except Jammu and Kashmir, Nagaland and Tripura.

Nonetheless, it has to be remembered that Orissa also has another face and therein lies the paradox. In spite of the rich natural resources, Orissa remains the poorest state in the country in terms of the ratio of urban and rural poor to the total population (44.1% and 57.6%, respectively). In the agricultural sector, out of the available 79 lakh

Table 3.1: Mineral Deposits of Orissa as on 1.4.2005

Sl. No.	*Mineral*	*Deposits (in million tonnes)*	*As Percentage of All India Deposits*
1.	Bauxite	1808.27	54.97
2.	Coal	61999.26	24.48
3.	Chromite	202.96	95.26
4.	Lime Stone	1738.36	0.99
5.	Manganese Ore	152.96	40.40
6.	Fireclay	176.49	24.90
7.	Nickel Ore	174.48	92.46
8.	Iron Ore	4760.63	32.54

Source: Economic Survey-2008-09, Government of Orissa.

hectares or arable land only 29 lakh hectares could be cultivated by 1990. Though the underground water potential has been estimated to be about 700 million cubic metres, only less than 1 per cent has been harnessed. The State also lacks adequate infrastructural facilities for sustained economic growth. On the industrial front, Orissa again emerges as a backward state. As per a survey conducted in 1990-91, Orissa has a share of only 3.19 per cent of the total investment, 1.33 per cent of the total number of factories, 1.85 per cent of factory workers and 2.24 per cent of value addition in the manufacturing sector of the country. The per capita investment in industry stood at Rs. 1,961 compared with the country average of Rs. 2,303.

With a huge amount of natural resources, Orissa is characterized as 'poverty amidst plenty'. In comparison to the rest of India, it stands out as one of the extremely poor state of India marked by low literacy rate, high infant mortality rate, poor health status, and other indicators of development such as rate of urbanization, per capita income, number of villages electrified etc. Table 3.2 presents some of the indicators of development in Orissa and India.

3.2 Situation of Displacement

After Independence, the process of socio-economic development was initiated in the state in the successive plans. The process of development

Table 3.2: Indicators of Development in Orissa and India

Sl. No.	*Items*	*India (2001)*	*Orissa (2001)*
1.	Literacy	75.85	63.08
2.	Urbanization	27.78	14.92
3.	Irrigated Area	35.50	26.20
4.	Per capita Income (in Rs.)	10254	5663
5.	Population below poverty line (%)	26.10	44.15
6.	Percentage of village Electrified	86.00	73.00
7.	Percentage of Agriculture in Gross State Product	32.20	60.50

Sources:
1. Govt. of Orissa (2001), Statistical Outline of Orissa, Director of Economics and Statistics, 2001.
2. Govt. of Orissa (2001), Statistical Abstract, Director of Economics and Statistics, Bhubaneswar, 2001.
3. Govt. of Orissa (2001), Statistical Economic Figures, Director of Economics and Statistics, Bhubaneswar, 2001.

was slow during the first three plans. In the 1950s, Orissa did not have any industry worth the name except few saw-mills and some ice factories near Cuttack. The state had only two large dams (1950) as against 149 in March 1990 (Fernandes and Anthony Raj, 1992). Exploitation of its natural resources began in the 1950s with the building of the Hirakud dam and Rourkela Steel Plant. Other mines followed in support of this plant and the medium Mandira dam was built to provide water to it.

However, beginning from the 1970s, more dams were constructed and more mines were opened. It resulted in building of a few industrial complexes like NALCO, some major multi-purpose irrigation projects like Balimela, Upper Kolab, Rengali, Upper Indravati, Subarnarekha, etc. and a number of medium irrigation projects. Though these development projects have brought manifold benefits to the state, yet these have resulted in large scale deforestation not only for raw material exploitation but also for acquisition of vast areas of land under cultivation for the establishment of factories and also for residential complexes. The unintended consequences of this action have been not only loss of habitat for the rural poor but also of their means of livelihood, which has been mainly agriculture and sale of forest produce. The groups displaced have been mostly of weaker sections of the society.

Table 3.3 below gives the detailed figures of displacement of people due to various development projects in Orissa from 1947 to 1995.

Table 3.3: Development Projects and Displacement Scenario in Orissa (1947-1995)

Sl. No.	*Different Sectors where Displacement has taken place*	*No. of Villages Displaced*	*No. of Families Affected*	*Percentage to Total Displacement*
1.	Mines	79	3,143	3.65
2.	Industries	113	10,704	12.43
3.	Thermal Power	73	2,426	2.81
4.	Wildlife Sanctuary	NA	142	0.16
5.	Urban Slums	NA	4,792	5.57
6.	Irrigation Projects	1191	64,903	75.38
	Total	**1,441**	**86,110**	**100.00**

Source: Records of various Departments, Government of Orissa.

3.3 Profile of Ganjam District

Ganjam is one of the 30 administrative districts of Orissa with its headquarters located at Chhatrapur. However, the principal city is Berhampur. The district is surrounded by Khurda, Kandhamal, Gajapati and Nayagarh districts in four different directions. The district derives its name from the word "Ganj-i-am" which means the Granary of the World. The district is named after the Old Township and European fort of Ganjam situated on the northern bank of river Rushikulya which was the then headquarters of the district.

The literal meaning of Ganjam is the source of foodgrain and as this district is famous for foodgrain production and trade, it is named as Ganjam. The inhabitants of this district are hardworking and painstaking. This district has contributed a lot to the making of Orissa state and its progress. It has played a great role in the politics of Orissa as four Chief Ministers of Orissa belonged to this district. The Rushikulya and Badanadi river pass through Ganjam district and there exists a 3,824 feet high mountain, named Barama. There are many important places like Gopalpur-on-sea, Narayani, Nirmalajhar, Tara-Tarini, Panchama, Jaugarh, Sidha Vairabi, Buddhakhol and Byaghra

Devi. There is a University and medical college located in the district which are known as centres for academic excellence. Ganjam is also known for its horn works, salt factory, silver works, appliqué works and spinning and silk weaving mills. The principal city of the district, i.e. Berhampur is famous for its silk saris known as Berhampuri Pata. Berhampur is also one of the important business hubs of Orissa.

Ganjam district is broadly divided into two divisions, the coastal plains in the east and hill and table lands in the west. The Eastern Ghats run along the western side of the district. The plains lie between the Eastern Ghats and the Bay of Bengal. Since the hills are close to the sea, the rivers flowing across the hills are not very long and are subject to sudden floods. The plains are narrow because of the absence of big rivers. The coastal plains in the east contain more fertile and irrigated lands. Towards the centre and south it is hilly with beautiful water valleys. The south eastern portion is fertile. The extreme north-east is occupied by a portion of the famous Chilika Lake.

3.3.1 Water

The Bay of Bengal touches the eastern frontier of Ganjam district and its coast extends over 60 kms. It provides unique opportunity for fishing and port facility at Gopalpur for international trade. The rivers like Rushikulya, Dhanel, Bahuda and Ghoda Hada are the prominent ones which govern the agriculture and power sectors of the district. The vast river basin of Rushikulya provides grand potential for exploitation of groundwater. However, the rivers are only navigable during the rainy season. The Chilika lake which attracts international tourists and known for its scenic beauty and marvellous birds sanctuary, is situated in the eastern part of district.

3.3.2 Soil

The district has alluvial soil in its eastern part (coastal region) and laterite soil in the west (hilly table land) with small patches of black cotton soil at the centre and in the north east close to Chilika.

3.3.3 Mineral Resources

The chief economic minerals found in the district are abrasives and grinding materials, limestone (kankar), manganese, monazite, sand and talc. Garnetiferous granitic gnashes and charanokites are used for manufacture of grinding stones in the district while clay deposits are also found in different areas of the district.

A profile of the district is depicted in the following tables.

Table 3.4: Position of Ganjam District in the State: Demographic Characteristics

Sl. No.	District/ State	Population			% of Urban Population to Total	Sex Ratio	Density of Population per sq. km.
		Total	S C	ST			
1.	Ganjam	3160635	586798	50919	17.60	998	385
2.	Orissa	36804660	6082063	8145081	14.99	972	236

Source: Census of India, 2001.

Table 3.5: Position of Ganjam District in the State: Religious Affiliation

Sl. No.	District/ State	Religion							Religion not stated
		Hindu	Muslim	Christian	Sikh	Buddhist	Jain	Others	
1.	Ganjam	3132628	10910	14818	325	39	86	49	1780
2.	Orissa	34726129	761985	897861	17492	9863	9154	361981	20195

Source: Census of India, 2001.

Table 3.6: Position of Ganjam District in the State: Literacy Status

Sl. No.	District/ State	Literacy Rate					
		Total		ST		SC	
		1991	2001	1991	2001	1991	2001
1.	Ganjam	46.72	60.77	19.98	35.54	28.01	44.56
2.	Orissa	49.09	63.08	22.31	37.37	36.78	55.53

Source: Census of India, 2001.

Table 3.7: Position of Ganjam District in the State: Worker Status

Sl. No.	District/State	Per cent of Total Workers				
		Total Workers	Main Workers	Marginal Workers	Cultivators	Agriculture Labour
1.	Ganjam	1306	62.79	37.21	24.65	38.59
2.	Orissa	14276	67.17	32.83	29.75	35.02

Source: Census of India, 2001.

Table 3.8: Classification of Forest Area by Legal Status in Ganjam district as on 31.3.2004 (Area in sq. kms.)

Sl. No.	Classification of Forests	Orissa State	Ganjam District	Percentage of all Orissa
1.	Reserve Forests	26329.12	1485.69	5.64
2.	Demarcated Protected Forests	11685.68	143.54	1.23
3.	Un-demarcated Forests	3838.78	1167.36	30.41
4.	Un-classified Forests	20.55	0.86	4.18
5.	Other Forests	16261.34	352.45	2.17
	Total	**58135.47**	**3149.90**	**5.42**

Source: Principal Chief Conservator of Forest, Orissa.

Table 3.9: Details of Small Scale, Cottage and Handloom Industries in Ganjam District

Sl. No.	*Items*	*2001-02*	*2002-03*	*2003-04*
A.	**Small Scale Industries**			
I.	No. of SSI Units Established	328	331	313
II.	Total Capital Investment (Rs. in Lakhs)	1078.06	1050.31	1329.55
III.	Employment Generated (in number)	1233	1050	13377
B.	**Cottage Industries**			
I.	No. of Cottage Industries Set up	2098	2458	1892
II.	Total Capital Investment (Rs. in Lakhs)	386.13	512.62	243.01
III.	Employment Generated (in number)	2256	3107	2867
C.	**Handloom Industries**			
I.	No. of Looms	2403	2105	NA
II.	Total Capital Investment (Rs. in Lakhs)	NA	NA	NA
III.	Production (in Lakh sq. mt.)	10.35	10.23	NA
IV.	Employment Generated (in number)	4806	4210	NA

Source: Directorate of Industries, Cuttack.
Directorate of Textiles, Bhubaneswar.
Directorate of Handicrafts and Cottage Industries, Orissa, Bhubaneswar.

3.4 Genesis of Tata Steel, Gopalpur Project

It is thus clear that there is a big gulf between 'what Orissa is and what Orissa can be'. To bridge this gap, Orissa's vast potential for economic growth has to be carefully nurtured and the natural resources optimally utilized. The steel plant project of Tata Steel proposes to do just and will prove to be an asset to the nation, a provider to its people and the beginning of fast economic growth in the entire region of Orissa. That is the promise of the Tatas.

Due to the process of liberalization and privatization in India since 1991, establishment of processing and manufacturing industries even in the core sector like steel, power, etc. are at present, allowed in the private sector. Economic Reforms were also introduced in India in the year 1991. Consistent with the policy of industrial dereservation and deregulation of complex regulatory policies, the state of Orissa made a bold attempt to usher in an era of industrial growth and modernization of Orissa's economy. The objectives were to spread economic growth in the state, transform the traditional agrarian economy into a modern one and to spread the benefits of development to the people. Taking advantage of this trend, Tata Steel planned to install a second steel plant. Since there is no satisfactory increase in demand for steel inside India, an export-based steel plant near a port was emphasized upon.

Tata Steel's Gopalpur project was one such initiative. In 1993, the private sector steel giant of the country proposed to expand its capacity and set up another steel plant with a capacity of 10 to 12 Mtpa. This was not possible at its Jamsehedpur location because of existing logistics. Orissa happened to be the ideal choice for setting up of an integrated steel plant due to proximity of raw material sources which belonged mainly to Orissa and the adjoining state of erstwhile Bihar. In the year 1996, Tata Steel designed a project for setting up a steel plant at Goplapur in Ganjam district of Orissa. This was their second steel plant in India and was designed to be a very modern and sophisticated plant.

As many as eighteen sites were examined within the state and ultimately, Gopalpur, a small coastal village in Ganjam district was identified. The most important reason for selecting this site was proximity to high grade iron ore from captive sources like

Mankadnacha and Beliapahar group of deposits located on the north-eastern part of the state. Another major factor was the potential Gopalpur had for being converted into a deep sea port and may be into SEZ in the long run paving the way for exports and competition in the global markets. It was in the year 1996 that Tata Steel could start the process of land acquisition.

Development of any major project related to dams for irrigation and hydel power, ports for creating opportunities for expanding external trade and commerce, industrial projects for setting up of automobile plants, steel plants and SEZs for export oriented activities invariably leads to displacement of a large number of households in large and mostly contiguous areas.

The twentieth century gave birth to one amongst the great personalities in the industrial field, like J.R.D. Tata who had lived through the entire span of upheaval and scientific progress. Though he had no part in any of the events all he could claim, was some influence on the development of the house which broadly synchronizes with growth of India as an industrial power. It was the year of 1908 that the Tata Iron and Steel Company Limited (TATA STEEL) began operations at Jamshedpur in undivided Bihar. It symbolizes the cherished memories of the growth of the Indian Steel Industry in the post-independence era; the great city bears the proud name of the founder, Jamshedji Tata. It was upon his dreams that the foundation was laid for the production of 1 lakh tonne per annum at the beginning.

3.4.1 Need for Expansion

The need for expansion of the existing steel plant at Jamshedpur beyond 3.2 million tonnes per annum (mtpa) of crude steel is constrained by certain factors by making quick snap of its market. Tata Steel's market share in the domestic market was about 15 per cent in 1996 with a production capacity of 2.7 mtpa of saleable steel. It was projected that by 1998, with the completion of the modernization programme, the anticipated production capacity would be 3.2 mtpa of saleable steel, the domestic steel demand would be about 28 mtpa and Tata's domestic market share dropped to about 20 per cent, without producing additional capacity. From the level of about 23 mtpa, domestic steel demand has been forecasted to grow to about 32 mtpa by 2001. It was likely to grow about 41 mtpa by 2005 and to about 57 mtpa by 2011. Further, during this time-frame, the steel demand in South East Asia was predicted to grow rapidly. In order to meet the domestic and global needs of steel, Tata's had the vision to increase it to around 20 per cent. Therefore, the capacity expansion of steel to around 15 mtpa was required during the next 15 to 20 years. Thus, the oldest steel plant of the country has been planning for the installation of a new large capacity integrated steel plant since 1993.

3.4.2 Choice of Coastal Location

India is rich in natural resources. It has sufficient reserves of good quality of iron ore. For low ash coking coal, we do depend on imports. The low ash coking coal is a vital ingredient for a globally competitive steel plant. For better import of raw materials and export of finished products, the natural choice was to locate the new steel plant on a coastal site.

The search for a coastal based location started in September 1993. A small task force consisting of members of Tata Steel as well as consultants of M.N. Dastur & Co. were pressed into action. The team drove along almost the entire coastline of India. Eighteen locations were identified and each of these locations were visited and assessed. The following factors were taken into account such as; availability of land and its terrain, availability of iron ore, power supply, population to be displaced, feasibility of building a port, assembly cost of raw material and distribution cost of finished products. Some of the potential locations include Mithivirdi, Marol, Saphale, Marg Tamhane, Pavas, Ankola, Nandikuir, Cheemeni, Paradeep and Gopalpur-on-sea. All the sites were examined for their suitability to locate the plant with an ultimate capacity of 10-12 mtpa. One factor which emerged as a constant in all the locations was that 5000 acres of land, just about adequate for a 10 million tonne steel plant was not available near the coast without involving displacement of its inhabitants. The population to be displaced in any location would have been within 2000 to 3000 families if 5000 acres of land were to be acquired along the coast. Among all the locations pruned, two were short listed, one at Ankola in Karnataka and the other at Gopalpur-on-sea of Orissa. And eventually, Gopalpur-on-sea of Orissa was selected for constructing the Tata's Steel Plant.

3.4.3 Locational Advantages of Gopalpur-on-Sea

Concomitant with the advantages of improved logistics in a coastal location, the possibility of using high grade iron ore from captive sources in nearby areas of Orissa made Gopalpur a preferred location. The required iron-ore for steel production would be mined from the Mankadanacha and Beliapahar group of deposits located in the North-Eastern part of the state. The mine site has proven resources of around 400 million tonnes. For selecting possible avenues for the steel plant, eight in the west coastal region and two locations in the east were searched. Compared to the sites on the western coast, this location was much closer to the sea port. Along with the locational advantage, the factors which strengthened 'Gopalpur-on-Sea' to be the most selective area for Tatas proposed plant were; availability of cheap land, presence of a working minor port, some degree of industrial culture in the vicinity with Indian Rare Earths Ltd. (IRE) as a neighbour, availability of abundant labour with cheaper wage and a sound civil society from the towns of Berhampur and Chhatrapur.

Tatas approached the State Government of Orissa. The Government of Orissa responded to the Tata Steel's proposal by agreeing to provide all infrastructure required in building a mega steel plant. The Memorandum of Understanding (MoU) with the Government of Orissa was signed in the month of August 1995.

Gopalpur-on-Sea is situated in the Southern part of Orissa. It is in the district of Ganjam. Gopalpur is close to the Andhra border, between the National Highway No. 5 and the Bay of Bengal. Berhampur town lies about 12 kms. to its west and the district headquarters of Ganjam at Chhatrapur is around 10 kms. to the north. This minor fair weather port has a history of trade since early Kalinga days and in fact, it was called the Gateway of Kalinga at a particular point of time.

The project displaced and affected people adjacent to Gopalpur-on-Sea mostly belong to the Reddika community. A well coherent rural based economy was strengthening those villagers both socially and economically. Agriculture was their prime occupation. In comparison to male counterparts, females had an excellent sense of work culture. Especially in the Reddika community, most were addicted to alcohol irrespective of their gender. They were earning through harvesting seasonal crops and selling it in the nearby town, Berhampur. The Gopalpur belt was one of the main sources of rice, vegetable, raggie, green gram, mango and cashew, to the nearby town. The people were very self-sufficient in maintaining their day-to-day lives. Village proximity, neighbourhood, interdependency, providing work for the villagers at lower echelons, rural infrastructure, cultural norms and values, community based activities and such other factors were responsible for maintaining an equilibrium both economically and socially in their respective villages. No doubt, there was a high degree of caste feeling in those villages, but most of them felt happy as they were able to earn their bread and butter. In the community, the sense of deprivation was not seen at least in getting their daily earnings. Though the villagers were struggling extrinsically to function democratically the Reddika community dominated over others. They were functioning autocratically. The Brahmins, Goudas and Scheduled Castes were succumbed to them.

Keora flower (Pondanus) was one of the vital sources of income for the local people. Even a sixty year old lady was able to earn by collecting and selling *keora* flowers to the local buyers. During rainy season, production of flowers was more in comparison to the winter and summer season. A specific perfume extracted from the flowers was used for preparing alkaloids. It was very costly in the global market. Gopalpur-on-Sea belt is the only area with nature's blessings for production of *Keora* in huge quantity. The entire area was most suitable for cultivation.

Tata House for their would be project at Gopalpur-on-sea committed to have a major positive impact on the state of Orissa in general and the Ganjam district in particular. The projected concrete benefits include improved standards of living, generation of employment, establishment of downstream small and medium scale engineering units, enhanced tourism, increased revenue to the state by way of taxes, and duties, improved green cover, superior communication and transport facilities and perennial water supply for improved agriculture. They had declared that the establishment of the plant would necessarily involve some amount of short-term inconvenience and "pain" but meticulous planning would bring long term prosperity of the local population and "gains" for Orissa.

From the industrial point of view, the district of Ganjam does not have many major industries (as can be seen from Table 3.9). It has only two medium scale industries, viz. the Chlor-Alkali plant called Jayashree Chemicals at Ganjam and the Indian Rare Earths (IRE) of the Government of India. It is quite clear that the industries are not the prime factors responsible for the current economic status of these people. The construction of steel plant would have brought opportunities for changing the lifestyles of the people nearby. At least, it would have provided scope for employment in a better way. They had made a version that what come from the people had to be given back to the people many times over and a new cycle would emerge at Gopalpur-on-sea. Following the same earlier project patterns since 1995, after a lot of propaganda through publications and media, Tata's project started their work by displacing villagers to the rehabilitation site. The displacement process has been studied in detail in the consequent chapters. The compensation paid to the displaced persons were incomplete till January 2001. The utilization of compensation, extension of houses as per suitability, uncertainties arising out of displacement to the Tata Rehabilitation Colony and the initial trauma faced by the oustees have been reflected in the forthcoming chapters. Since 1996 to date, Tata team starting from Chief at the helm of affairs to bottom including the various agencies who had worked for rehabilitation and resettlement of the people like Tata Consultancy Services (TCS), Environment Resources Management (ERM) were giving wrong portraits about Gopalpur steel plant. The political hegemony of Tata Steel gave a number of imaginative commitments like giving jobs to every family member just after shifting to the site, sanctioning loans from banks, making all arrangements for their better lives, were very pathetic. Tata's team made gullible the simple candid community. The upcoming Tata Steel Plant Project for the people has ended in a fiasco. The dreams inculcated in the minds of those kind-hearted people have collapsed. Over the two years (1998-2000) the entire jargon of "Tata Steel, Gopalpur Project" became a flying target as they shifted the Cold Rolling Mill (CRM) to Jamshedpur and created more questions about the future of this entire project. As a result, the steel plant has become a distant reality. The show of flights, helicopters, trains and other communication means of the Tata from Jamshedpur to Gopalpur-on-sea have eventually turned to zero. Perhaps the entire project seems to be a futile one. Burning exemplifications not only include Tata's Automobile Sector (Tata Sumo) but also Chilika (Orissa) prawn culture and aviation industries of Tata.

The main reason cited for the project not taking off is the lack of infrastructure which was promised by the State Government and indispensable for the project, but not provided at all. These include, water resources, railway and highway network, upgradation of port at Gopalpur to international standards etc. Due to people's agitation the Pipalpanka dam from which water was supposed to be supplied, had to be scrapped. By the time it was discovered that the State Government is not able to keep up its commitment, the land had been acquired and people displaced from their habitats.

In this dynamic Third World, changing of versions, decisions and commitments have become the strategies of Tata House. It has kept the people in a major paradox. Tata Steel makes pretensions of making something, diverting the larger community to a dilemma. This is a suspended animation in real sense for the state of Orissa. The much touted "social responsibility of business" concept has remained in philosophy only. Within the protected cocoons of this pious philosophy, Tata is making pretensions to people. The displaced people are remaining in non-proximity, non-coherent atmosphere. Entire neighbourhood relationship has been broken. The sentimental and emotional, sacrosanct linkages have been entirely withered. The project displaced persons are in a desert, awaiting for the conversion of a mirage into reality.

3.4.4 Villages and Households Affected or Displaced

Tata Steel had planned to displace a minimum number of persons. It was in order to satisfy the basic requirements of a contiguous land area. The steel plant complex at Gopalpur was likely to displace 2083 families comprising 10661 inhabitants in seven villages. The villages proposed to be displaced were: Badapur, Badaputti, Kalipalli, Laxmipur, Paikapada, Patrapur, Sindhgaon and Sri Ramchandrapur. Only the vacant land areas in four other villages in the plant site such as Basanputti, Chamakhandi, Jagannathpur and Mansurkota; two, namely Luhajhar, Sitapalli in the resettlement site and two in the township such as Aruapali and Dura were proposed to be acquired without displacing people from their households. The details of the entire land proposed to be acquired have been given in Table 3.11.

But in reality the villages of Badapur, Sindhigaon and Patrapur have been displaced totally. Only some families of Kalipalli and Paikapada village have been displaced till March 2001, but subsequently TISCO decided not to acquire the villages or displace the people. However, the families which had moved to the rehabilitation colony continue to occupy the houses and some have rented them out while maintaining their houses and property in their erstwhile villages. Sri Ramachandrapur village was also excluded from the land acquisition.

The inhabitants displaced from the plant area comprise various categories of people. This mainly includes cultivators, agricultural labourers and landless labourers. The demographic details of the other villages wherein only the land area is being acquired are presented in Table 3.10. Land belonging to villages, Kallipalli, Sri Ramachandrapur. Aruapalli and Dura were subsequently not acquired.

Table 3.10: Details of Families and Population Proposed to be Displaced

Sl. No.	*Villages*	*No. of Families*	*Total Population*
1.	Badapur	181	1200
2.	Badaputti	343	1491
3.	Kalipalli	283	1212
4.	Laxmipur	63	267
5.	Paikapada	257	983
6.	Sindhigaon	384	1907
7.	Sri Ramchandrapur	572	3601
	Total	**2083**	**10661**

NB: Patrapur is included as a hamlet under Sindhigaon.

Source: Resettlement and Rehabilitation at Gopalpur prepared by Tata Steel, 1996.

Table 3.11: Village-wise Different Types of Land Acquired by Tata Steel

Sl. No.	*Village*	*Land Acquired (in Acres)*		
		Private Land	*Govt. Land*	*Total*
I.	**Plant Site**			
1.	Badapur	398.211	84.879	483.090
2.	Badaputti	319.647	254.316	573.963
3.	Basanapurti	189.812	49.375	239.187
4.	Chamakhadi	377.793	58.553	436.346
5.	Jagannathpur	316.443	80.896	397.339
6.	Kalipalli	211.958	46.127	258.085
7.	Laxmipur	116.873	38.725	55.598
8.	Mansurkota	413.222	158.156	571.378
9.	Paikapada	769.628	147.235	916.863
10.	Sindhigaon	434.398	153.175	587.573
11.	Sri Ramchandrapur	881.695	148.668	1030.36
	Total	**4492.68**	**1220.105**	**5549.785**
II.	**Rehabilitation Town**			
1.	Luhajhar	284.118	18.577	302.695
2.	Sitlapalli	253.70	19.287	273.057
	Total	**537.888**	**37.864**	**575.752**
III.	**Township Site**			
1.	Arupalli	379.673	70.287	449.96
2.	Dura	482.977	12.945	495.922
	Total	**978.309**	**141.761**	**1120.070**

Source: Resettlement and Rehabilitation at Gopalpur prepared by Tata Steel, 1996.

3.5 Profile of Displaced Villages

As per the Tata Steel's Report, there was supposed to be local displacement of people from (i) seven villages for the plant site, (ii) two villages for resettlement and rehabilitation site, and (iii) two more villages for township. The land from four villages of the locality and one village which is in Berhampur town will be acquired without displacement. Only few acres of private land in Sindhigaon village of those residing in towns have been acquired by the Government without consulting the sharecroppers. These traders are most vocal supporters of the project due to their vested interest.

It is reported that around 82 per cent of the residents of the affected areas were engaged in agriculture. Fifty-six per cent of these people engaged in agriculture were landowners and others were landless labourers. People spoke either Telugu or Oriya and sometimes both languages. Only 28 per cent of the total population of the area were literate. The unique occupation of the area and people is extraction of *attar* (scent) from Keora plants grown abundantly. The demographic details of the area and villages is given in Table 3.12, depicted in the following pages.

3.5.1 Badapur

A keen observation of the demographic details reveals that the village Badapur was having 220.15 hectares of area and comprising 165 households. Total population was 881 of which 434 were males and 447 were females. A total of 280 people were belonging to Scheduled Caste category. So far the literacy rate is concerned approximately 43 per cent of the population was literate. From the families point of view 181 families had been affected by such displacement. Most of the villagers belonged to the working class category. In total, 249 workers (212 males and 37 females), 60 cultivators, 149 Agricultural labourers, 3 in forestry, livestock and fishing activities and 12 people were involved in allied activities occupationally. Mostly the milkman community was involved in dairy activities. The villagers belonging to lower echelon (Scheduled Castes were daily wage earners). Some of them had taken rickshaw pulling as the prime source of income in the nearby town, Berhampur.

3.5.2 Badaputti

The village Badaputti had 283 households in which 1491 villagers were there, comprising 774 males and 717 females. Around 5.5 per cent of the population belonged to Scheduled Caste category, 353 were literate comprising 264 males and 89 females. Most of the persons were cultivators. 138 villagers were agricultural labourers. Some villagers had also taken livestock, forestry and fishing activities as their occupation.

3.5.3 Kalipali

Most of the villagers belonged to the Reddika community. A total area of 104.19 hectares of land contained 237 households in which 1212 villagers (579 males and 633 females) existed and 114 belonged to the Scheduled Castes. Most of the villagers earned their livelihoods by cultivating their own lands while some were agricultural labourers. Approximately 31 per cent of the total population were literate.

3.5.4 Laxmipur

A total area of 62.97 hectares comprising 52 households having a population of 267 (117 males and 150 females) were to be displaced. Around 27 per cent of population was literate and 4 per cent were workers. Out of a population of 207; 44 were cultivators, 51 were agricultural labourers and 2 villagers were involved in household industry and allied activities.

3.5.5 Paikapada

Paikapada had a total of 371.87 hectares of land, comprising 223 households and a population strength of 983 (438 males and 545 females). In this village approximately 63 per cent of population were Scheduled Caste and 343 villagers were workers. Cultivation was the main occupation of the villagers. In this village 244 marginal workers were there.

3.5.6 Sindhigaon

This village had population strength of 1907 persons. Total land that was about to be acquired was 240.420 hectares. This is a Reddika dominated village with 408 households of which 893 were males and 1014 were females. It included 186 Scheduled Caste men and 225 Scheduled Caste Women. In this village, women were very hard working. Out of a total number of 876 workers, 290 were cultivators, 273 were agricultural labourers, 11 were involved in livestock, forestry and fishing activities and 15 were into manufacturing and processing in non-household industrial activities for their livelihood. So far as the working class was concerned 11 were involved in construction works, 47 in trade and 34 in transport, storage and communication related activities. There were totally 83 marginal workers in this village.

Patrapur, a hamlet coming under Sindhigaon was dominated by Brahmins. Most of its villagers were cultiyators. The lower caste people worked as agricultural labourers, daily wage earners, fishing, trade and commerce activities occupationally.

3.5.7 Sri Ramchandrapur

For the steel plant, total land of 1030.363 acres of land was supposed to be acquired by the Tatas. This village had 741 households with a population of 3601. From this village only agricultural land was planned to be acquired. In this village, 50 per cent of population belonged to the Scheduled Caste category. Most of the villagers numbering 1250 were main workers of which 578 were cultivators, 398 were agricultural labourers and 491 persons were marginal workers. Trade and commerce were pursued by 74 persons. Some had also taken up livestock, forestry, fishing, household industry and allied activities as their occupation.

The demographic details of the project's displaced villages show that cultivation was the main occupation of these areas. Population of Sri Ramchandrapur village was the highest followed by Sindhigaon. The female population is higher than the male in all villages. Maximum number of Scheduled Caste people are there in Sri Ramchandrapur village followed by Paikapada. Kalipalli has the lowest number of Scheduled Caste population. Overall female literacy is low. Sindhigaon and Laxmipur have more number of workers. Proportionately more number of female workers are there in Sindhigaon followed by Laxmipur. Kalipalli village has least number of female workers. Highest numbers of female workers in the form of cultivators are found in Paikapada, followed by Badaputti, whereas Badapur shows the lowest percentage of cultivators and has no female cultivators in the village. Sindhigaon possesses the highest numbers of agricultural labourers. The number of female agricultural labourers is the highest in Laxmipur followed by Sindhigaon.

The income of the local people was derived from natural sources. They earned their livelihood from agriculture, fishing and from sale of coconut, banana, cashew, keora flowers besides being employed in 59 keora scent distillation plants. This area which is densely populated (1041 per sq. km.) has the highest concentration of trees and groves. In Chhatrapur Block, the plant site of a large part of Tata Steel Gopalpur project, the land utilized for trees and groves is 3,152 acres which is the highest in Ganjam district and it is 25 per cent of the net area sown (Govt. of Orissa: 1993; Voice Gopalpur 1996). In fact, Kallipali Panchayat which was to be fully acquired has the highest

Table 3.12: Demographic Details of the Displaced Villages

Sl. No.	Villages	Area (Ha)	House-holds	Population									Total Workers	
				Total			SC		ST		Literate		M	F
				T	M	F	M	F	M	F	M	F		
1.	Badapur	220.15	165	881	434	447	139	141	--	--	262	114	212	37
2.	Badaputti	393.34	283	1491	774	717	42	44	--	--	264	89	386	120
3.	Kalipalli	104.19	237	1212	579	633	49	65	--	--	246	135	319	36
4.	Laxmipur	62.97	52	267	117	150	29	40	--	--	42	31	60	49
5.	Paikapada	371.87	223	983	438	545	166	215	--	--	122	37	226	117
6.	Sindhigaon	240.42	408	1907	893	1014	166	205	--	--	470	214	482	394
7.	Sri Ram-chandrapur	1005.71	741	3601	1745	1856	941	934	--	--	868	174	986	264

Table 3.12: (*Contd.*)

Sl. No.	Villages	Cultivator		Agr. Labour		Marginal Workers		Non-Workers		Trade and Commerce Workers	
		M	F	M	F	M	F	M	F	M	F
1.	Badapur	60	0	113	36	0	0	222	410	6	0
2.	Badaputti	261	44	72	66	3	32	385	565	8	6
3.	Kalipalli	214	14	89	19	28	339	232	258	4	1
4.	Laxmipur	40	4	12	39	0	27	57	74	3	1
5.	Paikapada	118	89	89	23	21	223	191	205	3	2
6.	Sindhigaon	172	118	140	233	18	65	393	555	37	10
7.	Sri Ram-chandrapur	551	27	208	190	12	479	747	1113	65	9

Source: Resettlement and Rehabilitation at Gopalpur prepared by Tata Steel, 1996.

concentration of trees and groves in Chhatrapur Block. The 10 kms width belt adjacent to the seacoast from Chamakhandi, of this area to Srikakulam of Andhra Pradesh spreading over 50 kms is known as the nature's garden, popularly as Udyanam. This garden belt is gradually developing due to nurturing by the local people particularly through plantation of trees like coconut, banana, mango, jack fruit, pine apple and keora.

In this affected area, around 2 crore of keora flowers were sold every year. Keora flowers blossom for six months and one sold a flower at Rs. 4.25. One family earned anywhere between Rs. 5,000 to Rs. 10,000 per month during the season. Around 60 traders from Kaunaj of D.P. were distilling *attar* (scent) from keora flowers. Moreover, ropes made out of the roots of keora plants are sold in Andhra Pradesh and Tamil Nadu. Around 750 acres of land were utilized for keora and 200 acres for cashew. The land in this area is very fertile. The paddy yield rate in the area is 34.15 quintals per hectare compared to 29.69 in Ganjam district and 14.53 in Orissa. Irrigation canals of Rushikulya also flow through this area where more than one crop is grown in a year.

In the name of the proposed Pipalpanka irrigation system, 25 million gallons of water was proposed to be taken to the Tata Steel plant daily. This, in consequence, may affect the Rushikulya irrigation system. The canal system may even dry up which will adversely affect the agricultural production of the district. Besides this, there will be also adverse environmental impact on the sea and marine life due to pollution, which would affect the livelihood of thousands of traditional fishermen of Gopalpur area.

3.6 Overall Profile of the Affected Villages

The demographic profile of the villagers proposed to be displaced for the Tata Steel, Gopalpur Project brings out the following features:

(a) Population of Sri Ramchandrapur village is the highest followed by Sindhigaon. The female population is higher than the male in all villages proposed to be displaced by the plant except in Badaputti.

(b) Sri Ramchandrapur has the highest number of Scheduled Caste population followed by Paikapada. Kalipalli has the lowest number of SC population.

(c) Female literacy rate is very low across all villages.

(d) Sindhigaon and Laxmipur have proportionately higher number of workers. Maximum number of female workers are found in Sindhigaon. It is followed by Laxmipur. Kalipalli village has least number of female workers.

(e) Highest number of female workers in the form of cultivators are found in Paikapada followed by Badaputti whereas Badapur shows the least percentage of cultivators with no females cultivators in the village. In Sindhigaon highest numbers of agricultural labourers are found to exist. The number of female agricultural labourers is highest in Laxmipur followed by Sindhigaon.

(f) Sindhigaon villagers represent highest rate of miscellaneous occupational holders.

(g) None in Badapur village is a marginal worker whereas the highest number of marginal workers is found in Paikapada.

(h) Large number of non-workers are found in Badapur of which females form the majority. One significant point to be made is that in almost all the villages proposed to be displaced relatively greater number of women have not taken to any occupation in comparison to their male counterparts. The Badaputti village stands as an exception to this.

(i) Though eight villages were proposed to be displaced, but hitherto only three villages have been displaced, namely Badapur, Sindhigaon and Patrapur which is a hamlet of Sindhigaon but for purpose of shifting is treated as a separate village. People from Kalipalli and Paikapada were shifted to the rehabilitation colony partially but subsequently a decision was taken not to acquire these villages.

(j) By making a comparative study of the number of households in the pre-displacement phase and the number of families in the post-displacement period, it clearly shows that most of the Sindhigaon people have been shifted to the rehabilitation colony. It is followed by Badapur village and the least number of Kalipalli villagers have been settled in the Tata Resettlement colony. So far as the number of households are concerned, 1033 number of households were there in erstwhile villages. This was reduced to 497 households. The major factor behind it was the ambiguity involved in the displacement of Paikapada and Kalipalli village as it was initially decided to displace them and few households were shifted to the rehabilitation colony but subsequently this decision was revoked but some household continued to stay in the rehabilitation colony.

(k) Inspite of an elapse of 12 years, the Tatas could not set up the proposed steel plant. Various kinds of reasons have been attributed; such as lack of infrastructure to be provided by the government in the form of water supply, railway network and port. There are talks going on with government for converting the land acquired for the purpose into a SEZ which may benefit the state and the affected people. In the meantime, some persons from affected families have been training and having jobs with TISCO at Jamshedpur, but the benefits that would have accrued had the plant come up, have been denied.

(l) Tata Steel, Gopalpur Project has kept the entire projected people's eyes in great suspense for getting more effective work reward. TISCO R&R team in Gopalpur project took a lot of initiative in shifting people to the rehabilitation colony but now some oustees claim that they are really facing terrible problems both mentally and physically. The oustees who are thinking of returning back to their villages are fearful of their once fellow villagers. By protesting against the villagers these people have come to the rehabilitation site. Now they are neither a part of the rehabilitation colony nor a part of the old village. The burning example is Kalipali village. From this village only 14 households have been shifted. Their other relatives are staying in their old village. Old cultural norms and tradition and emotional attachment with the villagers have been broken. As per their views they have lost everything by getting uprooted from their social and moral environment. These families are not in a position to go back to the old villages because of fear psychosis. These victims of ambiguous decisions have been deprived from getting any Government assistance, BPL facilities and such other facilities. This is really a big pathos story in this would be Steel

Plant Project. The project displaced people have taken the severe strains of displacement.

3.7 Brief Outline of Current Situation of Affected and Displaced Villages

A brief outline of the current situation as found from secondary sources is given below.

Affected Villages

1. Jagannathpur (Only Affected not Displaced)
2. Chamakhandi (Only Affected not Displaced)
3. Narendrapur (Only Affected not Displaced)
4. Laxmipur (Only Affected not Displaced)
5. Basanaputti (Only Affected not Displaced)
6. Sitlapalli (Only Affected not Displaced)
7. Bada Kusasthali (Only Affected not Displaced)
8. Sana Kusasthali (Only Affected not Displaced)
9. Madua (Only Affected not Displaced)
10. Luhajhar (Only Affected not Displaced)
11. Mansurkota (Only Affected, not displaced but some families have occupied houses at rehabilitation colony). Most of the families are staying at their original village and rented out the houses in rehabilitation colony. This village had a total of 150 households out of which hardly 5-10 households have lost land. Village was about to be displaced so some people shifted to rehabilitate. Later, decision was changed and TISCO did not acquire the homestead lands or shift the village. They are no longer cultivating the lands because their land falls under the boundary wall area.

Displaced Villages and Population now Residing at Rehabilitation Colony/Tata Colony

1. Sindhigaon—1336
2. Badapur—711
3. Patrapur—483

Villages and Population living in Rehabilitation Colony but not Displaced Nor Affected

They were shifted but TISCO decided not to acquire the villages. Neither agriculture nor homestead land was acquired but they continue to remain at the rehabilitation colony. Many have rented out the houses in rehabilitation colony too. They have not been included in the sample. Such villages and their population are as follows:

1. Paikapada—120
2. Kalipalli—75

Thus, villages and the population residing in the Rehabilitation Colony which include those effectively displaced as well as those neither project affected nor project displaced, are as follows:

1. Sindhigaon—1336
2. Badapur—711
3. Patrapur—483
4. Paikapada—120
5. Kalipalli—75

Total Population in Rehabilitation/Tata Colony—2725

Not included in the Sample/Study

(a) Affected Villages which continue to cultivate their lands in spite of getting compensation have not been included. Other villages are called genuinely affected.

Percentage of Affected Households still Cultivating the Lands

1. Chamakhandi—75 per cent
2. Basanaputti—40 per cent
3. Jagannathpur—25 per cent
4. Laxmipur—75 per cent

(b) Mansurkota—percentage of households who lost lands is very small

(c) From Rehabilitation Site/Villages which were not actually displaced:

1. Paikapada
2. Kalipalli

In short, the present context of our study is rather unique mainly because the project did not take off midway, and the sample has been chosen so as to have a proper representation of 'pre-project' and 'post-project' conditions. In any case Tata's R & R policy had been implemented to a sufficient extent to provide a basis for our study of the impact of displacement, R & R. Therefore the following Chapter IV examines in detail how the R & R Policy was implemented.

IV

Implementation of R & R Policies by the Tata Steel

This chapter provides a critical appraisal of the Resettlement and Rehabilitation (R & R) policies of Tata Steel against the background of the national policy and guidelines of the World Bank. Sections 1 and 2 give an overview of the national R & R policy and that of Government of Orissa. Policy guidelines for selection of displaced persons and villages are given in section 3 while section 4 provides a critical appraisal of the Orissa Policy, 2006. This is followed by a critical appraisal of the National Policy of 2007. In sections 5 and 6, World Bank Guidelines are examined, and issues and recommendations are discussed in section 7. A detailed assessment of Tata Steel's R & R policy is made in section 8 while the programmes implemented especially for the displaced persons to achieve the policy objectives are given in section 9 which happens to be the last section.

The modern development projects in both developed and developing countries including India have caused massive involuntary displacement of human population with little success of the rehabilitation measures adopted for the oustee population in the new resettlement areas. Evidence from the findings of many studies in India and other developed and developing countries, analyzed in the first two chapters of the present work confirms that in the past resettlement rarely worked well. This is mainly due to the absence of a well formulated resettlement and rehabilitation policy by the authorities responsible for the implementation of the development projects in these countries. Needless to say that, after independence, India has implemented many development projects such as large dams, water reservoirs, thermal, hydel and atomic power plants, excavation of mines for exploration of minerals and metals, setting up of large and key industries and the like. Interestingly, further, with a view to achieving the planned goal of balanced development of regions, many such development projects have been promoted in backward and tribal areas of Jharkhand, Bihar, Orissa, Madhya Pradesh, Assam, Uttar Pradesh, Rajasthan, etc. However, it has been observed that people who sacrificed their homes and hearths in the name of development and either willingly or unwillingly finally agreed to resettle in the new areas with the compensation package offered by the Government, have ultimately become the worst victims due to the *ad hoc* resettlement policies and a casual approach. The main reasons for the failure of the resettlement measures are that they deal too much with the technical and economic aspects and ignore the cultural, sociological and ecological aspects of rehabilitation. Even the technical and economic issues relating to resettlement of the oustee population are taken up in a hurry at the top level without any involvement and participation of the affected group in the policy making process.

For a policy of resettlement and rehabilitation, different principles and approaches are often used in policy proposals (Goyal, 1996). They are:

(i) Cash for land.
(ii) Land for land.
(iii) The standard of living approach requiring that standard of living of displaced persons is at least the same after resettlement as before displacement.
(iv) Bargaining approach seeking voluntary resettlement based on collective bargaining between displaced persons and the state (of the project authorities).

4.1 Resettlement and Rehabilitation Policy: The National Scenario

As mentioned earlier, after independence, several developmental projects including major dams, power plants, mining-operations etc. have been carried out to accelerate the tempo of economic development. As a result, millions of people have been displaced from their ancestral homes by these projects. Despite the magnitude of displacement and the longevity of the multiple traumas that most oustees face, one of the most glaring examples of successive Central Governments shunning their constitutional responsibility has been, the lack of a national policy for those who have been forcibly displaced in the 'national interest' (Kothari, 1996). In the last five years, only a Draft of National Rehabilitation Policy has been prepared by the Ministry of Rural Development (MRD) and Water Resources Department (WRD) of Government of India (Fernandes, 1985), which is yet to be made into a law.

In the absence of such a national level policy for rehabilitation, it is left for the project authorities to prepare the plans for rehabilitation and implement them in accordance with various circulars issued by the concerned State Governments. But of late, few State Governments, like Karnataka, Gujarat and Maharashtra, have prepared detailed resettlement and rehabilitation policies to resettle the displaced people.

In post-Independent India the Governments both at the Central and State level designed and launched many large development projects through Five Year Plans in order to accelerate the process of economic development in the country. These development projects basically aimed at strengthening of the infrastructure base and key industries in the public sector such as irrigation and hydro power, iron and steel industries, coal and thermal plants, aluminium and the like to develop and transform the traditional subsistence oriented agriculture and craft economy into a modern industrial economy. However, as discussed earlier, such mega projects especially building of multi-purpose river dams to generate hydro electricity and to provide flow irrigation facility to farmers for rapid agricultural growth, required massive involuntary displacement of human population and relocation of human settlements. In the early phase of the independence, as every citizen of the country was overwhelmed with the joy of freedom and everybody was under the impression that implementation of many such development projects relating to irrigation, power, basic industries and mines would solve the problem of poverty and economic backwardness of people at large, no serious thought was given to the proper resettlement and rehabilitation of the people displaced and negatively affected by such development projects.

As a result, the resettlement plans developed for such project affected persons were purely *ad hoc* and very casual in nature. They were not based on any detailed planning studies to focus on the members to be rehabilitated and the cost of resettlement. The project authorities did not view resettlement of the displaced persons as their responsibility and tended to offload the job to the local authorities. Also for the project authorities as well as the Government, the responsibility of rehabilitation and resettlement of the displaced persons was over the moment they were paid cash compensation for the property acquired by the project. As a result many landless and assetless poor dependant for their livelihood on the project area were deprived of their bread and butter. Secondly, the quantum of compensation on many occasions was determined arbitrarily by the Government and it varied from project to project depending upon the bargaining strength of the displaced people. Thirdly, such cash compensation was often not paid in time and in quite a few cases the oustees continue to fight for just compensation after 30/40 years of completion of the project as in the case of Hirakud Dam in Orissa (Baboo, 1992).

In the past, compensation for land and houses was grossly inadequate and none among the oustees was paid for loss of job/ employment or disruption of livelihood other than farmland. Many such development projects in the past have affected the livelihood of small and marginal farmers, landless labourers, share croppers, tenant cultivators and the collectors of minor forest produce. Even the displacement of the village artisans and other service castes has caused occupational displacement and the threat to survival of such categories of population. In the absence of a clear cut R & R policy in the past, the displaced families were harassed and thrown into a state of destitution by the unscrupulous elements including the project officials. Their illiteracy and ignorance often brought untold miseries and sufferings. In the case of Srisailam Project though the law provided for compensation at the market rate according to the latest land deals in the area, the compensation was arbitrarily fixed by the authorities. Similarly, in the case of Sardar Sarovar Project, it is alleged that terms of acquisition and other procedures were never orally explained to the people and in the process, the illiterate people were cheated by the officers and their intermediaries (CSE, 1985:104). Added to this, there were no clear cut guidelines for the partially affected persons such as individuals who were losing agricultural lands without being physically displaced or the individuals who were losing their houses and/or part of the portion of cultivable lands to the project.

Similarly, although "land for land" is considered a better resettlement measure than mere cash payment, in the past, no effort was being made by the project authorities to rehabilitate the displaced families in the nearby area of the project, particularly in case of irrigation projects where land in the command area could be made available for relocation. The displaced families were sometimes settled in an alien environment and culture. The oustees of Pong dam in Himachal Pradesh were settled in Anupgarh in Rajasthan bordering Pakistan. The policy for rehabilitation of the tribals displaced by Inchampalli and Bhopalpatnam Projects in Maharashtra and the Koel Karo project in Bihar had created similar type of problems for the outsees (CSE, 1985:105).

Till early 1970s, neither the Central Government nor the State Governments in India bothered much about resettlement. Maharashtra is the first State in India, which has a legislation that recognized the rights of the people displaced by irrigation, power and other utility projects to get land in the area benefited by the projects. According to the Maharashtra Resettlement of Project Displaced Persons Act, 1976, the displaced people are granted land in the command area of irrigation projects. While agriculturists get at least half of the land lost by them, agricultural labourers, artisans and other landless people also get one acre of land if they live along with other displaced persons. Under the Act when a project is executed in the State, the Government appoints a Resettlement Officer at the very inception to survey the families to be displaced and identify land in the benefited zone made available for resettlement (CSE, 1985:103).

However, although resettlement of the project displaced persons is now viewed seriously at the all-India level, only four States have enacted state-wise R & R policies for the displaced persons, namely Maharashtra, Madhya Pradesh, Punjab, Karnataka and Rajasthan. Apart from this, however, sector based policies in a number of States have been developed. West Bengal has developed a sector specific R & R policy for the coal mines and Andhra Pradesh, Orissa, Tamil Nadu and Gujarat have issued Government Orders/Resolutions to tackle the problem of displacement in various development projects executed in the respective States. Similarly, at the national level many large national companies like National Thermal Power Corporation (NTPC), Coal India Limited (CIL), and National Aluminium Company (NALCO) have formulated company wide and sector specific policies.

4.2 Resettlement and Rehabilitation Policy by Government of Orissa

With an objective to utilize the vast water resources and mineral resources and to achieve rapid economic growth, the Government of Orissa has undertaken various mega projects. As a result of these development projects about 5 lakh people (nearly 86,110 families) have been displaced. Despite the large scale displacement of people form various state sponsored projects, no uniform and concrete state level resettlement and rehabilitation policy had been formulated by the Government of Orissa till 1994 when the Water Resources Department of Government of Orissa came out with a detailed resettlement and rehabilitation policy due to tremendous pressure from the World Bank which is the major funding agency of various ongoing irrigation projects.

Before 1994 for development projects in Orissa, resettlement and rehabilitation activities were carried out by individual project authorities and were based on a broad set of guidelines issued by Government of Orissa. These Government guidelines have also been revised periodically. Even the criteria keep varying for identifying a person to be displaced and for being eligible to receive the rehabilitation benefits.

A displaced person, according to the Irrigation and Power Department Resolution No. 131619 dated 20.4.1977 means: "A person who on account of the acquisition of his/her lands for the purpose of the major and medium irrigation projects has been displaced from such lands, including any landless and homeless person, who is dependent for his livelihood, by manual labour, on agricultural lands immediately before the area comprising such land is taken up for acquisition by the project and who is being deprived of such livelihood on account of acquisition of the lands" (Circular and Orders, Department of Irrigation, p. 14).

And displaced family means "displaced persons and his or her spouse minor brother(s) or sister(s), father and mother and other members residing with him and dependent on him for their livelihood." In the year 1990, as per the Department of Irrigation Resolution No. 31888, dated 21.8.1990, two more clauses were incorporated in the definition of the family being displaced, viz. (i) a person who is more than 18 years of age irrespective of his marital status, and (ii) physically and mentally retarded person irrespective of their age.

Again in 1992, two more clauses were added to the definition of displaced family by two different resolutions of the irrigation department. As per the Resolution No. 13446 dated 20.4.1994 minor orphans who have lost both parents and have nobody to fall back upon (such orphans numbering more than one in a particular family will be clubbed together and counted as one family), and Resolution No. 25101 dated 14.7.1992 stipulated inclusion of divorcees with or without dependant children but having no source of livelihood. (For the purpose of treating women as divorcee, the claimant should make an affidavit and file her claim along with a copy of such affidavit. After receipt of the claim, the officer-in-charge of rehabilitation shall enquire into the matter and take a decision depending on the merit of the case).

4.3 Policy Guidelines for Selection of Displaced Person and Displaced Village

The R & R policy defines displaced person as "a person who since at least one year or prior to the date of publication of the notification under the section 4 of the Land Acquisition Act, 1894, has been ordinarily residing, and who on account of acquisition of his/her land including homestead land in the submerged zone for the purpose of the project is displaced from such land. This would also include landless labourers."

The policy guidelines also mentioned that for the purpose of selection of displaced village, village submerged will be taken us a unit. Any village where homestead land is not affected or partially affected; but more than 75 per cent of the total agricultural land is acquired, or it is found on due inquiry that partial acquisition of land and property in the submergence zone may lead to socially and economically unviable living, the entire village may be treated as fully submerged village and R & R benefits given to all the villagers as per resettlement and rehabilitation policy.

Again, a person who loses land for the project but is not displaced by the project, is entitled to get compensation for such acquisition, amounting to an equal area of land if unirrigated or half of the area if irrigated but not more than four acres of unirrigated land, as rehabilitation benefit along with reclamation cost.

A person losing his/her only house due to acquisition for the project, but the village is not displaced and who is entitled to get compensation, will be given an equal area of house site subject to maximum of 0.20Ac along with house building assistance as applicable to the oustees.

A person of the affected village who had no landed property whatsoever will not be entitled to any rehabilitation benefit, if the village is not evacuated due to construction of the project, but if the whole village gets relocated, he/she will get the rehabilitation benefits. In case of displacement from encroached government land, rules and procedures as in force in settlement of encroachment will be followed.

4.4 The Orissa Resettlement and Rehabilitation Policy, 2006

In order to ensure sustained development through a participatory and transparent process, the Government of Orissa has framed a comprehensive R & R policy, with the basic objectives of (i) to avoid displacement wherever possible and minimize it, exercising available options otherwise, (ii) to recognize voices of displaced communities emphasizing the needs of the indigenous communities and vulnerable sections, (iii) to ensure environmental sustainability through participatory and transparent process, and (iv) to help guiding the process of developing institutional mechanism for implementation, monitoring, conflict resolution and grievance redressal. The important features of the Policy are:

(i) A major son, unmarried daughter/sister more than 30 years of age, physically and mentally challenged person, minor orphan, a widow or a woman divorcee are treated as a separate family for the purpose of extending rehabilitation benefits.

(ii) Periphery means the district(s) in which the project is geographically situated.

(iii) A socio-economic survey for identification of displaced families; and a socio-cultural, resource mapping and infrastructural survey by an independent agency.

(iv) Consultation with Gram Sabha of Panchayat in scheduled area before initiating land acquisition.

(v) Identity card to displaced family.

(vi) Classification of development projects into five categories such as (a) industrial, (b) mining, (c) irrigation, national park and sanctuaries, (d) urban, and linear projects like roads and railways, power lines, and (e) other projects.

(vii) Rehabilitation assistance will be specific to the types of projects.

(viii) Compensation money through account payee cheque.

(ix) Construction of public property like school building, etc.

(x) Resettlement and rehabilitation after due consultation with displaced communities.

(xi) No physical displacement before the completion of resettlement work.

(xii) Additional compensation amounting to 50 per cent of the normal compensation payable when there are multiple displacements.

(xiii) Immediate declaration of the new resettlement habitat as a Revenue Village.

(xiv) Preference to local persons in the matter of employment.

(xv) In case of industrial projects, Displaced Families (DF) will be eligible for employment by the project causing displacement, the order of preference is as follows: (a) DF losing all land including homestead land, (b) DF losing more than 2/3rd of agricultural land and homestead land, (c) DF losing more than 1/3rd of agricultural land and homestead land, (d) DF losing only homestead land but not agricultural land, and (e) families losing all agricultural land but not homestead land. The upper age limit shall be relaxed by five years.

(xvi) DF and families can get one time cash assistance in lieu of employment/self-employment in the following amount: DF under (a) (as in xv) Rs. 5 lakh, DF under (b) Rs. 3 lakh, DF under (c) Rs. 2 lakh, and families under (d) and (e) Rs. 1 lakh.

(xvii) There are provisions for (a) training for self-employment, (b) convertible preference shares, (c) homestead land, (d) assistance for self-relocation, (e) house building assistance, and (f) shops and service units.

(xviii) In case of mining projects, provisions are very similar except for preference for categories of displaced families.

(xix) There are provisions for (a) homestead land, (b) house building assistance, (c) assistance for agricultural land, and (d) registration cost in R & R package of irrigation etc. projects.

(xx) In urban and linear projects, provisions for homestead land, house building assistance, etc., are available.

(xxi) Benefits are also available to landless and homesteadless encroachers common to all categories.

(xxii) There are various other assistance common to all categories of projects such as (a) maintenance allowance of Rs. 2,000 pm for one year, (b) assistance of Rs. 10,000 for temporary shed to each DF, (c) transport allowance or free transport.

(xxiii) Additional provision for assistance in specific nature of displacement.

(xxiv) Special benefits to displaced indigenous families and primitive tribal groups such as (a) respect to socio-cultural norms, (b) preferential allotment of land, (c) resettlement in a compact area close to their natural habitat, and (d) 25 per cent higher R & R benefits in monetary terms if resettled outside the district.

(xxv) Indexation of rehabilitation grant, periphery development, and many other provisions.

Critical Appraisal

No doubt, at present, the R & R policy of the Government of Orissa is the best in India. The classification of development projects into five categories having specific rehabilitation assistance, and provisions like completion of resettlement work before displacement, immediate declaration of resettlement habitat as a revenue village, special benefits to indigenous communities, preference to local people in matters of employment and special treatment to women, are highly appreciable. There is a strong focus on the modalities of implementation of this Policy. The State Government claims that the present policy draws its strength from the experiences of implementation of past policies, best practices in other states and Orissa Government's Industrial Policy Resolution, 2001. Consultation with various direct and indirect stakeholders including civil society from the state has been conducted, and the views of the academicians, and specialists in the field of resettlement and rehabilitation have been considered by the State Government before formulating this Policy.

The fact is that just four days after Kalinganagar police firing leading to death of 12 tribals on January 6, 2006, the State Government of Orissa (GoO) constituted a Ministerial Committee to finalize such an R & R Policy. The single R & R Policy of GoO has replaced the eleven different sectoral R & R Policies that were operational in Orissa. Compared to National R & R Policy, GoO's R & R Policy is better in many respects. One is that while the National R & R Policy is applicable only where 500 households are displaced in the plains and 250 households in the hilly and scheduled areas, the GoO's R & R Policy does away with any such limitations.

Commenting on the fact that Orissa's R & R Policy was considered to be among the best in the country, the President of Associated Chambers of Commerce and Industry of India (ASSOCHAM) said that it was so good on paper but it has not percolated to the field. The state should sharpen its policy implementation, be proactive in approach and remove road blocks to give much needed propellant to the industries while attracting more and more in the process. The Report, *Orissa Towards Industrialization*, of ASSOCHAM, submitted to the Chief Minister of Orissa, suggests setting up a Social Committee or Task Force to study the nature of the natives and recommend appropriate strategy taking into consideration the localized factors and ensure justice to all parties/stakeholders.

4.5 The National Rehabilitation and Resettlement Policy, 2007

The national policy was announced by Policy Resolution dated 31.10.2007 by Ministry of Rural Development (Department of Land Resources) (Land Reform Division). The aim is to minimize large-scale displacement, as far as possible. The major objectives of National R & R Policy are to (i) minimize displacement, (ii) ensure adequate rehabilitation package and expeditious implementation of the rehabilitation process with the active participation of the affected families, (iii) protect the rights of the weaker sections including SC and ST, (iv) provide better standard of living, and facilitate harmonious relationship between the requiring body and affected families.

Various welcome measures in the Policy are: (i) declaration of tenure holder, tenant, lessee, agricultural and non-agricultural labourers, landless persons, rural artisans, small traders or self-employed as 'affected family', (ii) need of Social Impact Assessment (SIA) and Environment Impact Assessment (if necessary) study of projects, and public hearing, (iii) A base-line survey and census for identification of the persons and families likely to be affected, and publication of the findings of the survey inviting objections and suggestions from all persons likely to be affected, (iv) draft R & R scheme and its discussion in *Gram Sabha* (village council) in rural areas, and in public hearing in urban and rural areas where *Gram Sabha* does not exist.

The benefits for the affected families for rehabilitation and resettlement are as follows: (i) allotment free of cost house site whose house has been acquired or lost, and affected BPL family without homestead land, (ii) allotment of agricultural land or cultivable wasteland whose entire land has been acquired or lost, (iii) preference in allotment of land-for-land in command area of the project, fishing rights in the reservoir, in case of irrigation or hydel projects, (iv) financial assistance for construction of cattle shed, for shifting of the family, building materials, belongings and cattle, for construction of working shed or shop of rural artisan, small trader or self-employed persons, (v) preference in providing employment in the project, allotment of outsourced contracts, (vi) training and scholarship for skill development, (vii) rehabilitation grant in lieu of agricultural land or employment, equivalent to 750 days minimum agricultural wage,

(viii) option to have shares and debentures of the company, (ix) monthly subsistence allowance for one year, (x) pension for life to the vulnerable affected persons, (xi) special provisions and preference for ST and SC, (xii) indexation of rehabilitation grant and other benefits, and (xiii) many others.

The National R & R Policy is silent on the needed overhaul of the L.A. Act. In fact, that Act is implicitly present behind the policy (Iyer, 2007). Compensation under the L.A. Act had to be paid for the land or property taken over, based on historical cost plus a solatium, but the concept of replacement cost was unknown. The compensation amount was not a negotiated sum, but a figure fixed by the government officials under certain rules. The figure could be contested under the Act. But, the 'public purpose' for which the state proposed to acquire private property and land was not open to contestation. There was great deal of dissatisfaction with the Act (*Ibid.*).

Of course, due to various problems arising out of L.A. Act, 1994 (such as acquiring land from farmers at very low price and leasing/ selling out plots out of it to industrial units or SEZ or in the contiguous SEZ at higher price, as in Kalinganagar), the Act is being amended. The major change proposed is to require companies seeking land to buy it from willing sellers by negotiations. The government will step in only after the company has acquired at least 70 per cent of the land needed. After which, the government will use the provision of the Act to acquire the land of the holdouts, if any. However, the holdouts will be paid the same price as that established by the negotiated sales with the willing owners of 70 per cent of land needed. This process is underway in a number of proposed SEZs in the country.

However, the amendment does not solve the problem of acquisition of land for infrastructure projects implemented by government departments such as the PWD, railways, or for strategic or defence purpose. In case of compulsory acquisition, the important change required is to pay the former the replacement cost of the asset being acquired at the time he receives the compensation.

The Government of Orissa has asked the Centre for some clarifications and raised some objections to National R & R Policy and the proposed amendment to L.A. Act. First, the provision in the L.A. Act that the government will step in only after the company has acquired 70 per cent of the land needed from the willing land owners will create problem in the state of Orissa. In Orissa, no one can purchase land directly from the tribals without the prior permission of the government. In this case, how the company will purchase land from the tribals is not explained. Second, it is not clearly mentioned in the National R & R Policy, whether rehabilitation and resettlement benefits will be available to the displaced persons of the villages involving involuntary displacement of less than 400 in plain areas, or 200 in tribal or hilly areas. Third, there is no clarification about the availability of R & R benefits to the willing sellers of 70 per cent of land needed for the project. The Government of Orissa, through the Chief Secretary has written a letter to the Secretary, Ministry of Rural Development asking to amend the proposed measures to rectify the defects and anomalies in the proposed Acts (*Samaj*: 16.5.08).

Various criticisms are levelled against National R & R Policy (e.g., Singh, 2006). First, the policy contains little that would operationalize the first objective of minimizing displacement. Second, the problem with the definition of 'affected family' is that the term 'substantially' has not been defined. So, the classification of families will be made by the acquiring authority on its discretion. Third, there is no R & R benefit except *ex gratia* cash payment to the persons displaced by linear acquisition of land. Fourth, there is also no credible method in the National R & R Policy by which the community can ensure that it is consulted, and that its views are given due importance. Fifth, though most of the issues are acknowledged, the policy appears to leave specific issues, such as grievances redressal and monitoring mechanism, etc., to the discretion of the acquiring bodies. The National R & R Policy is not only toothless but also unconvincing—for all its numerous politically correct statements are either accompanied by their own contradictions or unsupported by any concrete action plan (*Ibid.*).

4.6 The World Bank Guideline

The World Bank guidelines are intended to improve the livelihoods that Bank-financed projects will achieve through its objectives of Operational Policy on involuntary resettlement such as:

(i) to avoid or minimize adverse impacts and to conceive and execute resettlement activities as sustainable development programmes,

(ii) to give displaced persons opportunities to participate in the design and implementation of resettlement programmes, and

(iii) to assist displaced persons in their efforts to improve their livelihoods and standards of living, or at least to restore these to pre-project levels.

Some of the recurring lessons derived by the World Bank from its projects are (*Ibid.*):

(i) Systematic resettlement planning is important.

(ii) An early start is often the key to effective planning.

(iii) Effective plans should be crafted to fit the particular project context.

(iv) Effective plans should elicit positive response from the affected population.

(v) Resettlement plans should be conceived as development opportunities.

(vi) Resettlements should not be conceived as blueprints.

(vii) Early resettlement supervision should identify any need to make changes.

(viii) Close monitoring of resettlement should continue until the likelihood of achieving resettlement objectives is established.

(ix) Outstanding resettlement issues should be documented at project completion and discussed between the Bank and the borrower (*Ibid.*).

4.7 Issues and Recommendations

In the past, in the absence of a national policy on rehabilitation, different projects as well as different policies to resettle the displaced persons were followed by different State Governments. In Orissa also, we find different policy norms for different projects. There was no unambiguous policy of rehabilitation for the displaced people of Machhkund Hydel project. The *ad hoc* policy measures adopted in the case of Hirakud Dam, RSP, and Balimela project brought miseries to the displaced persons (Sahu, 2000). The rehabilitation policy followed by NALCO Angul Sector was one of the best in India because it directly provided employment to the members of the displaced families, and provided training facilities to the unemployed members of the displaced families to get training at the cost of the Company to get employment in NALCO complex. The people in the nearby area had a vested interest to be displaced and affected by NALCO, so that they could get various benefits. The policy of NALCO set a trend for provision of jobs to displaced persons by other companies like MCL.

The rights of the development project-induced displaced persons are also not guaranteed by the legal and constitutional framework of the country. Due to this, even the best intended rehabilitation and resettlement package has created some undue burden. Involuntary displacement, resettlement and rehabilitation is a complex process. The misunderstanding of this complex process by the authorities is appalling in India. But if the resettlement policy is implemented in a proper way, the socio-economic conditions of the displaced persons may even improve after displacement. For preparing a correct and suitable policy of resettlement and rehabilitation, rigorous economic research on displacement, resettlement and rehabilitation is absolutely necessary.

While tackling the problems of R & R Policy, in general, the following points may be considered favourably: (i) acquisition of land by the government/project authority on offer price basis, (ii) resettlement of people of a particular village en bloc in one resettlement colony, particularly in the same eco-cultural zone, (iii) an accurate baseline survey in the affected area, (iv) maintenance allowance for two years from the date of displacement, (v) compensation money in joint account of both the spouses in a scheduled commercial bank, (similarly joint holding in case of land-for-land rehabilitation), (vi) at least 10 per cent reservation for displaced persons at concessional price during sale/allocation of government land for houses in the capital/urban centre, (vii) independent evaluation of resettlement work by a research institute, (viii) universal application of the enhanced compensation under Sections 18 and 28(A) of the Land Acquisition Act to all individuals, where on the basis of court verdict and cases filed, one individual is awarded additional benefits by the government/project authority, (ix) afforestation in replaced land, earmarking land for burial ground, grazing land, cultural shrines, temples, community centres, etc., (x) economic rehabilitation plan in association with the displaced persons, and (xi) consideration of all types of costs and benefits during cost-benefit analysis.

In case of displacement by dams, (i) if land-based rehabilitation, (a) offering land free from all types of encumbrances to displaced persons, (b) final *patta* within three months, and (c) total land in a particular consolidated patch to a displaced person, and no forest land for resettlement, (ii) resettlement of displaced persons in command area by acquiring land at least 20 per cent from people living in the adjacent area (since their land value will rise), and on government land and wasteland in the potential command area, (iii) proper care of occupational displacement, (iv) free electricity for at least five years from the project-generated power, (v) transport of belongings, bovine population as well family members by government/ project authority, and (v) tent, medical facility, drinking water, cooked food in the transit period for three months.

At present, the major controversy is around mega industrial projects and SEZ, where the potential displaced persons are agitating against their displacement, though the people in Orissa were demanding a second steel plant in the state three decades ago. In case of industry, it is in better position to rehabilitate the displaced persons, compared to dam projects. It is to be mentioned that land is a valuable, productive and non-depreciating asset. The first-generation effect may not be harmful for displaced persons, if rehabilitated through employment in the project. But the second-generation effect will be harmful in the form of (i) fall in capability and power of entitlement, and (ii) land and environment pollution.

Therefore, it is desirable to find out regular and sustainable flow of income for affected people such as: (i) earmarking, every year, a certain percentage of the total net profit earned by the industrial project for social and economic infrastructure of the residential area of the displaced persons, (ii) offering certain number of shares to the affected persons on the basis of their annual earning from their land/assets and from common property resources (e.g., water bodies, forest, grazing land, etc.), or (iii) land on lease renewable every 10 years, annual lease value equal to the earning from the land and giving options to the land owner to sell if he likes at any time.

Secondly, exclusive preference must be given to the displaced persons of the industrial projects for (i) work and contract during the construction stage of the project, (ii) potential shops/establishments on lease/outright grant, near factory/residential area to be constructed by the project authority, (iii) all contracts (e.g., transport, supply of services, security, plumbing, milk supply, etc.), and (iv) ancillary development and downstream industries through provision of shed/capital/fund to start the units.

Third, all services (such as school, hospital, road, electricity, water supply) to be supplied to the project-displaced persons should be similar to that of the employees of the unit.

Fourth, classification of displaced persons is a must, as in the case of NALCO Angul sector, to determine the R & R package.

Fifth, the site for the industry should be selected at the place where the number of displaced persons will be the least. So, the land required for an industrial project must be seriously examined since it is seen from past experiences that the project authorities usually ask for more land than the required amount.

We should also remember that landlessness and improper R & R Policy after forceful land acquisition are some of the causes of Naxalite violence, as mentioned by a high power committee, set up by Planning Commission in 2006, headed by D. Bandhopadhyay. The other members are Prakash Singh, Ajit Doval, B.D. Sharma, Sukhdeo Thorat and K. Balgopal. The Committee has asked the government to first deal with the problem of landlessness, ensure livelihood, and have an effective land acquisition, rehabilitation and resettlement policy. It also recommended that landless poor occupying government land should not be treated as encroachers. Instead, they should be declared as deemed *patta* holders on "as is where is" basis (*TOI*, 2008).

The Report mentioned that "public purpose" in the Land Acquisition Act should be limited to national security and public welfare, and should not be stretched to acquisition for companies, cooperatives and registered societies. Moreover, the concept of 'public purpose', in the view of economists, is related to the provision of 'public good' which includes economic and social infrastructure.

Michael Cernea (2008) identifies the major causes of impoverishment and the types of benefit sharing with the affected and displaced population, followed in various countries, which are given as follows.

Causes of Impoverishment

1. Gap between compensation in theory and compensation in practice,
2. Limited resources of the project allotted for the affected population,
3. Absence of benefit sharing—share options to dividends to multiple incentives, and
4. Compensation is not a benefit only a restitution.

Five Mechanisms of Benefit Sharing which have been Adopted in Various Countries

1. Columbia, China and Brazil—Direct transfer of a share of the royalties from hydropower to finance specific post relocation area development schemes.
2. China, Brazil—Revolving development funds established through fixed allocation or augmented through replenishment rounds. While the principal of those funds is being saved and preserved, the interest generated from the principal is used for stimulating development after relocation.
3. Canada—Equity sharing in the new projects created enterprises (and other potentials) through various forms of co-ownership.
4. Norway—Special taxes paid to regional and local governments, additional to the general tax system. These are to supplement local development in the impacted demographic/geographic area by financing additional programmes and initiatives.
5. Several countries—Allocation of electric power on a regular and mandated basis; or the granting of preferential electricity rates; lower water fees; or other forms of access to in kind benefits.

4.8 Resettlement and Rehabilitation Policy of Tata Steel Project at Gopalpur

At the time of initiation of Tata Steel Project at Gopalpur, Orissa was among the first few states to bring out a comprehensive Resettlement and Rehabilitation Policy for water resources projects. However, at that time there was no such policy for industrial or other developmental projects either in the State or at the national level. In a way, this is understandable since R & R issues are site and project specific. As a result, the R & R plans for any project have to be evolved taking into consideration the needs of the local population, their socio-economic conditions and the available infrastructure facilities.

The Resettlement and Rehabilitation plan suggested for Gopalpur, which has been prepared after careful consideration to ensure total rehabilitation, could form a useful basis for the development of a State and National Policy for resettlement.

The R & R plan for the steel plant project of Tata Steel at Gopalpur forms a crucial component of the project and has been prepared after incorporating significant improvements over the earlier R & R plans implemented in other developmental projects as well as after drawing upon the past rehabilitation experiences of some of the completed projects. In preparation of this R & R plan, three major initiatives have been taken:

- On the policy front, a comprehensive plan has been prepared.
- On the institutional front, a structure is being established delineating responsibilities for individual R & R activities.
- Continued commitment of Tata Steel towards the long term sustainability of the resettled villages.

The Resettlement and Rehabilitation plan is aimed at making provisions for ensuring total Rehabilitation. The primary objective of the policy is that the economic condition of the project affected persons must improve significantly after resettlement and rehabilitation. The rehabilitation measures besides providing compensations, and means of livelihood, have included steps for physical, social, economic, educational, environmental, occupational and cultural development. For realizing these goals, the main thrust of the R & R programme has ensured:

- That the displaced people are physically resettled in a manner which represents their rights and takes cognizance of their dignity as individuals.
- The conversion of displacement into a potential beneficial opportunity for the economic betterment of the inhabitants.
- Full integration with the host communities on the basis of equality, mutual respect and understanding.
- Appropriate supporting community services.
- Ecologically self-sustainable resettlement site.

Towards these objectives, the R & R plan has envisaged:

- Expansion of definition of family to include: unmarried daughters, divorcee women, widows, physically and mentally retarded persons, and minor orphans.
- Empowerment of women by protecting their rights to property.
- Improved entitlements to those displaced and enhancement of rehabilitation and resettlement grants.
- Entitlements for homesteadless and landless encroachers.
- Providing access to training and employment opportunities in the new project and Government aided poverty alleviation programmes.
- Monitoring and evaluation including evaluation of the developmental impact by independent consultants.

The process of resettlement is being viewed in this exercise *as a short term inconvenience for some, for sustained long term benefit not only for those displaced but for the State and the Country as a whole*. The resettlement of any family from a well established household, however poor, brings in a feeling of a certain amount of trauma. It leads to the *fear of the unknown*. Issues like extent of benefits (fair and unfair), the suitability of the place of resettlement, ability to adjust to the new surroundings, uncertainty about the future income, overall peace and tranquillity in the new surroundings, etc., haunt the families. They dread the possible disintegration of their previous background, spiritual values and loss of individuality. These are often exploited by opportunistic groups to meet their own ends.

Lack of proper information often about the future adds to confusion and distress. Specific measures have been taken in this particular case to counter these misgivings by providing accurate information, establishing a communication centre at Chhatrapur and arranging widespread access to official communications by way of newsletters, audio-visuals, print media articles, etc. Several opinion groups comprising local youth, senior citizens and students from nearby educational institutions have also been formed to facilitate communication.

4.9 Implementation of Resettlement and Rehabilitation Policy by Tata Steel

Tata Steel, Gopalpur project formed a rehabilitation package for its project affected and displaced people. It has taken up a comprehensive rehabilitation policy brought out by the State of Orissa for various water resource projects, even though there are similar policies for industrial or other synonymous projects in the state. The Rehabilitation plan for this project has been evolved taking into consideration the needs of the local population, their socio-economic condition and the available infrastructure facilities as the needs differ from locality to locality.

- This proposed plan suggested for Tata Steel has been prepared after careful consideration to ensure total rehabilitation which could from a useful basis for development of the state policy. These measures for rehabilitation besides providing compensation and means of livelihood have taken steps for physical, social, economic and educational, environmental, occupational and cultural developments.

The rehabilitation plan has been widened to include unmarried daughters, divorcees, widow, physically and mentally retarded persons and minor orphans within the definitions of a family, empowerment of women by protecting their rights to property, improved entitlement to those displaced and enhancement of rehabilitation grants, entitlement for homesteadless and landless encroachers, providing access to training and employment opportunities in the new projects and Government aided poverty alleviation programmes. Monitoring and evaluation of development impact by independent consultants is also one of the components.

4.9.1 Rehabilitation Package of Tata Steel, Gopalpur

The whole package is as follows:

The family or person shall be eligible for rehabilitation benefit if:

- All the land of the family has been acquired;
- More than one-third of land has been acquired;
- Only homestead land has been acquired; and
- Disabled and mentally retarded persons and landless person residing in the village.

Committee consisting of representative of the Steel Plant, IDCO and the State Government (Collector of the district or his representative) shall conduct joint enquiry to determine the number of displaced persons on the basis of eligibility criteria.

Employment and Training

Effort would be made to facilitate employment of members of displaced families in the Steel Plant and ancillary industries to the extent possible. The Steel plant would give preference to the members of the displaced families for employment in the steel plant or in any other ancillary or auxiliary or service industries or activities under the aegis of the steel plant consistent with the skills of persons and the need of the job.

The Tata steel will soon establish a technical training school at Gopalpur and will train the youths of the area in this institute as well as in other public institutions in order to make them suitable for availing of the employment opportunities that will emerge during the construction and with the commissioning of the steel plant and several ancillary units. Subsequently employment preference will be given to the eligible youths of the displaced families.

During the initial period of construction of the rehabilitation colony and the plant, a number of people will be required by various constructing firms. The steel plant will ensure that preference is given to the persons of the displaced families for employment in these firms.

Definition of Family for the Purpose of Rehabilitation

The family in relation to a displaced family would mean: Husband and Wife as the case may be, and their sons and major unmarried daughters. All major sons of a family who are not separated as on the date of notification (i) of the Land Acquisition Act in respect of village shall be treated as one more family. The following categories of persons shall also be treated as separate family.

(i) The unmarried daughter who is more than 30 years of age.
(ii) The divorced or deserted women and widows having no source of livelihood;
(iii) Physically and mentally retarded persons irrespective of all age and sex; and
(iv) Minor orphans who have lost their parents and have nobody to fall back upon. Such orphans numbering more than one in a particular family will be clubbed together and counted as one family.

Homestead Land and Displaced Families

Each displaced family will be given 1/10th acre of land for homestead purpose free of cost with developed infrastructure.

Rehabilitation Colonies

Village community centre, school buildings, water supply facilities, electrical facilities, dispensary and other facilities of model colony are to be provided as a part of infrastructure development.

Assistance for Setting up of Temporary Shed

A sum of Rs. 3,000 is to be paid to each displaced family for setting up of temporary shed.

Facilities to be Extended for Homesteadless and Landless Encroachers

Encroachers who are homesteadless persons (as defined in Orissa

Public Land Encroachers Act) and not entitled for any compensation under the Land Acquisition Act will get gratia/one time solatium towards dwelling houses, constructed on Government land at the flat rate of Rs. 15,000 per family irrespective of the value of such dwelling houses. They will also get one-tenth acre of land per family for homestead purpose in the rehabilitation colony.

Encroachers who are landless (as defined under Orissa Public Land Encroachers Act) and not entitled for any compensation under the Land Acquisition Act will get *ex-gratia*/one time solatium equal to compensation to the maximum of one standard acre of land. The solatium will be proportionately less by the amount that the encroached land is less than the standard acre.

Maintenance Allowance

In order to ensure quick rehabilitation and resettlement a maintenance allowance of Rs. 500 per month per family shall be paid for a maximum period of one year from the date the family vacates the site. This will be admissible only to those families who vacate the site by the date fixed by the collector. While fixing this date, the Collector will take into account the payment of compensation and deadlines of the rehabilitation site.

Self-Rehabilitation

A grant of Rs. 300 will be provided towards self-rehabilitation on the option of the displaced persons.

Keeping in view the income of the local people out of the collection of keora leaves and flowers from the public land going to be acquired for the steel plant, it is proposed to carry out compensatory plantation of keora in the nearby vicinity.

Tata Steel will build in the rehabilitation colony dwelling houses for such families who would lose their houses in the land acquired by the steel plant on a house per house basis with a plinth area of approximately 250 sq.ft per house. If such families deposit the compensation they would receive the house. Any person getting a higher compensation for this house will also have the option to get such a house to be constructed by the steel plant.

The estimate of compensation would be made in a liberal and realistic manner. The expenditure in respect of rehabilitation packages as indicated above shall be borne by the steel plant.

The oustees had been assisted in availing of the announced rehabilitation package with the functional assistance of land acquisition office, Chhatrapur; revenue department, communication team and Rehabilitation and Resettlement team of Tata Steel and some agencies assigned for completing the task.

As per the earlier discussion in this chapter, the degree of effectiveness of such sensitive measures has to be analyzed against the evolution of the entire rehabilitation programme of Tata Steel and has been illustrated in the subsequent parts of the chapter. In addition to the declared rehabilitation package provided to the displaced persons, for implementation of various suitable innovative programmes Tata Steel had hired the services of some organizations on consultancy basis and whenever required, extra financial assistance was provided by the Tata Steel. In this way the most sensitive issue of this development project which was 'rehabilitation', had been given special attention.

4.9.2 Agencies Involved in Rehabilitation

For effective rehabilitation of the oustees, Tata Steel had appointed some agencies. In order to mitigate the socio-economic disparities caused by involuntary displacement of population, TISCO first chose 'Gram Vikas', a voluntary organization functioning at Mohuda, on the outskirts of Berhampur. This organization in its first step of intervention tried to give counselling in favour of self-sufficiency. It tried to form certain income generating groups as these projects displaced people were well acquainted with the group savings and expenditure system. But this organization could not meet the functionality requirement of Tata Steel for implementing the rehabilitation package properly. Tata Steel appointed evaluation machinery and then these sensitive responsibilities had to be bestowed to a consultancy. It was felt that things would be taken up with much more emphasis if they took one of their consultancy groups and eventually Tata Steel selected a consultancy of their own group, namely Tata Consultancy Services (TCS).

Role of Tata Consultancy Services (TCS) in Rehabilitation

Tata Consultancy Services played some logistic role in the sphere of rehabilitation for project displaced persons. It attempted to provide rehabilitation amenities in three major areas as per as the suitability of the oustees. TCS team first interacted with the displaced families. In the first phase of resettlement in the site these families suffered from maladjustment in the new environment. The team heard their suffering keenly with empathy, and counselled them. In the first six months of its functioning TCS conducted periodic surveys.

Procedure Adopted

Questionnaire and Survey formats of total family profile, their economic status, and immediate problems arising out of shifting, occupation and the details of current potential of the families were collected and collated. Taking the inputs of such survey, various plans were implemented in the rehabilitation site. Different responsibilities were given as per the potential of the members. The requirements of the project displaced persons were intimated to the Tata Steel through their monthly evaluation meetings.

Major Rehabilitation Programmes

Major areas in which TCS had intervened for proper rehabilitation of displaced persons on priority basis are:

(a) Land Based or Farm based
(b) Livestock Based
(c) Entrepreneurship based

Land Based Programmes

In the rehabilitation site, the villagers had been provided 10 decimals of land each, including residential house. The 10 decimal piece of land measuring 4357 sq.ft includes 267 sq.ft of a pucca house. The remaining land was utilized for cultivation, the yield of which would at least meet the daily consumption expenses. The cultivation of vegetables, horticulture trees and floral plants were encouraged by TCS. The proper maintenance of such programmes was sensitized within the minds of DP's in the immediate phase consequent to resettlement. Technical Support in the shape of insecticides from the horticultural department and other related activities were given by TCS. The oustees got other benefits from vegetable cultivation, besides meeting the household consumption needs. In few cases there was a domestic surplus too which could be marketed. During August 1999, the first monetary returns started coming in from the various seedlings which had been distributed in the rehabilitation site. The seasonal seeds were brought from reputed vegetable retailers. For floriculture cultivation tuberose bulbs, rose twigs and marigold seedlings were brought from the nearby village nurseries. The Horticulture Department of Berhampur provided wholehearted support in this context. Vegetables cultivation was not a new thing for the villagers of New Badapur and New Paikapada. Special care was taken so that the Scheduled Caste People would get at least part of their daily consumption from the kitchen garden activities.

By getting financial assistance from TISCO, TCS had raised a nursery in New Badapur village at the rehabilitation site. From the nursery, saplings were supplied to the displaced persons. Nursery raising was aimed as a permanent feature in the site so that it could be imbibed with cultivation besides their own occupations. Saplings from Government nurseries were supplied at a reasonable cost. For the floriculture programme, TCS had made marketing channels at Berhampur. All sorts of motivation and demonstration efforts had been taken up to create a sense of ownership of this programme. By getting special sanction from the District Rural Development Agency (DRDA) irrigation wells were dug on the concurrent opinion of the oustees.

Livestock Based

Employment through livestock based activities was one of the major rehabilitation programmes. All liaisoning and motivation efforts for this had been taken up by TCS and also for sanctioning of dairy loans and organizing health check-up camps at regular intervals of time.

Coordination was established with the Veterinary Department to ensure the identification of real beneficiaries among the displaced persons who would take ownership of the livestock activities. Identification of the dairy beneficiaries was done through base line survey and organizing meetings with the village members in the rehabilitation site in association with bank and blocks officials. Follow-up action was carried out by the block and bank (Indian Overseas Bank at Narendrapur) to identify the previous bank loans. Counselling was given to those defaulters to clear up the bank dues and to get the advantages of fresh loans as per their requirements. Due to the thrust given by the District Administration for the early distributing of dairy loans, six beneficiaries such as 3 from New Patrapur, 2 from New Badapur and 1 from New Kalipalli were sanctioned loans for cows in August 1998.

Village meetings were organized at regular intervals and in those public meetings the defaulters were not only motivated to clear up previous loans but also for organizing and constituting a dairy society in the rehabilitation colony. Disbursement of IRDP (Integrated Rural Development Programme) dairy loans created a demonstration effect in the site.

Assistance through Various Schemes

Discussions were held regarding the present loan position in the rehabilitation colony as also about prospects of other schemes apart from Government Subsidy schemes like IRDP and PMRY. Possibilities of providing loans under Differential Rated of Interest (DRI) were also discussed at length. With references to letters of Project Director of DRDA and consultation with manager of Indian Overseas Bank, Narendrapur, loans were provided for both dairy and non-dairy schemes. A meeting was also organized in August 1998 with AGM, NABARD to find out the possibilities of any funding for development of tiny and cottage industries as well as direct loans for the Business sector.

Dairy Society

A dairy society, namely 'Siddhabhairabi Milk Society' was formed by the oustees of the site. The society was being run by a committee formed with the displaced persons as members for smooth running of the dairy business. With the purpose of earning more profit in a streamlined manner, it was linked up with the Greater Ganjam Gajapati Milk Union (GGGMU) of the district. Timely collection of milk, repayment of loans by directing certain amount, maintaining quality, monthly health check-ups of the animals by the veterinary department were the main objectives being coordinated by the 'Siddhabhairabi Milk Society'. Most of the beneficiaries were allowed their preference for a second cow. The dairy beneficiaries supplied milk to the society.

Entrepreneurship Based Activities

To provide for daily livelihood for the displaced persons various entrepreneurship activities were explored. During the first six months after shifting emphasis was put on women empowerment by involving them in the different village and cottage industries activities. Women belonging to the same economic group were brought under one umbrella by forming certain saving and credit groups, namely SHGs. These groups were imparted training in various activities like Leaf Plate Making (Khali), Paper bag making (Thunga), Mushroom Cultivation, Papad Rolling, Spice Making, Agarbati (Incense Stick) making and kitchen gardening. Some of the displaced persons took up certain activities mentioned, by making their own investments. The various programmes have been illustrated briefly as follows:

Self-help group is a blending of members having homogeneity in their economic and social status. The members forming the group decide to save a certain amount at regular intervals weekly or fortnightly or monthly. The saving amount is determined on the basis of their family income. A daily wage earner's income would be less than the expenditure. Therefore, it would not be possible to go for long term saving. At the time of celebrating social functions like marriage, thread ceremony, local festival or in case of contingencies like medical treatment or funeral rituals etc. these people at the lower income levels seek loans from moneylenders at exorbitant interest rates and even sometimes the lands are deceptively usurped by such moneylenders.

By taking into account the problems of the people in the downtrodden especially in rural areas, Mohd. Yunus of Bangladesh started forming the groups from people of the same economic background. They were saving some amount and keeping in a common fund. At the time of requirement the member can take the requisite amount from the common fund collected from members. As per the common agreement made by the members, the loanee members have to repay the principal along with the interest within the stipulated time.

After getting a positive response for improving the economic status of the rural poor, this saving and credit group concept was adopted by other South East Asian countries. These groups are popularly known as Self-Help Groups or Saving and Credit Groups or Saving and Thrift Groups. They have been taken as one of the vital financial institutions for building the backbone of the rural economy.

SHGs in Tata Rehabilitation Colony

In the rehabilitation colony a total of 21 Self Help Groups were functioning out of which two groups had already started their activities prior to shifting to the site. In total 270 members within the age group of 18 to 35 years were brought under the arm of SHG. Each member was depositing Rs. 10 per week or Rs. 50 per month as per the decision taken by all members. Two old groups, one of them being Radhakrishna Nari Sangha of Sindhigaon, had been registered under the Societies Registration Act, 1860. For smooth and easy implementation of various plans an apex level body had been formed in Tata colony, namely 'Izzat Mahila Samitee'.

Izzat Mahila Samitee

By including the executive body members of every Self Help Group, 'Izzat Mahila Samitee' had been formed. From among the members, ageing executive body members had been selected on the basis of democratic election. They were working with the help of TCS during the first six months of its formation. In the subsequent stages they were organizing meetings, preparing agendas, discussing minutely about the day-to-day occupational problems in the rehabilitation site and in most cases they took the assistance of TCS members. The financial status of every SHG in the site was discussed in the meeting. They were trying to resolve the problems arising out of delay in depositing savings, repayment of credit, sanctioning of loans to kith and kin among members, misunderstanding among members and other issues without the intervention of male counterparts of their families.

Activities Undertaken by SHGs

(a) Leaf Plate (Khali) Making

Based on people's demand a training programme for 6 new persons was organized in New Patrapur and New Badapur village in the month of August 1998. In addition to this 10 new persons took up leaf plate making as an Income Generation Programme (IGP). Several attempts were made to make the beneficiaries self-sustainable in a phase-wise manner so that they could operate the whole production cycle independently. In the Initial Period they were motivated to deposit the leaf plates at a common place and from therewith help of the TCS members they were selling the products in the nearby markets in and around Berhampur. The price of this product varied from Rs.15 to Rs. 25 per 100 leaf plates according to the stitching quality and the size. Due to a lean season most of the women were engaged at the nearby villages and therefore, they were unable to prepare leaf plates. For easy supply of raw material stitched leaf plates were procured from the Tikabali co-operative Society at Berhampur.

(b) Paper Bag (Thunga)

From a preliminary market survey conducted, it was revealed that paper bags were very much in demand by shops in the rehabilitation site and the nearby areas. During August 1998, training was imparted to 11 persons from which five took paper bag making as an income generation programme. But after eight months of starting their activities, it did not pick up in the markets as most of the business enterprises were using polythene bags for their business. The people gradually withdrew from this activity.

(c) Mushroom Cultivation

Mushroom Cultivation was taken up for the first time in the colony. Required technical assistance was imparted by the experts and mushrooms were sold in the local market. One of the womens' groups took this activity for generating income. They got profits by producing three production cycles of mushroom.

(d) Spice Making

One of the Self Help Groups, namely 'Maa Thakurani Mahila Sanchay Dal' of new Badapur started making spices. The members were given access to a modern weighing machine by TCS for better weighing which helped them in reducing the weight loss during packaging. Initially the group purchased the raw materials but over a month, were unable to pack the products. Nearly all the SHG members were engaged in cultivation in the nearby villages. After observing profits in packing turmeric powder, they started preparing chilly and curry powder. These products were sold in the local markets.

(e) Papad Making

Papad making is one of the traditional activities in which many housewives in and around Berhampur are involved. This activity was explored for economically empowering the oustees. In the month of August 1998 training was imparted to two displaced persons (women) of new Badapur. On a trial basis they were supplied with the raw materials. A training-cum-demonstration programme was conducted for a week in the first phase. Due to bad weather, the profit incurred was very less. The oustees were unable to take up this activity in the first phase of four months.

(f) Financial Assistance

For women empowerment District Rural Development Agency (DRDA) through Rangeilunda Block had provided finance to 9 SHGs under Development of Women and Children in Rural Area (DWCRA) scheme. Each group was provided with Rs. 25,000 and from this amount the members were given their share who were to take up various occupations with a condition of returning the amount to the group fund so that the grant could be utilized by the other members of the group for taking up any alternate income generation programmes. By utilizing the fund, 39 members from 6 SHGs were motivated to take up these activities occupationally. But finally only 14 members showed interest. Some women trainees were taken to Bhubaneswar to explore the quality of Lizzat Papad and procure equipment for production. All the interested beneficiaries were provided with raw material and necessary equipment. Papad making was carried out at a particular training centre in the site. To centralize this activity one male oustee had been engaged for preparing the dough, its distribution, collecting rolled papad and drying and packing of papad.

A grand total of Rs. 45,000 DWCRA fund from 30 women members was invested out of which Rs. 15,000 went towards labour charges, Rs. 10,000 for producing fixed assets and Rs. 20,000 was utilized for purchasing raw materials.

(g) Implications

Due to certain reasons, the first phase of production incurred a loss of Rs. 1,000. The reasons were:

- Lack of quality even through several times effort was made to sell with a brand name of 'Izzat Papad' as compared with 'Lizzat Papad'.
- Papad making procedure was experimented with for seven times which brought fatigue within the minds of displaced persons engaged in this activity.
- The daily return from the production was not lucrative and was much less than their expectations. Although it was a part time income generation programme yet members who produced papad, involving themselves fully and expected high return of Rs. 30 to Rs. 35 per day.
- The beneficiaries were not interested in taking financial risks and they did prefer to produce individually. It did not get wholehearted support in spite of the fact that by getting good profits they could have at least added to their prime source

of income in the long run; rather the members wanted immediate returns.

- The marketing assurance given by TCS was found to be a distant reality. Full-fledged production led to dumping and towards the last part of the first phase of production papads were sold at a lower price incurring heavy loss. After a lot of starting trouble, desperation among the women members set in and this activity was abruptly stopped.

Activity under SGSY Scheme

In place of Development of Women and Children in Rural Area (DWCRA), Supply of Indigenous Tools for Rural Areas (SITRA), Integrated Rural Development Programme (IRDP) schemes, a new scheme was launched by the Government of India. The new scheme known as 'Swarnajayanti Gram Swarozgar Yojana' (SGSY) was implemented in Tata Rehabilitation colony for the first time in Ganjam District. Two self-help groups were linked up under these schemes. Each group was sanctioned an amount of Rs. 1,80,000 with subsidy of Rs. 1,25,000.

Women members had been provided training to manufacture cement products like well rings and sanitary wares. This was the first instance when the SGSY scheme was being initiated in the country and these groups were supposed to be the pioneers in this programme of Government of India, creating a new Swarozgari for carrying out different income generation programmes. But in the rehabilitation colony group activity was emphasized so that there would not be any sort of misappropriation or fraud.

Activities under NABARD Linking

In this programme two SHGs had been linked with NABARD for generation of income. Basing upon their amount saved in the common SHG fund, four times the amount was to be given as loan assistance. One of these groups had been sanctioned loans for promoting economic activities like cultivation of mushrooms and season's vegetables, vending shops and related activities.

Activities under M.A.S.S. Linking

To carry out the function of these self-help groups, Rangeilunda Block of Ganjam District had formed a Mahila Sanchayika Sangha (M.A.S.S.) on 20th May, 1999 at Kainisi. It was an apex level body overall the SHGs functioning under the block. It had an executive body which met at regular intervals whereas the general body meeting was held on 20th of every month. Two groups of this site were linked with M.A.S.S. and each group was given a loan assistance of Rs.12,000 for investing in various income generation programmes.

Coir-yarn Spinning

With assistance from the Coir Board, Cochin, training was imparted to women oustees on motorized coir-yarn spinning. All the women were members of self-help groups of the site. The training programme was scheduled to include 120 members in 8 batches. Each trainee received a stipend of Rs. 500 per month. At the end of training each trainee was supposed to be provided with a motorized ratt at the rate of 75 per cent subsidy of the machine cost. The coir-yarn produced had a good local market. There was a long term planning for producing coir mats and carpets but after three batches this activity was stopped.

Industry, Service and Business (ISB) Activities

For the displaced persons, Indian Overseas Bank at Narendrapur had given dry interest for financing loans under Industries, Services and Business (ISB) scheme. The bank was convinced by TCS about the need for such loans. The oustees availed loans to promote activities like carpentry, silver works, grocery shops, cycle marts, saloons, hotels, garment shops and electric shops. Not much interest was expressed towards repayment in spite of best efforts put in by the nodal agency hired for rehabilitation and resettlement. In some cases without making proper judgments, loans were disbursed under SC/ST financial scheme. It was sanctioned by Indian Overseas Bank after a lot of pressure from the District Administration.

Activities under Own Account Enterprise

Some oustees had been provided passenger rickshaws and trollies under the Differential Rates of Interest (DRI) scheme and they had to repay through Own Account Enterprise System. This enterprise system gave them a permanent source of livelihood. Women members of the loanee oustees had been motivated to save some of their daily income in saving boxes and it was to make them get into the habit of regular repayments.

Socio-Economic Survey

In every month socio-economic survey was conducted by TCS and it gave them the unique opportunity to interact with all the displaced persons. Based on the response of the oustees new strategies were formulated and adopted by Tata Steel. From this survey the economic status of displaced families was determined on the basis of their income from various sources of the different members of the family and thus the efficacy of persons was determined.

Renovation and Excavation of Tank

In order to duplicate the rural culture, tanks were excavated and some of them were renovated by utilizing the oustees. Through this activity they got employment and income for a particular span of time. In the bank excavation programme women members of the self-help group were involved for taking up vegetable cultivation on the banks of the tanks. They planted pumpkin seeds, coconut and papaya plants on the tank side. The entire activity was taken under Employment Assurance Scheme (EAS).

Fishery Activities

Fish cultivation is one of the most profitable income generation programmes in the rural areas. A number of meetings were organized with the villagers of New Sindhigaon and New Badapur who agreed for fish cultivation in their respective ponds and by taking the technical assistance of experts from the College of Fisheries, this activity was carried out.

Training Programmes

Capable youth from the site were selected for imparting training under Training of Rural Youth for Self Employment (TRYSEM) scheme. Out of 32 youth selected from New Badapur, New Patrapur and New Palikapada, 24 joined in different training institutes while the other eight candidates selected did not join due to personal reasons cited. TCS team members visited different training institutes like I.T.I. Berhampur; Community Polytechnics, Women I.T.I., Chhatrapur and ET&T, Berhampur on the joining dates of the candidates to facilitate the process. Meetings of the trainers were organized in order to sort out their problems relating to training.

Rural Awareness Programmes

Alcoholism was a major problem in the site. Most of the families in New Badapur and New Paikapada were suffering a lot due to this problem which increased the burden of the women who faced the brunt. At the same time some of the male counterparts were dependent upon the income of their wives. In New Sindhigaon village almost all the oustees were addicted to alcohol. But, because of their better economic status in comparison to the New Badapur and New Paikapada villagers their suffering was comparatively less.

An alcohol awareness programme was organized by 'Izzat Samittee' followed by a rally, protesting against alcoholism. Eventually at the right time a drama 'Suna Sabha Jane' was enacted to sensitize the oustees about the evils of alcoholism. This was attended by most of the project displaced persons. The 'Izzat Mahila Samitee', an apex level body of all SHGs in the rehabilitation township, made a success of this campaign with the help of TCS.

Miscellaneous Activities

Applications were generated for providing old age pension to the oustees. For providing financial assistance under PMRY (Prime Minister's Rozgar Yojana, liasoning with the government officials was carried out by TCS. For giving loan assistance under DRI scheme to get soft loans for initiating small income generation programmes,

20 cases were recommended by TCS to the Indian Overseas Bank, Narendrapur. It was done after getting clearance from Rangeilunda Block, for providing nursery sapling to the schools and for initiating any sort of new economic programmes about which villagers were consulting TCS from time to time.

Technical (Job-based) Training and Employment

Even though a period of 12 years have elapsed since the people were displaced in 1996, there is no sight of the Steel Plant. The proposed CRM and subsequent steel plant to be set up were shifted to Jamshedpur. However, since the year of shifting of the oustees, Tata Steel has identified youth based on their capabilities and imparted technical training through various institutions belonging to the government sector like the I.T.Is. as well as private institutions. Amongst the persons trained very few have been absorbed at Tata Steel Jamshedpur and at other facilities of Tata's in and outside the state. In the next Chapter we undertake a qualitative assessment of the rehabilitation policy of Tata Steel.

V

Evaluation of Tata Steel's R&R Policy vis-à-vis the R&R Policies of the Government of Orissa

To assess the strengths and weaknesses of the Tata Steel's resettlement and rehabilitation policy a comparative analysis has been made in this chapter between Tata Steel's R&R Policy and R&R Policies of the Government of Orissa which is regarded as the best resettlement and rehabilitation policy formulated till today. An attempt has also been made to compare the gaps between the proposed policy of Tata Steel and governmental norms and the actual implementation at the grassroots level.

The differences in eligibility criteria between the policies of Government of Orissa and those of Tata Steel have been discussed in section 1, with specific attention to gender issues. The provisions of Tata Steel's project and gaps relating to restoration and reconstruction of livelihoods, provision of civic amenities and compensation package are given in detail in section 2. This section also provides the actual picture of employment and training *vis-à-vis* the ideal scenario given to the oustees at the inception of the project. As the main steel plant project could not be set up due inherent constraints, its adverse impact on training and employment potential, have also been outlined in this section. Section 3 discusses the implementation process as regards roles of government, NGOs, community organizations, project authorities and monitoring and evaluation. Tata Steel's rural development activities have been outlined in section 4.

5.1 Eligibility Criteria

Ideally a person who loses his/her livelihood directly or indirectly should be considered as Project Affected Person (PAP) or Displaced Person (DP) and should be provided with rehabilitation assistance. But an oustee who is only a PAP and not a DP under the Tata Steel's R&R policy, has not been eligible for any rehabilitation assistance. As per the resettlement and rehabilitation policy of Orissa Government, DP means, "a person who since at least one year or prior to the date of publication of notification under section 4 of the Land Acquisition Act, 1984, has been ordinarily residing, and who on account of acquisition of his/her land including homestead land in the submergence zone for the purpose of the project is displaced from such land." This definition of a DP as in Government of Orissa is limited because it recognizes only those affected by submergence and those actually displaced from their homestead lands, as the displaced. This would simply mean that people affected and lost their agricultural lands and thereby sources of livelihoods under the Tata Steel project in the following areas will not be eligible for rehabilitation assistance. They are:

(i) People from villages like Sitlapalli, Madua, Bada Kusasthali, Sana Kusasthali and Narendrapur villages where only agricultural lands have been acquired and people have not displaced.
(ii) People whose lands have been acquired for construction of roads.
(iii) People whose lands have been acquired for building of offices, and quarters.

The differences in eligibility criteria do not end here but widen further when we look at the definition in greater details. Even to be identified as DP, the cut-off percentage of total land holding acquired is different. The arbitrary fixation of cut-off percentage varying one-third to two-third of total land holding to be eligible for getting rehabilitation assistance thus creates tremendous dissatisfaction amongst displaced people though they have been displaced in a similar nature of project and for the national development.

The Tata Steel R&R Policy and R&R Policies of Government of Orissa have also defined the 'family' which will be eligible for the rehabilitation package. According to the Government of Orissa resolution, a family means "Displaced person and his or her spouse, minor brother(s) or sister(s), father and mother and other members residing with him/her and dependent on him/her for livelihood." Later on, the policy was modified and included the following category of persons in the family (i) a person more than 18 years of age irrespective of marital status, (ii) physically and mentally retarded person irrespective of age (Resolution No. 31888, dt. 21.8.1990), (iii) minor orphan who has lost both parents and has no body to fall back upon (Resolution No. 13446 dt. 20.4.1994), and (iv) divorcee with children or without children but having no source of livelihood (Resolution No. 25101, dt. 14.7.1992).

The definition of a family adopted in Government of Orissa, seems wider than Tata Steel Project. In Tata Steel Project, though certain categories of persons have been included in the definition of family, the project authorities did not provide rehabilitation assistance to them. For example as per the revised rehabilitation and resettlement policy every person who is more than 18 years of age irrespective of marital status should be eligible for rehabilitation benefit. Despite this provision, adult single unmarried daughters/women were not treated as separate families. A family with more than one adult daughter has received only one rehabilitation package. An instance in which the adult daughter has lost her father and is dependent on her brother has been ignored even if none of her brothers are willing to support her. This policy measure seems to be discriminatory and gender-biased. Unmarried women are still not being given the same status as adult sons. Though much is being said about improving the status of women, in actual practice, women have no place in the project's scheme of things.

The rehabilitation policy also speaks of providing rehabilitation assistance to divorcees. As per the Resolution No. 25101, dt. 14.7.1992 for the purpose of woman to be treated as a divorcee, the claimant should make an affidavit and file her claim along with a copy of the affidavit. It is too much of a task expected out of an illiterate divorcee woman to get an affidavit after all the traumas she has undergone from family separation, and run from pillar to post to get the affidavit. It would be much wiser to consider some simpler method, such as conducting inquiry at the village level to identify if the woman is a divorcee.

5.2 Provisions of Resettlement and Rehabilitation Policy

The resettlement and rehabilitation policies formulated by Tata Steel's Gopalpur Project to resettle the oustees can broadly be divided into two parts. Part one of the policy deals with reconstruction and restoration of economic activities and livelihoods, and part two deals with providing civic amenities necessary for a decent community living and for strengthening community organizations. The following segment analyses the two aspects of the Resettlement and Rehabilitation Policy.

5.2.1 Policy Relating to Restoration and Reconstruction of Economic Activities

To restore the standards of living, the policy laid down that displaced people should be provided with agricultural land, homestead land, house building assistance, and maintenance allowance to regain their previous economic position in new site.

Before formulation of rehabilitation and resettlement policy to restore their income and standards of living, first of all a proper and systematic study of the socio-economic system and culture of the oustees was called for, to know their needs and background. A base line survey was also conducted for the Tata Steel Project at Gopalpur to know, (i) the exact total impact of the project, (ii) the number of people going to be affected by the project, their socio-economic characteristics, and (iii) the extent of resources and finances and institutional mechanisms required for resettling the displaced.

The displaced families were resettled near the Sitlapalli and Luhajhar villages in a Rehabilitation colony, commonly called 'Tata Colony' comprising an area of about 540 acres. The rehabilitation site had similar surroundings and identical socio-economic and cultural background as the pre-displaced villagers so that the amicable integration of the project-displaced persons with the host population becomes easy. Though the resettlement and rehabilitation policy spoke of land based rehabilitation, these policies could not be implemented as the project authorities failed to provide governmental land to all the displaced people. Without trying to understand the psychology and cultural habits of the oustees, a patch of land at Badapur, Patrapur and Sindhigaon were offered to the oustees for resettlement.

Even then, no effort was made to purchase private land as is usually done by the Orissa Government. To avoid the responsibility, the authorities chose an easy method of resettlement, and cash in lieu of land was announced, which was much below the market price. As a result, displaced people were forced to purchase private lands by paying huge amounts for purchasing of homestead land and agricultural land. Most of the displaced people were of poor category and they definitely needed help for economic rehabilitation, but were left to fend for themselves.

The present policy also did not take into account the needs of various occupational groups among the oustees, there was provision for planned economic rehabilitation that will ensure economic development. The fate of the artisans, barbers and blacksmiths, farm labourers, cattle grazers became uncertain. The present source of livelihood of these categories of people was destroyed by the project, as the policy provisions did not take into account the economic interest of the poorest among the poor oustees. There was no special provision for economic rehabilitation of these poor people.

The principal assistance was in the form of cash compensation for PAPs and DPs and maintenance allowance given to the DPs for a year. Attempts for employment and training covered both the groups but other form of rehabilitation assistance was limited to the DPs inhabiting the Rehabilitation Colony. Given the fact that the Steel Plant could not be set up and the limited skill level of the oustees, the promises made for providing employment on a large scale could not be kept up. As the rehabilitation was not land based, in spite of attempts made to ensure that the DPs take up other occupations, it was very difficult to convert them to new non-land based occupations.

Employment and Training

The scope of employment of unskilled manpower is nil since only engineers and skilled workers are employed in TISCO Gopalpur Project. It is to be pointed out that there were 13 categories of employees in Tata Steel Jamshedpur plant but there are only three categories of employees in Gopalpur Project. There is no direct employment in the company's services sector like education, health, sanitary, maintenance and repair, etc. After modernization of Tata Steel at Jamshedpur, the school formerly managed by TISCO is going to be given to DAV management and hospital to Apollo group (Pattnaik: undated). So, direct employment in the Gopalpur project has automatically been squeezed. Whatever little direct employment opportunities are there for engineers and skilled workers are limited due to replacement of TISCO's staff from Jamshedpur to Gopalpur project consequent upon modernization of the plant in the former place. Particularly, Oriya employees have been transferred from Jamshedpur to Gopalpur to create an impression in the minds of Government of Orissa and the local people that TISCO Gopalpur project is employing local Oriyas. Of course, TISCO has promised to provide special training to candidates above matriculate from the displaced families to join the plant since the lowest rank employee in the plant is an ITI trainee.

Details of training and employment are given in the following tables, based on latest data furnished by the Project Office at Berhampur.

From Table 5.1.a, it can be observed that a total of 306 persons have been imparted technical training of which 236 persons actually belong to the oustees category while a substantial number, i.e. 70 belong to the non-affected category and villages like Aruapalli, Dura and Ankuli. It may seem strange as to why such a large number of persons have been trained from peripheral non-affected villages but the reason cited by Tata Steel is that the villages were initially to be acquired but later the plans were changed. The affected people now claim that these are grave irregularities committed and have been done solely for populist measures and to satisfy the troublesome elements in the peripheral areas. The dissatisfaction extends to employment also as these persons from non-affected villages have been given jobs with the Tata owned companies and assisted in getting jobs in other organizations. It is also claimed that 3 persons from one undivided family of Basanaputti have been given jobs which goes against the norms that only one person of each undivided family should be given one job.

Table 5.1.a: Categories of Oustees Imparted Training

Sl. No.	*Category of Trainees*	*Numbers*
1.	Affected Persons	141
2.	Displaced Persons	95
3.	Non-Affected	70
4.	**Total**	**306**

Table 5.1.b: Employment/Engagement* of Trained Persons

Sl. No.	*Employed/Engaged* by*	*Numbers*	*%age*
1.	Tata owned Companies	95	31.05
2.	Other Corporate Houses	10	3.26
3.	Central Government Bodies	5	1.63
4.	Other Private Sector	92	30.06
5.	Self-Employed	71	23.20
6.	Not Employed	33	10.78
7.	**Total**	**306**	**100**

*Contractual through an outside agency.

Source: Tata Steel, Project Office, Berhampur-May, 2009.

Table 5.1.b represents the employment status of persons trained. The words employed and engaged have been used interchangeably because in some cases instead of directly being employed people have been engaged through third-party contractors. Till May 2009, out of total 306 persons trained, 202 were employed by various sectors like the Tata owned companies, other corporate houses, the government and also employed in their own businesses. Around 31 per cent (95) were engaged by the Tatas, 3.26 per cent by other corporate houses, 30.06 per cent by other private sector, around 2 per cent by the government bodies and 23.2 per cent were self-employed. Around 11 per cent of the trainees are not engaged at all.

TISCO had also claimed that employment will be available to local people in the ancillary industries but no clear policy has been announced by the project authority in this respect. Though direct and indirect linkage effects both forward and backward of a steel plant is higher than that of an aluminium plant (Samal: 1995, 1997, 1998), the linkages of TISCO Gopalpur project in Orissa is very similar to that of NALCO since both are export-oriented units having no significant linkage effects inside the state or in the local periphery except a little boost to trading activities due to demand emanating from the income of the employees. So, there is little possibility of any dramatic development of ancillary industries around TISCO Gopalpur project. Hence employment opportunities in ancillary industries of the proposed steel plant at Gopalpur may not have been sufficient in order to directly accommodate the displaced persons. Though 95 persons have been engaged with the Tata owned companies it is a very small number as compared to the fact that more than 3000 people have been affected by the project. Even the number of persons trained is very low but reasons cited by Tata Steel is that persons are not eligible as per their educational qualifications and skill levels.

Tata Steel had also declared that "Project Affected Persons (PAPs) who have lost their land" will get various benefits. Compensation for acquisition of land was fixed at the price which was 30 per cent higher that the market rate. In some cases, cash compensation of one lakh rupees was paid per acre. The other facilities to be given were: (i) imparting training, skill development and evaluation of employment facilities in future and (ii) *ex gratia* payment of Rs. 30,000 to the poor people (Tata Steel: 1996). Besides the above-mentioned facilities to the 'displaced persons who have lost their land', every displaced family was supposed to get some benefits which were very minor.

5.2.2 Policy Relating to Provision to Civic Amenities

Besides economic rehabilitation, to strengthen community life and for a decent life, the resettlement and rehabilitation policy also speaks of providing various civic amenities to the newly settled clusters. As per the guidelines, one primary school (with 2 rooms) for 100 families, one dispensary for 500 families, drinking water facility, linked all weather road, village ponds, electrification and other civic amenities should be provided for self-sustainable community life.

In comparison to Government of Orissa (GoO) Policy, the provision for civic amenities in the Tata Steel Project seems to be less than adequate. While the Government of Orissa Policy has laid down provisions for community centre, seed store, children's park, construction of one platform, and religious place of worship for every 500 families, there is no such provision to be found in Tata Steel's resettlement and rehabilitation policy.

As per the Government of Orissa policy the resettlement site should be planned as a model town and should serve an as example for others to emulate. The highlights of the township should be:

- Planned colony with fully developed infrastructure like approach roads, internal roads, electricity, running water, ponds, cattle grazing area, etc. with nearly 50 per cent open area for a better environment.
- Community facilities like schools, panchayat ghar, seeds store, community centres, TV dish antennae, children's play-ground, village tank, vocational training centre, health centres, cremation ground, etc.
- Religious places like temples for the village deities.

However, like Government of Orissa Policy, the Tata Steel Project Resettlement and Rehabilitation Policy laid down that certain basic civic amenities be provided for healthy and comfortable living of the displaced people at the new site. In the following section, an attempt has been made to assess various civic amenities provided at the new site. As per the Tata Steel's report the following facilities have been provided by the project authority at the Rehabilitation Colony.

The civic amenities have been only provided at the Rehabilitation colony where the displaced people reside and to the affected villages who have lost agricultural land. In those villages attempts have been made for restoration of livelihood through providing training and employment.

From Table 5.2 it can be seen that the total population of the Rehabilitation site is 2725 which comprises 5 clusters created from the displaced people from erstwhile villages. Each cluster has been named after the erstwhile village as in case of Badapur called as New Badapur of Rehabilitation Colony or Tata Colony. All the clusters are also geographically compact which becomes easier to access common civic amenities.

Table 5.2: Amenities Provided at Rehabilitation Colony

Sl. No.	Description	Details	Remarks
1	Total Population	Number of Clusters-5	Sindhigaon-1336, Badapur-711, Patrapur-483, Paikapada-120 and Kalipalli-75 Total Population of Rehab colony-2725.
2	Number of houses built in the colony area	939 + 5 = 944 Nos. (5 houses up to roof level)	Plinth area of House = 262 Sq.ft (Including Toilet)
3	Number of house Allotted	587 Nos.	
4	Number of House Plots	3022 Nos.	Size of Plot = 53′-5″x82′-8″ = 4418.67 Sq.ft (16.29x25.2M) = 410.50 Sq.Mt.
5	Number of Plots Allotted	871 Nos.	
6	Roads	47 Km.	All over the colony area
7	Drains	102 Km.	Both road-side drains all over the colony area.
8	Ponds	5 Nos.	All the ponds are being used by the colony residents.
9	Tube/Bore Wells	85 Nos.	Presently 51 nos. in running condition and are in regular use.
10	Open Wells	12 Nos.	
11	Micro Irrigation Project (Well)	126 Nos.	Through DRDA, Ganjam
12	Community Centres	8 Nos.	Sindhigaon-Boys-148, Girls-154, Total-302

(Contd.)

Table 5.2 *(Contd.)*

Sl. No.	Description	Details	Remarks
13	U.P. School (Run by Govt.)	4 Nos.	Paikapada-Boys-20, Girls-8, Total-28 Patrapur-Boys-29, Girls-24, Total-53 Badapur-Boys-52, Girls-40, Total-92
14	M.E. School	3 Nos.	Lying vacant
15	High School (Block grant school)	1 No.	Boys-118, Girls-84, Total-202
16	Health Centre	1 No.	Taken over by CDMO, Ganjam.
17	Temples	12 Nos.	
18	Cremation Ground	1 No.	Being used by the colony residents.
19	Work Shed	1 No.	
20	Sub-stations	12 Nos.	Handed over to South Co. in April 2005
21	Anganwadi Centre	2 Nos.	Run by Govt.
22	Veterinary Dispensary	1 No.	Run by Govt.
23	Police Beat House	1 No.	Run by Govt. under SP, Berhampur
24	Post Office	1 No.	Run by Govt.
25	Milk Society	1 No.	Run by Milk Society, Ganjam
26	Panchayat Office (Run by Panchayati Raj Department)	1 No.	
27	Plantation of trees	1,20,000 Nos.	Coconut, Saplings, Avenue Plantation, Fruit Bearing Saplings and Kewda Plantations etc.
28	Mahila Samitee (Women's Group)	2 Nos.	Given plot for construction of samitee
29	Technical Training Institute	1 No.	Running at Mandipalli from the year 2005 for 3 years. Diploma course and multi-skill programme for DP/PAP and residents of Orissa students.
30	Yuvak Sangh (Youth Club)	3 Nos.	Badapur, Patrapur and Sindhigaon (House allotted by Tata Steel at Rehab colony)
31	Kothaghara (Community Centre)	5 Nos.	Badapur, Patrapur and Sindhigaon (House and Plot allotted by Tata Steel at Rehab colony)

5.2.2.1 Drinking Water

As per the policy, new clusters should be provided with one village pond irrespective of number of families, drinking water well with though as per norms prescribed by Government of India. In case displaced people resettle, in-groups or clusters of 10 and more number of families, water wells, and tank should be provided.

It is found that adequate numbers of tube wells have been provided in new clusters but only 51 out of 85 are functional and in regular use. Most of the tube-wells provide water with contain high percentage of iron, which displaced people do not use as drinking water. In some clusters, tube-wells are not properly installed and therefore lie in defunct state putting oustees in a miserable condition. Tanks provided in newly settled clusters are not deep enough and get dried up even before the summer sets in. Thus availability of portable water, for the resettlers as well as the animals domesticated by them, is a great problem in the newly resettled villages.

Unlike in a village, the houses at the Rehabilitation colony are at a distance from each other so in spite of norms being followed for tube-wells, the accessibility has not been looked into. Sometimes the villagers have to walk almost half a kilometre or more to access tube-wells and drinking water. Those who are relatively affluent have dug open wells in their own compounds. Wells provided under the micro irrigation have also proved to be a failure right from the inception stage as well as regarding maintenance.

5.2.2.2 Primary School

As per policies, primary schools were to be made available for every 100 families. Though some primary school buildings have been provided in some clusters they are non-functional due to non-availability of teachers. The education department has failed to provide any teacher to those project-made schools. As an obvious consequence, these schools are now in dilapidated condition in absence of any care. Some schools are now being used as cowsheds. As a result, there is total loss of education for the children of the oustees. Though some of the oustees' children are attending primary schools existing in host villages, their attendance is very thin as they have to travel 2 to 3 kms and are sometimes facing the problem of 'social isolation'.

5.2.2.3 Primary Health Centre and Veterinary Centre

Though the Policy speaks of providing PHCs and Animal Care Centres for every 500 families, not a single Primary Health Centre and Animal Care Centre has been provided at any of the new sites. The oustees are still dependent on the existing health care centre available at Berhampur city, the headquarters of the project which is approximately 20 kms away from some of the new clusters. In July 2004 Chief District Medical Officer, Ganjam had appointed 2 health workers (one Female and one Male) in the Rehabilitation Colony for providing health facilities to the inhabitants. In addition to that, the Tata Steel sends a Doctor and staff who run a dispensary 5 days in a week for two hours daily with medicines and in some cases refer to the hospital. Apart from this time to time various medical camps are also being organized.

5.2.2.4 Other Facilities

(1) Other facilities like internal roads and all weather roads were constructed ten years back. In the absence of maintenance, most of these roads are in bad shape. Earlier the landless labourers who were travelling to Berhampur and Chhatrapur for daily wage jobs, were facing communication problems and other problems while returning at night. After shifting to the Rehabilitation colony they are getting easy and faster modes of communication round the clock as the colony is situated by the side of main road and one police beat house is also functioning inside the colony.

(2) As per the policy community centres in every cluster, kothaghars, panchayat, temples or shrines have been provided in the new site. Free electricity was provided for 10 years and the facility has been withdrawn only recently. Electric meters have now been installed in the houses and people have started paying for electricity and taking up their own responsibilities. However, electricity which was supplied to

street lights has also been withdrawn and until June 2008, it had not been supported by the state government due to which the entire Rehabilitation Colony was being considered unsafe by the inhabitants and especially the women folk who hesitated to move around in the dark.

(3) Provisions for free electricity, irrigation and self-employment programme, agro-forestry, vocational training, as promised in the policy have been fulfilled to a limited extent.

(4) A package of benefits planned for host villages to avoid conflict between host and displaced people has proved to be non-starter.

(5) A Technical Institute was started at Mandipalli in April 2005 and special preference is being given to children of displaced and affected families.

(6) After the super cyclone occurred on 17th October, 1999, a team of Tata officials estimated the damages incurred by the inhabitants in the colony. Accordingly efforts were made for restoration of electricity supply by changing poles, transformers and conductors. All complaints of damaged houses were addressed. Road and drains were also repaired and relief materials provided to the families. Five years back the Luhajhar (under which the Rehabilitation Colony lies) Panchayat Office and Godown buildings were constructed and have been functioning at the Rehabilitation colony.

(7) Kewda plantation has been introduced on both sides of *nala* (drains) passing through the Rehabilitation colony. Presently the village committee is earning money through contract for kewda flowers. In addition to kewda plantations, fruit and flower bearing trees have been planted in and around the colony. Forest plantation was taken up in total more than one lakh trees comprising teak, sisal, eucalyptus etc. were planted. Every house and allotted plot owner was supplied with fruit bearing saplings like mangos, coconuts etc., free of cost.

(8) The women of the colony were trained for self-employment in Agarbati making, leaflet making, mushroom cultivation, tailoring and motorized coir yarn spinning. There were 18 Mahila Samitis (SHGs) functioning in the colony supported by different agencies.

Of the total estimated Rs. 9,300 crores for the Steel Plant only a meagre amount of Rs. 170 crores (18.26%) have been spent for compensation, rehabilitation and resettlement of the displaced persons. On the other hand, Tata Steel does not give any guarantee for jobs to the displaced persons on a priority basis, since employment in the proposed plant and its ancillaries is strictly based on eligibility and qualifications. But the local people say that an acre of land in their erstwhile villages which gave an annual income of not less than Rs. 1 lakh was a better option than a job in the Steel Plant as it could sustain the entire family. They feel that even if one job is provided per family it will not be enough to compensate for the loss in livelihoods of all members of the family.

5.2.3 Compensation Package

In January 1996 the then District Administration examined the R&R package based on the policy of 1994 followed by the Orissa Government for irrigation projects. The Government and Tata Steel discussed about the various irrigation and industrial packages for resettlement and rehabilitation.

Finally on 19th March, 1996 the R&R package for project Gopalpur was announced by the Government of Orissa. According to Tata Steel such a package largely was based on the World Bank norms. The World Bank stipulated that all efforts must be made to restore the minimum standard of living enjoyed by the persons prior to displacement and Tata Steel adopted the same philosophy reiterating that the economic condition of the displaced persons must improve significantly in the long run.

In all village meetings in the erstwhile villages for selling price of lands/houses, orchards and immovable properties were discussed. The villagers thought that by selling their lands and immovable properties to Tata Steel at a higher price at least they could go for hiring other lands or deposit the amount for getting higher interest as an alternative they were neither likely to get any sure shot employment in the plant nor be able to purchase such high yielding agricultural lands what they possessed earlier. The increased amount would meet their mobility and transition expenses in the first phase of displacement. A strong point which came out during the meetings held with the village group was that the land prices were undervalued and hence the registered sales document should not form the basis for fixing the rate of compensation. Similar messages had been received by the District Administration during their informal talks with people of the area. The recorded sale transactions revealed that agricultural land was registered between Rs. 25,000 to Rs. 35,000 per acre. Given the background of Gopalpur commercial transactions were not alien to the people.

Based on the feedback received from various quarters the Government of Orissa after due consultation with Tata Steel declared that irrespective of the classification the minimum compensation payable for agricultural land would be Rs. 100,000 per acre. The implementation of this decision was not possible under the law. The Land Acquisition Act stipulated that the value of land would be based on a method of compensation which in most cases did not reach the minimum declared value. Ultimately after renewed negotiations with the State Government and the villagers Tata Steel decided to buy land at the rate of Rs. 1 lakh per acre. The land was bought through IIDCO as under the rules corporate houses could not buy land directly from the villagers.

The fruit bearing trees were valued liberally. The compensation for one coconut tree worked out to Rs. 600. Executive instructions issued by Government of Orissa for implementation of Land Acquisition Act for valuation of houses stated that houses in rural areas were generally not sold and hence market price could not be the basis of compensation. Rather, compensation should be determined on the basis of ability to construct a similar house in a different location. The house and structures were valued on the basis of 1994 schedule of rates determined by Public Works Department (PWD). Where compensation was payable for immovable assets a liberal view was taken to ensure a better economic return.

5.3 Implementation Process

Not only are the policies on resettlement and rehabilitation inadequate, but the implementation of these policies has also been shoddy. A serious attempt has not been made to implement these policies holistically. No separate organization or body was created to carry out the rehabilitation and resettlement works. Initially the

Land Acquisition Department was created which looked after both and acquisition, evacuation and rehabilitation work with the help of four zone officers. Resettlement and rehabilitation of the displaced persons is a time bound activity. It is essential that the various departments of the Government are associated from the very beginning for effective rehabilitation, so that assistance to the resettled villagers is maintained even after the R&R activities are completed by the project authorities.

5.3.1 Government

The Government of Orissa has set up a separate cell with a Special Land Acquisition Officer with adequate staff to co-ordinate all the activities involved in resettlement and rehabilitation. Further, representatives from other departments like Agriculture, Industries, Animal Husbandry, Forests, etc. have also been involved in assisting the Special Land Acquisition Officer, who reports to the Collector of Ganjam.

Further, a Resettlement and Rehabilitation Advisory Committee with the Revenue Divisional Commissioner as its Chairman has been formed whose function was to assess the suitability of the resettlement site, examine the rehabilitation schemes prepared for the displaced persons, review the implementation schedules and results and recommend improvements.

5.3.2 Community Organization

To ensure the active participation of the people from the displaced families it was proposed to form village-wise Groups who would assist in organizing the resettlers, educate and motivate them to provide group support and help them to choose any vocation which could be used by them productively. These Groups have assisted in helping the resettlers get accepted by the host villages. It was intended that these Community Groups act as internal bridges between the project authorities and the displaced persons for furthering the activities of resettlement and rehabilitation.

5.3.3 Non-Governmental Organisation (NGO)

The organizational capabilities of the R&R establishment could be gainfully enhanced by the active participation of well meaning and dedicated NGOs. The NGOs have been involved right from the start of resettlement process. NGOs who have adequate staff, experience in the execution of similar projects, and knowledge of the needs of the local people were selected for this purpose. The activities of the NGOs was closely monitored and reported to the R&R Advisory Committee regularly.

5.3.4 Project Authorities (Tata Steel)

The project authorities have executed the resettlement and rehabilitation plan under the overall guidance of the R&R Advisory Committee. Further, a Steering Committee comprising senior executives was formed at Tata Steel to review the progress, guide and render assistance to the executive staff in effective resettlement and rehabilitation of the displaced families befitting their rights and dignity, and in consonance with the traditional values and culture of the House of Tatas.

5.3.5 Monitoring and Evaluation

Periodic monitoring and evaluation of the progress of resettlement and rehabilitation was undertaken by an independent consultant who was appointed to prevent any aberrations creeping in due to weaknesses in implementation and also to ensure the welfare of the project affected families. A set of measurable indicators of progress comprising physical, economic, social and cultural aspects of rehabilitation were continuously evaluated by the consultant. The progress was also reviewed by the Resettlement and Rehabilitation Committee for redressal of grievances. The Steering Committee has also been reviewing the R&R progress every month and providing assistance to the executive authorities.

5.4 Tata Steel's Rural Development Activities at Gopalpur

The ceremonial foundation stone for the integrated steel pant at Gopalpur was laid on the 30th of December, 1995. Way back in August 1995 the Company, entrusted Tata Steel Rural Development Society (TSRDS) to undertake a survey of the villages proximity to the proposed site for the steel plant with a view towards initiating its rural development activities amongst the rural population. As a result of this survey, it was clear that despite the existence of primary health centres run by the Government, additional medical facilities were required in the villages and, accordingly, Tata Steel development activities in the form of a Mobile Medical Unit was initiated which helped establish cordial relationships with the local people who themselves voluntarily made premises available for the weekly clinics where the doctors and other team members regularly treated patients. The medical team has already treated nearly 6000 patients, but now the focus of this activity has been extended to include; curative intervention, regular health check-ups for school going children, large scale immunization programme, treatment of and other rehabilitation inputs for patients living in the Damien Nagar Leprosy colony in Chhatrapur, three eye cure camps in collaboration with the local NGOs and medical colleges and general health education for the villagers.

From the above analysis it may be concluded that in Tata Steel Project without proper database and sufficient investigation, resettlement and rehabilitation policy has been formulated and guidelines have been issued by the Government. Even though some aspects of the policies were good and supported reconstruction of economic activities and strengthening of community life, these polices were not implemented properly. Civic amenities provided in new sites have been inadequate. 'After care' facilities are totally absent. There have been gaps in inter-departmental coordination, and implementing organizations have been found lacking in specialized skills to understand the intricacies of rehabilitation and have thus failed to carry out the rehabilitation and resettlement work effectively.

The next chapter which is based on the primary survey data will help in providing a representative picture of the resettlement and rehabilitation process and its impact on the oustees over a period of 11 years framework.

VI

Economic Impact of Displacement: An Assessment

After analyzing the R&R Policy, its implementation pattern, strengths and weaknesses, in this chapter an effort has been made to study the perceived and quantifiable changes in the socio-economic aspects of life of the oustees in the post-displacement period as compared to the pre-displacement period, in order to assess the impact of displacement and resettlement.

This chapter is divided into 7 sections. The first section outlines the details of the demographic profile of the sample households on a comparative basis between the pre- and post-displacement periods while section 2 represents the education and skill profile. The comparative changes observed in the socio-economic status of the affected households are presented in section 3. Section 4 deals with details of the pattern of utilization of compensation money and its implications. Other non-economic aspects of impact are studied in section 5. Risk Factor Analysis has been carried out in section 6 and critical areas of concern have been discussed in section 7.

Induced displacement has several consequential impacts perhaps more unintended than intended, and it brings many changes in the lives of the PAPs. These changes are economic, social, cultural as well as psychological in nature. While social and cultural impacts are the results of the relocation and resettlement arrangement of the societies and communities within the project affected areas, often leading to lack of integration, the economic effects are the outcome of the changes in the livelihood base and production system.

Therefore, it is imperative and significant to study the changing dimensions of socio-cultural and economic life of the oustees in the pre- and post-rehabilitation periods.

To assess the socio-economic conditions of life, the present study covered a wide spectrum of indicators for investigation. For the assessment of social conditions, it covers family structure, living pattern, housing pattern as indicators and for assessment of economic conditions, it covers land holding pattern, occupational pattern, cropping pattern, dependence on forest, livestock, asset structure and various sources of income (both main and subsidiary) as indicators of study.

6.1 Demographic Profile

Before analyzing the socio-economic conditions of the oustees in the pre-and post-rehabilitation period, a brief demographic profile of the sample households has been presented. The demographic profile of the sample households can broadly be classified in terms of caste, gender, and literacy levels and age structure of the respondents. These variables are important indicators for the study of displacement and rehabilitation because they help us to assess the impact of displacement on different socio-economic and age groups.

6.1.1 Gender Composition

The survey has covered a total of 1044 persons out of which 546 (52.30%) are male and 498 (47.70%) are female, from the three categories of oustees under study (Table 6.1). As can be seen from this Table, there is not much difference in the gender composition of the surveyed population across the three categories, and in each case, there is a deficit of female population.

6.1.2 Caste Structure

Out of the 200 sample households in this present study, 16.50 per cent households belong to Scheduled Castes, 2.50 per cent are Scheduled Tribes, 48.00 per cent households are Other Backward Classes and the rest 33.00 per cent households are General Castes. The percentage of Other Backward Classes is highest followed by General Castes,

Table 6.1: Gender Composition of Surveyed Households

Sl. No.	*Categories of Oustees*	*Total Population Surveyed*		
		Male	*Female*	*Total*
1.	Lost Agriculture Land only	140 (51.47)	132 (48.53)	272 (100.0)
2.	Lost Home/Homestead Land only	118 (51.53)	111 (48.47)	229 (100.0)
3.	Lost both Home/Homestead Land and Agriculture Land	288 (53.04)	255 (46.96)	543 (100.0)
	Total	**546 (52.30)**	**498 (47.70)**	**1044 (100.0)**

NB: Figures in parentheses represent percentage to the respective total.

Scheduled Castes and Scheduled Tribes. As the sample area is in the coastal belt, the majority belong to OBC and General Households' category (Table 6.2). However, it should be noted that the caste composition varies a great deal across the three categories of oustees: whereas the General Caste population dominate the sample households who have lost agricultural land only, SC population dominate amongst those who have lost homes/homestead land only, while OBC population are the most prominent amongst those who have lost both home/homestead land and agricultural land (Table 6.2).

Table 6.2: Social Group-wise Distribution of Sample Households

Sl. No.	*Categories of Oustees*	*Percentage of Households*				
		SC	*ST*	*OBC*	*General*	*Total*
1.	Lost Agriculture Land only	11.11	0.00	31.11	57.78	100.0
2.	Lost Home/Homestead Land only	54.55	4.55	18.88	22.73	100.0
3.	Lost both Home/Homestead Land and Agriculture Land	3.60	2.70	66.67	27.03	100.0
	Total	**16.50**	**2.50**	**48.00**	**33.00**	**100.0**

6.1.3 Types of Households

To assess the social aspect of the oustees, the study covers family structure in the pre-displacement period and post-rehabilitation period, and this has been depicted in Table 6.3.

Table 6.3: Type of Family in Pre- and Post-Displacement Period of the Sample Households

Sl. No.	*Category*	*Pre-Displacement*		*Post-Displacement*	
		Nuclear	*Joint*	*Nuclear*	*Joint*
1.	Lost Agriculture Land only	14 (31.11)	31 (68.89)	37 (82.22)	8 (17.78)
2.	Lost Home/Homestead Land only	9 (20.45)	35 (79.55)	34 (77.27)	10 (22.73)
3.	Lost both Agriculture land and Home/Homestead land	48 (43.24)	63 (56.76)	76 (68.47)	35 (31.53)
	Total	**71 (35.50)**	**129 (64.50)**	**147 (73.50)**	**53 (26.50)**

Note: Figures in parentheses refer to percentage.

From the data on family structure before and after displacement it is clear that there has taken place a significant break-up of joint families and formation of nuclear families. This is particularly true of households who have lost agricultural land only where per cent of joint families has come down from about 69 per cent to about 18 per cent. Similarly, in the case of those who have lost homes/homestead land only, proportion of joint families has come down from about 57 per cent to 32 per cent. This seems to be induced by joint landed property and offer of monetary compensation.

6.1.4 Marital Status

The marital status of the displaced population has been depicted in Table 6.4. It is observed from the table that out of 1044 total sample population, 51.44 per cent of oustees are married and 41.38 per cent of oustees are unmarried which shows that marriage as a socio-religious institution is well appreciated by them. Besides this 6.80 per cent of people are widows/widowers and 0.38 per cent comprises divorced/separated persons.

6.1.5 Age Structure of the Family Members

Regarding the demographic picture of sample study population, it is found that the area has a relatively unfavourable sex ratio *vis-à-vis*

Table 6.4: Marital Status of the Total Surveyed Population

Sl. No.	*Categories of Oustees*	*Married*	*Un-Married*	*Widow/ Widower*	*Divorce/ Separated*	*Total*
1.	Lost Agriculture Land only	152 (55.88)	102 (37.50)	18 (6.62)	0 (0.00)	272 (100.0)
2.	Lost Home/Homestead Land only	115 (50.22)	95 (41.48)	18 (7.86)	1 (0.44)	229 (100.0)
3.	Lost both Home/Homestead Land and Agriculture Land	270 (49.72)	235 (43.28)	35 (6.45)	3 (0.55)	543 (100.0)
	Total	**537 (51.44)**	**432 (41.38)**	**71 (6.80)**	**4 (0.38)**	**1044 (100.0)**

Note: Figures in parentheses represent percentage to the respective total.

the total average sex ratio of population of India. According to 2001 Census, the number of females per 1000 males in India is 972, whereas it is 912 for the sample population of the surveyed area which could be due to excess outmigration. Indeed, the 0-6 age group is as low as 733 and the same is 787 for 6-14 age group population. This implies that the female mortality rate in study area is higher in 0-6 age group and also in 6-18 age group as compared to the males. The field data further show that the number of females per 1000 males in the 0-6 age group is abysmally low. This may be due to better life expectancy rate of males *vis-à-vis* females. It is also implied from the findings of the survey data that the female child in 0-14 age group does not get adequate health attention of parents as compared to male child and as a result, the sex ratio which is very low (at the rate of 769 females per 1000 males) in this age group, immediately shows an adverse trend of 782 females per 1000 males in 14-18 age group population in the surveyed area. Interestingly, it is found from the Table that in 60 and above age group the sex ratio is as high as 1173.

Another important feature of the sample households and the percentage of working age group population in 14-60 years are as high as 62.93 per cent or say three-fifth of the total and in 18-60 years age group, it is more than 50 per cent of the total (55.08%). This implies that dependency load of the working population on earners in the study area is relatively better than the Ganjam area as a whole.

Table 6.5: Distribution of Sample Population According to their Age and Sex

Sl. No.	Category	0-6 Yrs		6-14 Yrs		14-18 Yrs		18-45 Yrs		45-60 Yrs		60 and Above		Total		
		Male	Female	Male	Female	Male	Female	Male	Female	Male	Female	Male	Female	Male	Female	Total
1.	Lost Agriculture Land only	9 (3.31)	9 (3.31)	20 (7.35)	14 (5.15)	15 (5.51)	9 (3.31)	67 (24.63)	65 (23.90)	15 (5.51)	12 (4.41)	14 (5.15)	23 (8.46)	140 (51.47)	132 (48.53)	272 (100)
2.	Lost Home/Homestead Land only	15 (6.55)	8 (3.49)	20 (8.73)	19 (8.30)	9 (3.93)	7 (3.06)	43 (18.78)	42 (18.34)	13 (5.68)	20 (8.73)	18 (7.86)	15 (6.55)	118 (51.53)	111 (48.47)	229 (100)
3.	Lost both Home/Homestead Land and Agriculture Land	21 (3.87)	16 (2.95)	49 (9.02)	37 (6.81)	22 (4.05)	20 (3.68)	123 (22.65)	102 (18.78)	36 (6.63)	37 (6.81)	37 (6.81)	43 (7.92)	288 (53.04)	255 (46.96)	543 (100)
	Total	**45** **(4.31)**	**33** **(3.16)**	**89** **(8.52)**	**70** **(6.70)**	**46** **(4.41)**	**36** **(3.45)**	**233** **(22.32)**	**209** **(20.02)**	**64** **(6.13)**	**69** **(6.61)**	**69** **(6.61)**	**81** **(7.76)**	**546** **(52.30)**	**498** **(47.70)**	**1044** **(100)**

Note: Figures in parentheses represent percentage to the respective total.

6.2 Levels of Education and Skills

The socio-economic condition of the oustee population can be studied by looking at educational status and this has been analyzed in Tables 6.6 and 6.7. As compared to pre- and post-displacement period, it is a very distressing fact that 32.92 per cent of pre-displaced oustees are illiterate while the corresponding figure among post-displaced oustee's records at 25.26 per cent. As per the Resettlement and Rehabilitation Policy project authorities provided educational facility to the oustees after displacement in order to reduce the illiteracy rate of the study area. The percentage of just literate in pre- and post-displaced period is 27.54 and 26.68 respectively. This figure shows that there is very little impact of the resettlement. As regards Matriculates, 3.41 per cent belong to the pre-displaced period and 5.70 per cent to the post-displaced period. Only 1.24 per cent people were graduates in pre-displaced period while in the post-displaced period the corresponding figure is 2.05 per cent. The percentage of people who received technical education is 0.41 per cent in pre-displacement period while the corresponding figure in the post-displaced period is 2.18 per cent, which is most pitiable as it has prevented them from availing job opportunities from the development project. It is found that there are no post-graduate in the pre-displaced period as well as post-displaced period among the sample study oustees. With such low standard of education, it becomes very hard to raise their skill and efficiency. The steps taken by the project authorities towards the improvement of educational level of the oustees are quite inadequate. As per the R&R Policy, the project authority should take steps to provide technical education to the oustees for acquiring jobs. Tata Steel Company has not taken sufficient measure in this regard.

6.3 Economic Profile

The oustees in all the pre-displaced villages comprised a close-knit society and represented the existence of an integrated, self-sufficient and essentially a non-monetized economy. Agriculture, cattle-rearing, forests and rivers were the main source of sustenance. Keeping their economic condition of life in view in the pre-displacement period, this section attempts an assessment of the economic condition of the oustees in the post-rehabilitation period.

Table 6.6: Distribution of Sample Population According to their Level of Education in Pre-Displacement Period

Sl. No.	Categories of Oustees	Illiterate		Just Literate		Primary		Middle		HSC	
		Male	Female	Male	Female	Male	Female	Male	Female	Male	Female
1.	Lost Agriculture Land only	23 (9.06)	36 (15.35)	28 (11.02)	38 (14.96)	26 (10.24)	22 (8.66)	31 (12.20)	19 (7.48)	9 (3.54)	4 (1.57)
2.	Lost Home/Homestead Land only	26 (12.62)	48 (23.30)	37 (17.96)	35 (16.99)	27 (13.11)	16 (7.26)	12 (5.83)	2 (0.97)	1 (0.49)	1 (0.49)
3.	Lost both Home/Homestead Land and Agriculture Land	65 (12.85)	117 (23.12)	73 (14.43)	55 (10.87)	51 (10.08)	35 (6.92)	54 (10.67)	23 (4.55)	14 (2.77)	4 (0.79)
	Total	**114 (11.80)**	**204 (21.12)**	**138 (14.29)**	**128 (13.25)**	**104 (10.77)**	**73 (7.56)**	**97 (10.04)**	**44 (4.55)**	**24 (2.48)**	**9 (0.93)**

(Contd.)

Table 6.6: (*Contd.*)

Sl. No.	*Categories of Oustees*	*Intermediate*		*Graduation*		*Post-Graduation*		*Technical*		*Total*		
		Male	*Female*	*Male*	*Female*	*Male*	*Female*	*Male*	*Female*	*Male*	*Female*	*Total*
1.	Lost Agriculture Land only	9 (3.54)	1 (0.39)	4 (1.57)	0 (0.00)	0 (0.00)	0 (0.00)	1 (0.39)	0 (0.00)	131 (51.57)	123 (48.43)	254 (100)
2.	Lost Home/Homestead Land only	0 (0.00)	1 (0.49)	0 (0.00)	0 (0.00)	0 (0.00)	0 (0.00)	0 (0.00)	0 (0.00)	103 (50.00)	103 (50.00)	206 (100)
3.	Lost both Home/Homestead Land and Agriculture Land	2 (0.40)	2 (0.70)	5 (0.99)	3 (0.59)	0 (0.00)	0 (0.00)	3 (0.59)	0 (0.00)	267 (52.77)	239 (47.23)	506 (100)
	Total	**11** **(1.14)**	**4** **(0.41)**	**9** **(0.93)**	**3** **(0.31)**	**0** **(0.00)**	**0** **(0.00)**	**4** **(0.41)**	**0** **(0.00)**	**501** **(51.86)**	**465** **(48.14)**	**966** **(100)**

Note: Figures in parentheses represent percentage to the respective total.

Table 6.7: Distribution of Sample Population According to their Level of Education in Post-Displacement Period

Sl. No.	*Categories of Oustees*	*Illiterate*		*Just Literate*		*Primary*		*Middle*		*HSC*	
		Male	**Female**	**Male**	**Female**	**Male**	**Female**	**Male**	**Female**	**Male**	**Female**
1.	Lost Agriculture Land only	12 (4.72)	35 (13.78)	27 (10.63)	35 (13.78)	17 (6.69)	14 (5.51)	46 (18.11)	26 (10.24)	11 (4.33)	6 (2.36)
2.	Lost Home/Homestead Land only	22 (10.68)	43 (20.87)	41 (19.90)	41 (19.90)	16 (7.77)	7 (3.40)	21 (10.19)	9 (4.37)	2 (0.97)	2 (0.97)
3.	Lost both Home/Homestead Land and Agriculture Land	40 (7.91)	92 (18.18)	61 (12.06)	54 (10.67)	41 (8.10)	30 (5.93)	76 (15.02)	45 (8.89)	26 (5.14)	8 (1.58)
	Total	74 (7.66)	170 (17.60)	129 (13.35)	126 (13.33)	74 (7.66)	51 (5.40)	143 (15.13)	80 (8.28)	39 (4.04)	16 (1.66)

Contd.

Table 6.7: *(Contd.)*

Sl. No.	Categories of Oustees	Intermediate		Graduation		Post-Graduation		Technical		Total		
		Male	Female	Male	Female	Male	Female	Male	Female	Male	Female	Total
1.	Lost Agriculture Land only	8 (3.15)	2 (0.79)	5 (1.97)	3 (1.18)	0 (0.00)	0 (0.00)	5 (1.97)	2 (0.79)	131 (51.57)	123 (48.43)	254 (100)
2.	Lost Home/Homestead Land only	0 (0.00)	1 (0.49)	1 (0.49)	0 (0.00)	0 (0.00)	0 (0.00)	0 (0.00)	0 (0.00)	103 (50.00)	103 (50.00)	206 (100)
3.	Lost both Home/Homestead Land and Agriculture Land	3 (0.59)	5 (0.99)	8 (1.58)	3 (0.59)	0 (0.00)	0 (0.00)	12 (2.37)	2 (0.40)	267 (52.77)	239 (47.23)	506 (100)
	Total	**11 (1.14)**	**8 (0.83)**	**14 (1.45)**	**6 (0.62)**	**0 (0.00)**	**0 (0.00)**	**17 (1.76)**	**4 (0.42)**	**504 (51.86)**	**465 (48.14)**	**966 (100)**

Note: Figures in parentheses represent percentage to the respective total.

6.3.1 Occupation, Skill and Livelihood

Since the project was set up in rural areas it was predominantly the agricultural people who were displaced by the project. The study of the occupational pattern of the oustees shows that due to loss of agricultural land (which was not fully replaced by land for land policy), the oustees have shifted to other sectors of employment. Although they are interested to continue with their agricultural occupation and allied activities, the compensation money and rehabilitation assistance that they received was too meagre to help them to purchase land, given the artificially induced increase in land prices in the neighbourhood. It was found that most of the displaced people were not able to buy more than two acres of agricultural land; on the other hand, for some displaced people, compensation money appeared as a windfall. It was for the first time they were in possession of a large amount of cash. In absence of any guidance to help them to invest the money in proper manner, they squandered it on unwanted consumption.

6.3.2 Occupational Pattern

As all the projects are located in rural areas, the people affected by the projects mainly hailed from agricultural base. Besides agricultural activities, they were also engaged in other activities. Their occupational pattern is broadly classified into two heads, viz. Main occupation and Subsidiary occupation.

6.3.2.1 Main Occupation

In the pre-displaced period, most of the oustees were engaged in agricultural activities. A bulk of them were working in large landowners' farms as daily wage agricultural labourers and some of them were engaged in construction activities and others were daily wage labourers. In the post-rehabilitation period, since the land holding pattern has changed, there has been changes in occupational pattern also. Following tables present the main occupational pattern and their engagement in various activities during the year.

The main occupational profile of the sample households as compared between pre- and post-displacement period reveals that majority of them earn their livelihood by doing wage work in the informal economic sector of the city. It is found out from the field data shown in Tables 6.8 and 6.9 that nearly half (54.96%) of the sample households report cultivation as their principal means of livelihood in the pre-displaced period but in post-displaced period it is reduced to 12.97 per cent. In the pre-displacement period only 11.37 per cent are skilled and semi-skilled category wage earners working as masons, carpenters, mining and quarry, etc., 1.07 per cent are regular service and the rest (38.60%) are exclusive wage workers of unskilled category doing manual physical labour mainly as non-agricultural workers. In the post-displaced period, 12.97 per cent have main occupation as cultivation, 18.65 per cent are agriculture labourer, 37.57 per cent are skilled and semi-skilled category wage earners working as masons, carpenters, mining and quarry, etc., 7.30 per cent are regular service and the rest others are exclusive wage workers of unskilled category doing manual physical labour mainly as non-agricultural workers. Only 3.76 per cent of the households report as being engaged in self-employed occupations in pre-displaced period and 19.73 per cent in post-displaced period like small and petty business in the informal economic sector such as small grocery and stationery shops, vegetable vending, running tea stalls, sweet meat shops, jhompri hotels and eateries, betel shops and the like. Followed to that 6.79 per cent of the households in pre-displaced period and 37.57 per cent of post-displaced households earn their bread by working in informal service sector economy of the city somehow in self-employed or in contractual piecemeal work capacity such as plumbers, electricians, painters, laundry man, barbers and other service providers. 1.07 per cent of the households in pre-displaced period and 7.30 per cent of the households in the post-displacement period report government services as their principal source of earning, 4.56 per cent in pre-displaced period and 3.78 per cent in post-displaced period earn their livelihood by working as informal sector transport workers such as automobile drivers, rickshaw pullers and cart pullers, etc., 0.27 per cent in pre-displaced period and 0.27 per cent in post-displaced period by following traditional craft occupation and working in non-household sector small and tiny manufacturing industries. It is also found that households reporting government service as their principal source of earning are found employed mostly in the Class IV category jobs such as peons, messengers, sweepers, watchmen or as drivers.

Table 6.8: Main Occupation of the Sample Households in Pre-Displacement Period (1996)

Sl. No.	*Categories of Oustees*	*Cultivation*		*Agr. Labour*		*Cottage Industry*		*Large Scale Industries*		*Construction Worker*	
		Male	*Female*	*Male*	*Female*	*Male*	*Female*	*Male*	*Female*	*Male*	*Female*
1.	Lost Agriculture Land only	53 (67.09)	19 (24.05)	0 (0.00)	2 (2.53)	0 (0.00)	0 (0.00)	0 (0.00)	0 (0.00)	0 (0.00)	0 (0.00)
2.	Lost Home/Homestead Land only	5 (5.38)	2 (2.15)	33 (35.48)	33 (35.48)	0 (0.00)	0 (0.00)	1 (1.08)	0 (0.00)	6 (6.45)	0 (0.00)
3.	Lost both Home/Homestead Land and Agriculture Land	82 (40.80)	44 (21.89)	7 (3.48)	15 (7.46)	1 (0.50)	0 (0.00)	3 (1.49)	0 (0.00)	8 (3.98)	3 (1.49)
	Total	**140** **(37.53)**	**65** **(17.43)**	**40** **(10.72)**	**50** **(13.40)**	**1** **(0.27)**	**0** **(0.00)**	**4** **(1.07)**	**0** **(0.00)**	**14** **(3.75)**	**3** **(0.80)**

(Contd.)

Table 6.8: *(Contd.)*

Sl. No.	Categories of Oustees	Mining and Quarry		Trade/Business		Transport		Service		Total		
		Male	Female	Male	Female	Male	Female	Male	Female	Male	Female	Total
1.	Lost Agri. Land only	0 (0.00)	0 (0.00)	2 (2.53)	0 (0.00)`	0 (0.00)	0 (0.00)	3 (3.80)	0 (0.00)	58 (73.42)	21 (26.58)	79 (100)
2.	Lost Home/Homestead Land only	0 (0.00)	0 (0.00)	8 (8.60)	2 (2.15)	2 (2.15)	0 (0.00)	1 (1.08)	0 (0.00)	56 (60.22)	37 (39.78)	93 (100)
3.	Lost both Home/Homestead Land and Agriculture Land	15 (7.46)	6 (2.99)	2 (1.00)	0 (0.00)	14 (6.97)	1 (0.50)	0 (0.00)	0 (0.00)	132 (65.67)	69 (34.33)	201 (100)
	Total	**15 (4.02)**	**6 (1.61)**	**12 (3.22)**	**2 (0.54)**	**16 (4.29)**	**1 (0.27)**	**4 (1.07)**	**0 (0.00)**	**246 (65.95)**	**127 (34.05)**	**373 (100)**

Note: Figures in parentheses represent percentage to the respective total.

Table 6.9: Main Occupation of the Sample Households in Post-Displacement Period (2008)

Sl. No.	Categories of Oustees	Cultivation		Agr. Labour		Cottage Industry		Large Scale Industries		Construction Worker	
		Male	Female	Male	Female	Male	Female	Male	Female	Male	Female
1.	Lost Agriculture Land only	33 (35.48)	9 (9.68)	11 (11.83)	11 (11.83)	0 (0.00)	0 (0.00)	0 (0.00)	0 (0.00)	5 (5.38)	0 (0.00)
2.	Lost Home/Homestead Land only	0 (0.00)	0 (0.00)	12 (12.12)	6 (6.06)	0 (0.00)	0 (0.00)	0 (0.00)	0 (0.00)	38 (38.38)	23 (23.23)
3.	Lost both Home/ Homestead Land and Agriculture Land	6 (3.37)	0 (0.00)	13 (7.30)	16 (8.99)	1 (0.56)	0 (0.00)	8 (4.49)	0 (0.00)	53 (29.78)	11 (6.18)
	Total	**39** **(10.54)**	**9** **(2.43)**	**36** **(9.73)**	**33** **(8.92)**	**1** **(0.27)**	**0** **(0.00)**	**8** **(2.16)**	**0** **(0.00)**	**96** **(25.95)**	**34** **(9.19)**

(Contd.)

Table 6.9: *(Contd.)*

Sl. No.	Categories of Oustees	Trade/Business		Transport		Service		Total		
		Male	Female	Male	Female	Male	Female	Male	Female	Total
1.	Lost Agriculture Land only	16 (17.20)	0 (0.00)	2 (2.15)	0 (0.00)	6 (6.45)	0 (0.00)	73 (78.49)	20 (21.51)	93 (100)
2.	Lost Home/Homestead Land only	11 (11.11)	3 (3.03)	5 (5.05)	0 (0.00)	0 (0.00)	1 (1.01)	66 (66.67)	33 (33.33)	99 (100)
3.	Lost both Home/Homestead Land and Agriculture Land	37 (20.79)	6 (3.37)	7 (3.93)	0 (0.00)	14 (7.87)	6 (3.37)	139 (78.09)	39 (21.91)	178 (100)
	Total	**64** **(17.30)**	**9** **(2.43)**	**14** **(3.78)**	**0** **(0.00)**	**20** **(5.41)**	**7** **(1.89)**	**278** **(75.14)**	**92** **(24.86)**	**370** **(100)**

Note: Figures in parentheses represent percentage to the respective total.

From the above occupational profiles in the pre- and post-displacement periods, it can be seen that there has occurred a significant shift away from agriculture and allied activities to unskilled informal sector wage work. As majority of them are wage workers, there is high risk of employment insecurity. It is reported that the average days of wage employment of a regular wage worker varies between 20 to 22 days during a month and during rainy season, sometimes it comes down to 15 days in a month. Owing to lack of skill and minimum level of education, the quality of human capital is very low and very few among them are capable of earning a minimum and stable level of income to cross the barrier of poverty.

6.3.2.2 Subsidiary Occupation

Besides main occupation, there are marginal workers also who are engaged in different subsidiary activities which provides them additional avenues of employment and this is considered as subsidiary occupation. Tables 6.10 and 6.11 represent the households engaged in subsidiary occupation in both pre- and post-displacement periods. Out of 200 surveyed households 115 persons in pre-displaced period and 38 persons in post-displaced period have subsidiary occupation. Out of 115 persons in pre-displaced period, 16 (13.91%) are engaged in agriculture, 64 (55.65%) are agriculture labourers, 21 (18.26%) are non-agriculture labourers and 14 (12.17%) are engaged in petty business. Similarly out of the 38 persons in post-displaced period, 17 (18.42%) are engaged in agriculture, 19 (50.00%) are agriculture labourers, 9 (23.68%) are non-agriculture labourers, 2 (5.26%) are in petty business and 1 (2.63) is engaged in private service on part-time basis. The oustees are mainly non-agricultural labourers engaged in road construction works like NREGS work introduced by Government of India. As compared to pre-displaced period, the post-displacement period shows no other new subsidiary occupation of the oustees because of non-availability of subsidiary work. As no forest area is found in the post-displacement period, the number of families who took to Minor Forest Produce (MFP) as a subsidiary occupation in the pre-displacement period, have been compelled to take up other avenues as their subsidiary occupation or remain idle at home without any work.

Table 6.10: Subsidiary Occupation of the Sample Surveyed Population in Pre-Displacement Period (1996)

Sl. No.	Categories of Oustees	Cultivation		Agr. Labour		Cottage Industry		Large Scale Industries	
		Male	Female	Male	Female	Male	Female	Male	Female
1.	Lost Agriculture Land only	4 (19.05)	0 (0.00)	13 (61.90)	3 (14.29)	0 (0.00)	0 (0.00)	0 (0.00)	0 (0.00)
2.	Lost Home/Homestead Land only	0 (0.00)	0 (0.00)	4 (25.00)	3 (18.75)	0 (0.00)	0 (0.00)	0 (0.00)	0 (0.00)
3.	Lost both Home/Homestead Land and Agriculture Land	11 (14.10)	1 (1.28)	26 (33.33)	15 (19.23)	0 (0.00)	0 (0.00)	0 (0.00)	0 (0.00)
	Total	**15 (13.04)**	**1 (0.87)**	**43 (37.39)**	**21 (18.26)**	**0 (0.00)**	**0 (0.00)**	**0 (0.00)**	**0 (0.00)**

(Contd.)

Table 6.10: (*Contd.*)

Sl. No.	Categories of Oustees	Construction Worker		Trade/Business		Transport		Total		
		Male	Female	Male	Female	Male	Female	Male	Female	Total
1.	Lost Agriculture Land only	0 (0.00)	0 (0.00)	1 (4.76)	0 (0.00)	0 (0.00)	0 (0.00)	18 (85.71)	3 (14.29)	21 (100.00)
2.	Lost Home/Homestead Land only	6 (37.50)	2 (12.50)	1 (6.25)	0 (0.00)	0 (0.00)	0 (0.00)	11 (68.75)	5 (31.25)	16 (100.00)
3.	Lost both ome/Homestead Land and Agriculture Land	12 (15.38)	0 (0.00)	10 (12.82)	2 (2.56)	1 (1.28)	0 (0.00)	60 (76.92)	18 (23.08)	78 (100.00)
	Total	**18 (15.65)**	**2 (1.74)**	**12 (10.43)**	**2 (1.74)**	**1 (0.87)**	**0 (0.00)**	**89 (77.39)**	**26 (22.61)**	**115 (100.00)**

Note: Figures in parentheses represent percentage to the respective total.

Table 6.11: Subsidiary Occupation of the Sample Households in Post-Displacement Period (2008)

Sl. No.	*Categories of Oustees*	*Cultivation*		*Agr. Labour*		*Cottage Industry*		*Construction Worker*	
		Male	*Female*	*Male*	*Female*	*Male*	*Female*	*Male*	*Female*
1.	Lost Agriculture Land only	4 (33.33)	0 (0.00)	5 (41.67)	2 (16.67)	0 (0.00)	0 (0.00)	1 (8.33)	0 (0.00)
2.	Lost Home/Homestead Land only	0 (0.00)	1 (10.00)	3 (30.00)	4 (40.00)	1 (10.00)	0 (0.00)	1 (10.00)	0 (0.00)
3.	Lost both Home/ Homestead Land and Agriculture Land	2 (12.50)	0 (0.00)	3 (18.75)	2 (12.50)	0 (0.00)	0 (0.00)	3 (18.75)	3 (18.75)
	Total	**6** **(15.79)**	**1** **(2.63)**	**11** **(28.95)**	**8** **(21.05)**	**1** **(2.63)**	**0** **(0.00)**	**5** **(13.16)**	**3** **(7.89)**

(Contd.)

Table 6.11: *(Contd.)*

Sl. No.	Categories of Oustees	Trade/Business		Service		Total		
		Male	Female	Male	Female	Male	Female	Total
1.	Lost Agriculture Land only	0 (0.00)	0 (0.00)	0 (0.00)	0 (0.00)	10 (83.33)	2 (16.67)	12 (100)
2.	Lost Home/Homestead Land only	0 (0.00)	0 (0.00)	0 (0.00)	0 (0.00)	5 (50.00)	5 (50.00)	10 (100)
3.	Lost both Home/Homestead Land and Agriculture Land	0 (0.00)	2 (12.50)	1 (6.25)	0 (0.00)	9 (56.25)	7 (43.75)	16 (100)
	Total	0 (0.00)	2 (5.26)	1 (2.63)	0 (0.00)	24 (63.16)	14 (36.84)	38 (100)

Note: Figures in parentheses represent percentage to the respective total.

6.3.3 Type of Workers

In this study, the workers are mainly grouped under two heads viz. main workers and marginal workers. Out of 488 people, 373 are main workers comprising 76.43 per cent, while 22.60 per cent belong to marginal workers in pre-displacement period. In the post-displacement period, out of 408 cases, 370 are main workers comprising 90.69 per cent while only 9.31 per cent are marginal worker (Table 6.12). Clearly there has been a squeeze or supplementary employment in the post-displacement period.

A significant observation is that among the pre-displaced families in the category 'lost homes/homestead land only' the proportion of main workers is very high (85.32%) and among post-displacement oustees the higher proportion of main workers consist of 91.75 per cent which belongs to 'lost both agriculture and home/homestead land' category oustees. In pre-displaced period the highest percentage of marginal workers is 27.96 per cent in 'lost both home/homestead and agricultural land category' and in post-displacement the highest percentage of marginal workers, i.e. 11.43 per cent belongs to 'lost agriculture land only' category.

6.3.4 Child Labour

In recent years the Government of India in collaboration with the ILO (International Labour Organization) has been taking proactive measures for the elimination of child labour. It is found that despite Supreme Court strictures and running of many child labour schools by the NCLP (National Child Labour Project) for the rehabilitation of child workers, quite a few children in the study resettlement area are found working at present. When making an enquiry with the households having child labour and focus group discussions conducted in the localities revealed that due to acute poverty and insufficient level of earning of the principal earner of the households many children are forced to work in order to supplement the meagre income of the family. In some cases the parents feel it wiser to send the children to work for earning their bread instead of putting them under food insecurity conditions faced by the family off and on. It may be seen from Table 6.13 that out of a sample of 200 households,

Table 6.12: Distribution of Workers in the Sample Households in Pre-and Post-Displacement Period

Sl. No.	*Category*	*Pre-Displaced (1999)*			*Post-Displaced (2008)*		
		Main	*Marginal*	*Total*	*Main*	*Marginal*	*Total*
1.	Lost Agriculture Land only	79 (79.00)	21 (21.00)	100 (100.00)	93 (88.57)	12 (11.43)	105 (100.00)
2.	Lost Homes/Homestead Land only	93 (85.32)	16 (14.68)	109 (100.00)	99 (90.83)	10 (9.17)	109 (100.00)
3.	Lost both Home/Homestead Land and Agriculture Land	201 (72.04)	78 (27.96)	279 (100.00)	178 (91.75)	16 (8.25)	194 (100.00)
	Total	**373 (76.43)**	**115 (23.57)**	**488 (100.00)**	**370 (90.69)**	**38 (9.31)**	**408 (100.00)**

Note: Figures in parentheses represent percentage to the respective total.

14 (7.00%) households send their children to work as those households are suffering from the problems of acute poverty and insufficient level of earning in the post-displaced period and the same was four (2.00%) in pre-displaced period. Of the total households having child labour only one household has reported that because of expensive education system it is better to send the children to work instead of sending them to the school. Interestingly none of the households having child labour has reported that they send the children to work in order to earn more or to acquire skills to enable the child to earn more in future. Also, it was observed that the parents in the resettlement colonies were conscious about the usefulness of education for a bright future of their children but were compelled to send them to work due to acute poverty.

It was also observed from the data that out of 8 (5.03%) children in 6-14 age group out of a total of 159 do not attend any school and they belong to completely illiterate category. It is quite possible that all such children presently not attending any school are either workings as child labour or doing domestic chores including taking care of their younger siblings at home to enable both the parents to work as wage workers. As child labour is now banned by the Government some of them might have preferred to hide the fact that their children work to earn for the family. As regards child workers' nature of employment and occupations, the query held with people revealed that many work as food vendors in family-owned informal eateries, some work in traditional caste based occupations like laundering and washing of clothes and some others work in small garages and *dhabas*.

Table 6.13: Causes of Child Labour

Sl. No.	*Causes of Child Labour*	*No. of HHs*	
		Pre-displaced	**Post-displaced**
1	Acute Poverty and insufficient earning	4 (2.00)	13 (6.50)
2	Expensive education	0 (0.00)	1 (0.50)
3	Less usefulness of education for poor children to earn a livelihood	0 (0.00)	0 (0.00)
4	To earn more	0 (0.00)	0 (0.00)
5	Others	0 (0.00)	0 (0.00)
	Total	**4 (2.00)**	**14 (7.00)**

Note: Figures in parentheses refer to percentage.

6.3.5 Land Holding Pattern

Due to acquisition of agricultural land, all the land owning displaced families became landless. Some persons from 'lost agriculture land only' category could purchase agricultural land by utilizing the compensation money, received against the acquisition of land. Some have squandered the money. But all the oustee's families including landless get an opportunity to purchase a patch of agricultural land from the rehabilitation assistance that has been provided by project authorities. This was an opportunity for all the families including landless to become landed. Thus it is imperative to know whether all the families have purchased land and became landed.

Table 6.14: Category-wise Percentage of Farmers in Sample Households

Sl. No.	*Category of Farmer*	*Agriculture Land only*		*Home/Homestead Land only*		*Both Agr. Land and Home/Homestead Land*	
		Pre-	*Post-*	*Pre-*	*Post-*	*Pre-*	*Post-*
1.	Landless	0.00	26.67	97.73	100	0.00	94.59
2.	Small	82.22	48.89	0.00	0.00	79.28	3.60
3.	Marginal	6.67	13.33	0.00	0.00	12.61	0.90
4.	Medium	8.89	8.89	2.27	0.00	8.11	0.90
5.	Large	2.22	2.22	0.00	0.00	0.00	0.90
	Total	**100**	**100**	**100**	**100**	**100**	**100**

Table 6.14 shows that maximum households in the category of 'lost both agriculture land and home/homestead land' are landless farmers (94.59%) in post-displaced period due to no compensation for land against land. In this area no more agriculture land was available for land based rehabilitation. As per the R&R Policy, the project authority should have provided 2 acres of irrigated land or 4 acres of non-irrigated land to the oustee's family. But due to non-availability of agriculture land, land based rehabilitation was not possible. In the category of 'lost agriculture land only', only 26.67 per cent households became landless after displacement and the percentage of small farmers was 48.89 per cent, medium farmers was 8.89 per cent and large farmers, only 2.22 per cent. As compared to pre-displacement period there were no farmers in landless family, 82.22 per cent were small farmers, 6.67 per cent were marginal farmers, 8.89 per cent were medium farmers and only 2.22 per cent farmers were large farmers.

Table 6.15: Average Land Holding Size of the Sample Households in Pre- and Post-Displacement Period

Sl. No.	*Category*	*No. of HHs*	*Agriculture Land*			
			Pre-Displaced		*Post-Displaced*	
			Qty.	*Annual Income*	*Qty.*	*Annual Income*
1.	Lost Agriculture Land only	45	1.96	13689	2.05	9733
2.	Lost Homes/Homestead Land only	46	0.14	1136	0.00	0.00
3.	Lost both Home/Homestead Land and Agriculture Land	109	1.61	11530	0.13	505
	Total	**200**	**1.36**	**9729**	**0.54**	**2470**

Note: Figures in parentheses represent average.

Table 6.15 shows that the category of 'lost agriculture land only' possesses an average of 1.96 acre of land, while an average of 0.14 acre of land is possessed by the category of 'lost homes/homestead land only' households and the category of 'lost both homes/homestead land and agriculture land' possesses an average of 1.61 acres in the pre-displaced period. In the post-displacement period average land holding has increased in the category of 'lost agriculture land only', i.e. 2.05 acre but in the rest of the two categories it has been reduced to 0.00 acre and 0.13 acres respectively. In comparison to pre-displacement period, the average income from agriculture land in all the categories of households has been reduced substantially in the post-rehabilitation period.

Several reasons could be attributed for the considerable reduction in average land holding size and in the number of medium and large farmers in the post-displacement period.

(i) Initially when the agricultural land of the displaced people was acquired for the development projects, there was a huge gap not only between date of issue of notification of land acquisition and the date of payment of compensation of money but also between the date of payment of compensation money and date of physical shifting of the displaced people. As a result, the displaced people continued to cultivate the agricultural land in the acquired villages and paid little attention to purchasing land in new villages. By the time evacuation took place most of the displaced people had spent the compensation money on luxurious and other items without purchasing land in new villages.

(ii) As per the R & R policy the project authorities should provide land based resettlement. But the authorities could not provide stipulated amount of agricultural land to displaced people, and cash in lieu of land was announced.

When the cash payment was announced, at first the displaced people showed extra enthusiasm. They were carried away by the prospects of possessing heavy cash in preference to permanent gain of land and spent the rehabilitation assistance on other heads. They could not utilize the money in a proper manner and spent money mostly on liquor, purchase of fashionable items like Transistors, Watches, Dress materials etc. As a result, they could not purchase the amount of land prescribed in the R & R guidelines, i.e. 4 acres of unirrigated land or 2 acres of irrigated land.

(iii) When the displaced people spent the rehabilitation assistance on other items and not on purchase of land, the project authorities could have opened savings bank accounts in the name of each entitled displaced people and directed that money will be released if the displaced peoples purchase agricultural land and the amount will be disbursed at the time of actual registration of land. This was an innovative idea. Instead of paying dividends, this could act in a more productive way. Taking this opportunity, the Revenue Inspectors, officers-in-charge and the local middlemen and other unscrupulous elements take the benefit from this innovative policy. Several false land transactions could be made without proper verification and money released to the displaced people and the middlemen, Revenue Instructor and officers-in-charge can take their share. Even in some cases, the same patch of land was sold to different displaced people and the rehabilitation assistance was released by the R & R Unit.

(iv) The rehabilitation assistance for purchasing agricultural land in new villages was too less in comparison to market prices of the land. When the people in the new villages came to know that the displaced people would purchase land the price of various categories of land was hiked over night. This sudden artificial hike in land prices forced the oustee families to purchase less amount of land. This picture is almost identical among all the caste groups, which clearly indicates that displacement has drastically affected the economic condition of the displaced people irrespective of caste groups in terms of land holdings.

6.3.6 Cropping Pattern

The project affected villages fall under the Rushikulya river basin. Most of the families in these villages are involved primarily in agricultural activities for their sustenance. Their land holdings are small, with many families owning less than an acre each. Among those families dependent on agriculture, 56 per cent are land owners and the rest are landless agriculture labourers. Paddy is the major crop grown during the Kharif season since irrigation facilities are not available and only one major crop can be harvested in a year during the monsoons. The mode of agriculture is still primitive and the use of modern agricultural implements is unknown.

Before displacement, a variety of crops such as paddy, pulses, ragi, millet, maize, various types of oil seeds, vegetables and tobacco were grown by the people in different categories of land such as plain land, low land etc. At this time Kewra (also known as Kewda, Ketaki and Kia), a shrub plant whose flowers are used for the extraction of perfume was grown on public land in the area and along the boundaries of the agricultural fields. In the past decade, Kewra has emerged as one of the important sources of income for the villagers. Its flowers bloom mainly between June and December; they are collected by the villagers and sold to the local distillers for extracting crude perfume which is then further processed into a variety of value added products in Uttar Pradesh. Although Kewra as an industry has leapfrogged in India both in volume and in value with ever increasing popularity of Pan Masala, the benefits of this growth have not reached the rural poor of Orissa. The major part (over 90%) of the value addition is carried out outside the State. Further, the income from this industry is seasonal and does not provide any sustained employment to the villagers. Thus, to some extent, Kewra in its present state is not the boon the Ganjam district dwellers perceive it to be; yet, it has the potential of being a panacea for the region if scientific methods of growth and distillation within Ganjam are introduced.

But in the post-displacement period, most of the displaced people have been resettled in plain areas. Types of land under cultivation at present are thus totally different. Due to change in the variety of land under cultivation, there is a drastic change in the cropping pattern in the post-rehabilitation period. The cropping pattern is almost becoming monocrop one with paddy as the principal crop. And production of other crops is very minimal. As a result, there is total change of cropping pattern and production of pulses, oilseeds is almost *nil*. The table below shows the cropping pattern and production of different crops, their value in post-rehabilitation period. The value of crops is estimated over the local market prices and yield of crops is for the year 2008.

Table 6.16: Average Output of Different Crops in Post-Displacement Period

Sl. No.	*Category*	*Total Agr. Land (in Acre)*	*Cereals*	*Pulses*	*Vege-table*	*Others*	*Total Output (in Qtl.)*
1.	Lost Agriculture Land only	92.27	15.41	0.56	0.25	0.50	16.72
2.	Lost Homes/ Homestead Land only	0.00	0.00	0.00	0.00	0.00	0.00
3.	Lost both Home/ Homestead Land and Agriculture Land	14.80	0.87	0.00	0.00	0.00	0.87
	Total	**107.07**	**16.28**	**0.56**	**0.25**	**0.50**	**17.59**

Table 6.16 shows that, rice has become the principal crop and production of other crops is very negligible. The table shows that in the post-rehabilitation period, the category of households who 'lost agriculture land only' is dependent upon agriculture sources. Due to that, their agriculture production is highest among all other categories. There is no agriculture land in the category of 'lost home/homestead land only' after the displacement. So there are no crops grown in this category after the displacement.

6.3.7 Household Income

The income, expenditure and savings data of households has been adjusted for inflation according to the GSDP (Gross State Domestic Product) of Orissa State where the project is based. Deflator has been calculated as per details given below and adjustments made to arrive at comparative figures. The GSDP data was obtained from the Bureau of Statistics of Government of Orissa.

Data for the pre-displacement period was collected for the year 1996-97 and for the post-displacement period for the year 2007-08. Adjusting to the base year 1999-2000, this data for 1996-97 and 2007-08 have been expressed in terms of 1999-2000 base year prices so as to make them comparable in real terms.

(a) GSDP Implicit Deflator 1996-97

$$\frac{\text{Nominal GSDP}}{\text{Real GSDP}} = \frac{\text{GSDP at Current Price}}{\text{GSDP at Constant Price}}$$

$$= \frac{2913335}{3499604} = 0.832476$$

The nominal income of 1996-97 has been divided by the deflator to express it in terms of 1999-2000 prices.

b) GSDP Deflator for 2007-08

$$= \frac{12216467}{7841012} = 1.558022$$

The income of 2007-08 has been divided by the deflator to convert it to real income at 1999-2000 prices.

By comparing the average per capita income of oustees for the pre-displaced periods (1996-97 and 2007-08), we find that there has been a considerable decline in income following displacement—by as much as 42.88 per cent (Table 6.17), implying significant impoverishment.

Table 6.17: Average Income per Month/Annum of the Sample Households, Pre- and Post-Displacement Periods

Sl. No.	*Category*	*No. of HHs*	*Income (in Rs.)*			
			1996-97		*2007-08*	
			Monthly	*Annum*	*Monthly*	*Annum*
1.	Lost Agriculture Land only	45	2965	35580	1728	20736
2.	Lost Homes/Homestead Land only	46	1688	20256	1021	12252
3.	Lost both Home/ Homestead Land and Agriculture Land	109	3787	45444	2126	25512
	Total	**200**	**3141**	**37692**	**1794**	**21528**

Note: The income of both pre-displacement and post-displacement years, i.e. 1996 and 2008 has been adjusted to 1999-2000 values with base year. The Gross State Domestic Product (GSDP) deflator has been used for the purpose.

A comparison of income range between pre- and post-displacement period shows that there is also little change in the high income group due to the employment provided by project authority to the oustees in the post-displacement period. The agriculture income is reduced due to lack of agricultural land in the post-displacement period. This shows that before displacement agriculture was the main source of income of majority of people. They were cultivating either settled land, un-settled land or encroached land. The economy was mostly based on land and people depended heavily on natural resources. Low income has been generated from agriculture after displacement because oustee families have lost considerable amount of land and have less dependence on forests and livestock. After displacement also, labour income has declined. Before displacement, annual average income of a labourer was Rs. 4,263 and after displacement this has reduced to Rs. 2,865, a decrease of 32.80 per cent. At the time of focused group discussion with oustees, it was found that as there is limited source of non-agriculture work in the new resettlement area, the number of days of employment has reduced drastically.

6.3.8 Expenditure Pattern of Sample Households

The average consumption expenditure of the sample households on food and non-food related items are 57.45 per cent and 42.55 per

Table 6.18: Distribution of Sample Households According to their Size of the Annual Income

Sl. No.	*Income Range (In Rupees)*	*Lost Agriculture Land Only*		*Lost Home/Homestead Land Only*		*Lost both Agr. Land and Home/Homestead*	
		Pre-	*Post-*	*Pre-*	*Post-*	*Pre-*	*Post-*
1.	Upto 10,000	1 (2.22)	1 (2.22)	12 (26.08)	9 (19.56)	5 (4.59)	13 (11.93)
2.	10,000-12,000	3 (6.67)	4 (8.89)	9 (19.56)	4 (8.69)	1 (0.92)	3 (2.75)
3.	12,000-15,000	6 (13.33)	7 (15.56)	2 (4.34)	1 (2.17)	9 (8.26)	6 (5.50)
4.	15,000-18,000	10 (22.22)	7 (15.56)	5 (10.86)	8 (17.39)	3 (2.75)	5 (4.59)
5.	18,000-21,000	3 (6.67)	5 (11.11)	9 (19.56)	5 (10.86)	9 (8.26)	10 (9.17)
6.	21,000-25,000	5 (11.11)	4 (8.89)	1 (2.17)	0 (0.00)	9 (8.26)	5 (4.59)
7.	25,000-30,000	5 (11.11)	1 (2.22)	3 (6.52)	6 (13.04)	10 (9.17)	7 (6.42)
8.	30,000-40,000	4 (8.89)	5 (11.11)	3 (6.52)	11 (23.91)	27 (24.77)	25 (22.93)
9.	40,000-50,000	1 (2.22)	2 (4.44)	0 (0.00)	2 (4.35)	12 (11.01)	10 (9.17)
10.	50,000-60,000	2 (4.44)	0 (0.00)	0 (0.00)	0 (0.00)	7 (6.42)	8 (7.34)
11.	60,000-80,000	6 (6.67)	4 (8.89)	1 (2.17)	0 (0.00)	10 (9.17)	8 (7.34)
12.	80,000-1,00,000	0 (0.00)	2 (4.44)	1 (2.17)	0 (0.00)	6 (5.50)	4 (3.67)
13.	1,00,000 and Above	2 (4.44)	3 (6.67)	0 (0.00)	0 (0.00)	1 (0.92)	5 (4.59)
	Total	**48 (100)**	**45 (100)**	**46 (100)**	**48 (100)**	**99 (100)**	**109 (100)**

Note: Figures in parentheses represent percentage to the respective total.

cent respectively in pre-displaced period and 55.48 per cent and 44.52 per cent respectively in post-displaced period. The modal consumption expenditure of the households on food and non-food related items are Rs. 2,562 per month, out of which 57.00 per cent is spent on food only in pre-displaced period and in post-displacement period; Rs. 1,629 per month, out of which 55.00 per cent is spent on food only. Interestingly, the average monthly consumption expenditure of the sample households is less than the average monthly income. But, this does not indicate better living condition of the sample households. It has been found that the majority of the sample households in the surveyed locations are perpetually reeling under debt incurred from both formal and informal sources. Such debts are incurred mostly to meet basic subsistence needs of the households and unforeseen immediate needs like medical expenditure in case of sickness of family members. Also, social obligatory needs like marriage of sons and daughters or close relatives and birth, death rituals in the family force many among them to borrow from informal sources. It is because of payment of high interest for the debt incurred from informal sources like moneylenders or chit fund agencies, the households of the sample are not able to meet the essential consumption needs of the family in majority of the cases.

A detailed analysis of the consumption pattern of the sample households further reveals that consumption of cereals mainly rice constitutes bulk of the household expenditure made on food related items. Among the other food related items, amount spent on fuel constitutes the major chunk of expenditure. As a result, very few of the households are able to access adequate protein in their diet. The main vegetables consumed by the households are edible leaves, onion, and potato. For many pulses and non-vegetarian food like meat, fish, eggs, etc. are a luxury which they afford to consume only on special occasions. In this situation, amount spent on clothing, shelter, education, etc. are much less. Rather, it has been observed that among the non-food related expenditure, forced expenditure on medicine and frequently occurring endemic diseases such as diarrhoea, malaria, scabies, gastroenteritis, etc. constitutes the major share. Due to unhygienic living environment people frequently fall sick, mainly the vulnerable groups like small children and elderly people in 60 plus age group. This leaves little money for meeting the clothing and shelter related expenditure. The houses where they live in, remain un-repaired and ill-maintained, as only a very nominal amount is left out after meeting all other non-food related basic necessities. To add further to their miseries, it has been found that the principal earners of the households are slave to their bad personal habits like consumption of country liquor, smoking, chewing of tobacco, betel leaf, etc. It is found that quite a few of them spend more than one-fourth of their monthly earnings on non-food related personal habit goods.

Table 6.19: Average Expenditure per Annum of the Surveyed Oustee Households

(in Rs.)

Sl. No.	Category	No. of HHs	1996 Food	1996 Non-Food	1996 Total	2008 Food	2008 Non-Food	2008 Total
1.	Lost Agriculture Land only	45	16449 (55.59)	13142 (44.41)	29590 (100)	11405 (57.98)	8266 (42.02)	19670 (100)
2.	Lost Homes/Homestead Land only	46	11493 (63.02)	6744 (36.98)	18237 (100)	7892 (67.12)	3866 (32.88)	11757 (100)
3.	Lost both Home/Homestead Land and Agriculture Land	109	20612 (56.96)	15575 (44.04)	36187 (100)	11784 (52.19)	10796 (47.81)	22581 (100)
	Total	**200**	**17669** **(57.45)**	**13085** **(42.55)**	**30754** **(100)**	**10843** **(55.48)**	**8702** **(44.52)**	**19545** **(100)**

Note: Figure in parentheses represent average.

6.3.9 Poverty Status: Post Displacement

The official poverty line estimated for Orissa during 2004-05 and based on MPCE (Monthly Per Capita Consumption Expenditure) was Rs. 325.79 for rural areas and Rs. 528.49 for urban areas (Mahendra Dev and C. Ravi, 2008). After including per capita expenditure on health and education, the revised estimates are Rs. 348.68 for rural Orissa and Rs. 585.39 for urban Orissa (*ibid.*). As the oustees under the study inhabit rural Orissa, the figure of Rs. 348.68 has been used to calculate the poverty line of the households. The average size of family for the sample households was 5.22. Therefore, the poverty line works out to Rs. 21,841 (Rs. 348.68*5.22*12) per household per annum.

Applying this estimate and rounding off the BPL (Below Poverty Line) income to Rs. 21,000 per annum it can be found from Table 6.18, that almost half, i.e. 44 per cent of the oustees presently live below the poverty line. However, this would be an underestimate of the extent of poverty since it is based on poverty line income of 2004-05 and not on that of 2007-08 and also poverty line income has been rounded off downwards. As against this, it is found that according to NSS, 2004-05 (Mahendra Dev and C. Ravi, 2007) 47.76 per cent of the people in rural Orissa live below the poverty line based on a uniform recall period. As compared to the incidence of poverty in rural India at 29.18 per cent, that of Orissa at 47.76 per cent is very high and indeed the highest in India. The condition of oustees is almost at par with that of Orissa and indicates the acute nature of poverty.

As per the standard norms, ultra poor households are identified by those falling below 75 per cent of the BPL level of income, which in this case works out to Rs. 16,381 and is rounded off to Rs. 16,500. It is found from Table 6.18 that 29 per cent of the total oustees or around 65.9 per cent of the BPL households are categorized as ultra poor households. These figures are higher than the state estimates of ultra poor at 25.16 per cent and 52.68 per cent of the population and all poor (Mahendra Dev and C. Ravi, 2007). This clearly reflects the precarious living condition of the oustee families at present compared to the state as a whole after displacement.

6.3.10 Savings

The analysis of income, expenditure and asset position of the oustee households in the sample shows that very few among them are left with substantial sum of unspendable income in the form of savings. Hardly 10 per cent among them regularly save some money either on monthly or yearly basis to meet unforeseen needs. It is found that the households, where the earners are employed in Government services or in organized sector private establishments, make regular savings for the welfare and development of the family members. Among such households, many of them have retained their compensation money intact in the form of fixed savings and time deposits in nationalized banks and Post Offices. But the majority lives a life of hand-to-mouth existence and quite a few of them live in perpetual debt.

6.3.11 Savings and Insurance Particulars

It is found that low income level coupled with employment and earning insecurity for majority of the households hardly enable the urban poor to go for regular savings and insurance schemes for the social security measures. Only of late, thanks to the initiation of micro savings through the formation of Self-Help Groups (SHGs) by the government agencies and NGOs quite a few among them are now being covered under the SHGs.

Table 6.20: Savings and Insurance Particulars

Sl. No.	Monthly Savings/Insurance (in Rs.)	Savings (No. of HHs)	Insurance (No. of HHs)
1	Up to Rs. 100	82 (56.94)	25 (49.02)
2	100-150	29 (20.14)	10 (19.61)
3	150-200	18 (12.50)	7 (13.73)
4	200-300	4 (2.78)	2 (3.92)
5	300-500	7 (4.86)	4 (7.84)
6	500-700	4 (2.78)	3 (5.88)
	Total	**144 (100.00)**	**51 (100.00)**

It may be seen from Table 6.20 that out of a total of 200 households covered under the survey, 144 (72.00%) households are now doing regular monthly savings and 51 (25.50%) households have been covered under life insurance schemes. However, it is seen from the Table that due to low income base, majority of the households (56.94%) save up to Rs.100.00 per month. Next to them 20.14 per cent of the households save around Rs. 100-150 per month, 12.50 per cent save between Rs. 150-200, 2.78 per cent between Rs. 200-300, 4.86 per cent between Rs. 300-500 and 2.78 per cent between Rs. 500-700 per month. It has also been revealed from the discussions held with the people that the households who save up to Rs. 100.00 per month, save through SHGs and mostly use that savings money among the group members as short term loans to meet contingent and unforeseen needs such as, for medical purpose or for meeting basic consumption needs of the households.

Similarly, out of 51 households covered under insurance policies near about 50 per cent of them contribute up to Rs. 100 per month towards insurance premium. Of the rest, 19.61 per cent pay monthly insurance premium between Rs. 100-150, 13.73 per cent between Rs. 150-200, 3.92 per cent between Rs. 200-300, 7.84 per cent between Rs. 300-500 and 5.88 per cent between Rs. 500-700 per month.

6.3.12 Indebtedness

Although debt is manifestation of negative savings and weak

economic position of a household or nation at the macro level, debts and loans are not bad if these are utilized for productive investment or expansion of economic activities of a household or nation. Under the poverty alleviation programmes, especially, after the nationalization of commercial banks the Government has taken steps to advance loans to the weaker sections in order to enable them to earn decent form of livelihood by investing the loan money in productive income generating activities and micro enterprises. These loans from the formal type financial institutions are made available to the poor at a very low level of interest with adequate subsidy component. So, if such loans are made available to the poor and channelized for gainful occupations and activities, we may not characterize such loans as increasing indebtedness of the poor.

However, in the case of resettlement colonies and cluster villages it is found that although loans from the formal sector financial institutions are made available to oustee families under more liberal terms and conditions because of their weak and vulnerable socio-ecological positions in the place of resettlement, they have become loan defaulters with increasing debt burdens. In addition to the Government, the oustee families borrow from informal sources at higher level interest of 60 to 120 per cent per annum depending upon the collateral securities offered by them to the private moneylenders in the village. The informal loans are incurred to meet immediate consumption needs and other socio-economic and medical needs such as marriage, birth and death rituals, illness of family members and the like. As these loans are made in a scenario of low and uncertain income of the household, the high level interest put the loanee households into the debt trap.

Although savings habit has, of late, developed among the sample households due to formation of SHGs by the Government agencies and NGOs, it is found that people living in rural area invariably borrow from informal sources as many of them suffer from employment insecurity problem coupled with inadequate level of earning. It is seen from the data shown in Table 6.21 that out of a total of 200 sample households, 120 (60.00%) of them were indebted at the time of survey. The average amount of debt incurred by the sample households for various purposes is found to be Rs. 11,644. The enquiry with the respondents further revealed that such loans were mostly obtained from informal sources as it was difficult for majority of them to meet formal paper needs and collateral security obligations insisted by the formal public lending institutions like banks and co-operative societies. It has been found that among the borrower households, the majority (40.00%) borrow from the informal source or from the SHGs to meet basic subsistence needs of the households and the average amount of loan incurred for such purpose is found to be Rs. 6,964. Next to this, it is found that people borrow for the purpose of pursuing one's own occupation and the average amount borrowed by such category of households is Rs. 12,691. Apart from that it is found some of the households (16.67%) in the sample are highly indebted due to reckless spending made on marriages and other social rituals of their close kin and the average amount of loan taken for such purpose by the debtor households is Rs. 21,948. Another major cause of indebtedness is unforeseen health expenditure that compels many of them (15.00%) to knock the door of moneylenders. It is seen that the average amount of loan taken by the sample households for productive economic activities like pursuing one's own occupation or for making investment on education of children is much less than the loan obtained for unproductive economic activities. Among the debtor households, only one (0.83%) has borrowed for the education of the principal earners or family members and the average amount of debt incurred for such purpose is Rs. 17,000. At the time of focus group discussion held with different sections of people in the sample, it was found that the debtor households borrow not only to meet emergent contingent needs, but also they often borrow to clear old debts or for the purpose of constructing illegal hutments for their shelter. In the sample the researcher came across seven (5.83%) households who had borrowed money from one moneylender to repay the debt of another moneylender or to repay the money borrowed from SHG on scheduled time. This shows that indebtedness of the rural poor households is a perennial problem and the present credit policies followed by the public lending institutions is mostly unfriendly and unreachable for the rural poor.

Table 6.21: Causes of Incurring Debt by the Sample Households

Sl. No.	*Causes of Debt.*	*No. of HHs.*	*Average Amount (in Rs.)*
1	For Business/Occupation	26 (21.67)	12691
2	For Subsistence needs	48 (40.00)	6964
3	For Diseases and Sickness	18 (15.00)	11373
4	For Education of Self/Family Members	1 (0.83)	17000
5	For Social obligations/rituals	20 (16.67)	21948
6	Others	7 (5.83)	10336
	Total	**120 (100.00)**	**11644**

6.3.13 Asset Structure

In the pre-displacement period the displaced people possessed various kinds of assets like agricultural land, homestead land, farm equipments, livestock, consumer durables etc. Thus, it is imperative to analyze the asset structure of the oustees in the pre- and post-rehabilitation period and Table 6.22 below presents the asset structure and average value of assets.

The poverty of the sample households has made them vulnerable in all aspects of life. The poor households in the sample are hardly left with any valuable assets to bale them out from unforeseen disasters and calamities that affect them off and on in a disaster prone locality of the area where they reside. Needless to say, coastal Orissa is frequently affected by the problem of floods and cyclones almost every alternate year. As most of the resettlement colonies of the sample households are located in low lying and unhygienic areas, the poor households become the double victims of disaster and post-disaster problems that visit them off and on in the forms of spread of epidemic, destruction of shelter and measly family assets. The analysis of assets position of the households in the sample households reveal that the average value of assets owned by households is Rs. 32,290 only. This includes all consumer durables including gold and silver ornaments in majority of the households. More so, it is found that due to high level of disparity in the earning and skill level of the different households, there exists wide disparity in the assets position of the households also. It may be seen from Table 6.22 that almost one-fifth of the households in the sample possess less than Rs. 10,000 worth value of assets, whereas almost one-fourth among them possess assets valuing more than Rs. 50,000. The average values of assets owned by the latter category households is Rs. 77,000 and interestingly this is the modal value of assets owned by the sample households. This type of disparity reflected in the assets position of the households, of course, implies the unintended effects of the resettlement policies followed by the Government for the rural poor. It has been observed that quite a few non-poor category households presently reside in the resettlement colonies meant for the rural poor.

Table 6.22: Assets Position of the Households

Sl. No.	*Value of Assets (in Rs.)*	*No. of HHs*	*Per cent*	*Avg. Value (Rs.)*
1	Below 5000	10	5.00	3071
2	5000-7000	21	10.50	5324
3	7000-10000	5	2.50	7964
4	10000-15000	23	11.50	10857
5	15000-20000	16	8.00	15528
6	20000-30000	35	17.50	22608
7	30000-40000	33	16.50	32137
8	40000-50000	8	4.00	42083
9	50000 and above	49	24.50	77358
	Total	**200**	**100**	**32290**

Displacement not only brings about changes in lifestyle and standards of living of the oustees but also changes in the asset structure. Shifting to a new location directly affects the movable as well as immovable properties. In most of the cases fewer people are likely to have land as an asset after displacement due to:

(i) Acquisition of their land forcing them to shift to other occupations.

(ii) Prohibitive price of land elsewhere which they cannot pay because of inadequate compensation money they had received.

(iii) The absence of land for land principle in the rehabilitation policy as already pointed out above.

There is of course an increase in the holding of financial assets. The extent of livestock asset also changes as it depends on the availability of space for maintenance and of fodder. In contrast to this, there is a possibility of increase in the possession of durable goods, as the oustees for the first time were exposed to outside markets.

The average quantity of agricultural land per oustee family is only 0.54 acre in post-rehabilitation period. But in pre-displacement period, the oustee family occupied 1.36 acres of agriculture land which shows 60.29 per cent decline in agricultural land. Similarly, there is a decline in the quantity of homestead land from 1.11 acre to 0.18 acre per family in post-rehabilitation period. There is a decline in possession of livestock in post-rehabilitation period. The average value of livestock has declined from Rs. 3,411 in pre-displacement period to Rs. 961 per oustee family in post-rehabilitation period to the extent of 71.82 per cent reduction due to selling of livestock during transit period or death of some livestock for want of acute shortage of fodder and drinking water.

There is a reduction in the extent of ownership of farm equipments like sickles, axes, spades, and wooden plough due to reduction in the size of agriculture land after rehabilitation. As stated above there is of course an increase in the financial assets. The oustee families get cash compensation in lump sum and some of them deposit the money in financial institutions. There is an increase of consumer durables as the oustees for the first time were exposed to outside markets. The average value of consumer durables per oustee family increased from Rs. 1,332 in pre-displacement period to Rs. 2,643 in post-rehabilitation period showing an increase of 98.42 per cent. The value of other assets like gold, silver, watch, bicycle, radio which was Rs. 779 per family during pre-displacement period, became Rs. 3,427 per family after post-displacement period and such an increase in the average value of assets is due to the fact that displaced people received cash compensation in lump sum and purchased various household assets. However, all the non-land physical assets acquired by the oustee households are unproductive and do not contribute anything to the current income stream.

6.3.14 Housing Pattern

The housing pattern of the displaced people was very simple as it was in pre-displacement period. Mostly they were residing in double or single room kutcha houses made of mud, bamboo, thatch, straw etc. They had constructed their houses in their own land. Table 6.23 shows the housing pattern in the pre-displacement period.

Table 6.23: Type of Houses Owned by Oustees (Pre-Displacement)

Sl. No.	*Categories of Oustees*	*Percentage of Households*			
		Kutcha	*Semi-Pucca*	*Pucca*	*Total*
1.	Lost Agriculture Land only	55.56	22.22	22.22	100
2.	Lost Homes/Homestead Land only	72.73	27.27	0.00	100
3.	Lost both Home/Homestead Land and Agriculture Land	42.34	38.74	18.92	100
	Total	**52.00**	**32.50**	**18.50**	**100**

In the pre-displacement phase, out of 200 sample households, 52.00 per cent were staying in kutcha houses. Of the sample, 32.50 per cent households used semi-pucca (tile/asbestos) houses. Only 18.50 per cent households used pucca concrete houses in the sample.

In the post-displacement phase, out of 200 sample households, only 5.50 per cent households are staying in kutcha houses. Of the sample, 8.50 per cent households used semi-pucca (tile/asbestos) houses and 56.00 per cent households are staying in pucca/concrete houses as revealed in Table 6.24. The percentage of kutcha houses has reduced and that of pucca/concrete houses has increased in the post-displacement period because the compensation money has been used towards construction of new houses of the oustees. These figures show the development of the housing pattern of the oustees after the displacement.

Table 6.24: Type of Houses Owned by Oustees (Post-Displacement)

Sl. No.	*Categories of Oustees*	*Percentage of Households*			
		Kutcha	*Semi-Pucca*	*Pucca*	*Total*
1.	Lost Agriculture Land only	20.00	35.56	44.49	100
2.	Lost Homes/Homestead Land only	0.00	0.00	100.00	100
3.	Lost both Home/Homestead Land and Agriculture Land	1.80	0.50	97.30	100
	Total	**5.50**	**8.50**	**56.00**	**100**

In comparison to pre-displacement period, as far as the housing pattern of all three categories are concerned, the displaced people are better off in the post-displacement period as there is an increase in number of pucca and semi-pucca/asbestos houses. This could be attributed to the rehabilitation assistance which all the displaced people got in post-rehabilitation period which provided an opportunity to construct better houses of their own choice.

6.3.15 Size of Living Rooms

The families were living in single, double or three rooms kutcha houses before displacement and this has been depicted in Table 6.25. So far as size of living room of the households was concerned, out of 200 sample households, 2.00 per cent households were staying in single room houses, 23.00 per cent were residing in double room houses and 59.00 per cent were living in three to five room houses and the rest 16.00 per cent were staying in more than 5 room houses (Table 6.25).

Table 6.25: No. of Living Rooms of Oustees (Pre-Displacement)

Sl. No.	*Categories of Oustees*	*Percentage of Households*				
		Only 1	*1 to 2*	*3 to 5*	*5 and Above*	*Total*
1.	Lost Agriculture Land only	6.67	17.78	64.44	11.11	100
2.	Lost Homes/ Homestead Land only	0.00	47.73	45.45	6.82	100
3.	Lost both Home/ Homestead Land and Agriculture Land	0.90	15.32	62.16	21.62	100
	Total	**2.00**	**23.00**	**59.00**	**16.00**	**100**

In the post-rehabilitation period it is observed that out of 200 sample households, only 0.50 per cent households are residing in single room house, 2.50 per cent households are staying in double roomed houses, 122 (61.00%) households are living in three to five roomed houses and 36.00 per cent households are residing in more than five roomed houses (Table 6.26).

In post-rehabilitation period it is found that the number of houses with double rooms and single rooms has decreased and three to five and more than five rooms houses have are increased due to the compensation money being invested towards the construction of good houses.

Table 6.26: No. of Living Rooms of Oustees (Post-Displacement)

Sl. No.	*Categories of Oustees*	*Percentage of Households*				
		Only 1	*1 to 2*	*3 to 5*	*5 and Above*	*Total*
1.	Lost Agriculture Land only	2.22	11.11	66.67	20.00	100
2.	Lost Homes/Homestead Land only	0.00	0.00	90.91	9.09	100
3.	Lost both Home/Homestead Land and Agriculture Land	0.00	0.00	46.85	53.15	100
	Total	**0:50**	**2.50**	**61.00**	**36.00**	**100**

6.3.16 Dwelling Condition

It is needless to mention that the socio-economic condition of people of a particular place or region gets reflected in their dwelling set up. Food, shelter and cloth are three basic necessities of life and man always tries to fulfil and improvise these three basic necessities in order to improve the quality of life. However, when we made an observation of the dwelling units of the oustees in resettlement colonies and the cluster villages at the time of field study, those were found to be no better than any other poor rural households of the region. Due to lack of capital, they have failed to develop the homestead plots for residential purposes. In the case of poor households, the houses were found to be hurriedly and haphazardly erected, as makeshift arrangement of mud, bamboo and straw. Since the cash compensation received was for the loss of house only, in the case of rural landless household it was too low, and they failed to utilize the compensation money towards construction of house in the place of resettlement. Rather the compensation money was spent on meeting basic consumption needs of the households in the process of their transition from the place of original inhabitations to the resettlement areas. Table 6.27 shows that out of total 200 samples, 65.00 per cent houses are in good condition, 10.50 per cent are in moderate condition and 24.50 per cent are in bad condition of the oustees households.

Table 6.27: Quality of House Construction of the Oustees (Post-Displacement

Sl. No.	*Categories of Oustees*	*Percentage of Houses*			
		Good	*Moderate*	*Bad*	*Total*
1.	Lost Agriculture Land only	77.78	4.44	17.78	100
2.	Lost Homes/Homestead Land only	20.45	2.27	77.27	100
3.	Lost both Home/Homestead Land and Agriculture Land	77.48	16.22	6.31	100
	Total	**65.00**	**10.50**	**24.50**	**100**

6.3.17 Sources of Fuel for Cooking Purpose

Fuel is a major issue and one of the important requirements of villagers in the study area. Table 6.28 shows that during the pre-displaced period 94.00 per cent of the families were using wood for cooking purpose, only 1.00 per cent of families used Liquefied Petroleum Gas (LPG) and 5.00 per cent families used other source of fuel for cooking purpose. Table 6.29 shows sources of the fuel used by post-displaced oustees in the study area. It shows that 94.00 per cent families are using wood, 25.00 per cent are using LPG and 33.00 per cent are using other sources of fuel like cow dung, straw etc. for cooking purpose. There are no major changes in the source of fuel for cooking purpose in post-displacement period.

Table 6.28: Sources of Fuel for Cooking (Pre-Displacement)

Sl. No.	*Categories of Oustees*	*Percentage of Households Using*			
		Wood	*LPG*	*Other*	*Total*
1.	Lost Agriculture Land only	91.11	4.44	4.44	100
2.	Lost Homes/Homestead Land only	88.64	0.00	11.36	100
3.	Lost both Home/Homestead Land and Agriculture Land	97.30	0.00	2.70	100
	Total	**94.00**	**1.00**	**5.00**	**100**

Table 6.29: Sources of Fuel for Cooking (Post-Displacement)

Sl. No.	*Categories of Oustees*	*Percentage of Households Using*			
		Wood	*LPG*	*Other*	*Total*
1.	Lost Agriculture Land only	64.44	20.00	15.56	100
2.	Lost Homes/Homestead Land only	88.64	6.82	20.45	100
3.	Lost both Home/Homestead Land and Agriculture Land	97.30	34.23	45.05	100
	Total	94.00	25.00	33.00	100

6.3.18 Sources of Drinking Water

Another major issue and one of the important requirements of villagers in the study area is availability of safe drinking water. It was revealed from the study that families mainly depend on either tube well or open well for drinking water purpose. It has been observed that in all the villages the families indicated that water level of tube wells as well as the open well goes down considerably during summer and they face great deal of difficulty in fetching drinking water. The river water is also polluted with sewerage and effluents from nearby industries and affects health of persons taking bath in the river water. During summer season, these tube wells dry up creating lot of difficulty for the villagers.

The analysis of the data (Table 6.30) collected on sources of drinking water for the oustee families in pre-displacement period, reveals that about 66.00 per cent of families depended on open well, 2.00 per cent on hand pumps, 31.00 per cent on tube wells and only 1.00 per cent were depending on rivers for drinking water purpose. But as compared with post-displaced period Table 6.31 shows that 59.00 per cent of the families depend upon open well, 4.00 per cent of family on hand pumps and the rest 37.00 per cent depend upon tube wells for drinking water purpose. The families also indicated during the study that water level of tube wells as well as the open well goes down considerably during summer and they face some difficulty for fetching drinking water.

Table 6.30: Sources of Drinking Water (Pre-Displacement)

Sl. No.	*Categories of Oustees*	*Percentage of Households Using*					
		Open Well	*Hand Pump*	*Tube well*	*Pond*	*River*	*Total*
1.	Lost Agriculture Land only	64.44	0.00	31.11	0.00	4.44	100
2.	Lost Homes/Homestead Land only	72.73	2.27	25.00	0.00	0.00	100
3.	Lost both Home/Homestead Land and Agriculture Land	63.96	2.70	33.33	0.00	0.00	100
	Total	**66.00**	**2.00**	**31.00**	**0.00**	**1.00**	**100**

Table 6.31: Sources of Drinking Water (Post-Displacement)

Sl. No.	*Categories of Oustees*	*Percentage of Households Using*					
		Open Well	*Hand Pump*	*Tube well*	*Pond*	*River*	*Total*
1.	Lost Agriculture Land only	46.67	0.00	53.33	0.00	0.00	100
2.	Lost Homes/Homestead Land only	54.55	2.27	43.18	0.00	0.00	100
3.	Lost both Home/ Homestead Land and Agriculture Land	65.77	6.31	27.93	0.00	0.00	100
	Total	**59.00**	**4.00**	**37.00**	**0.00**	**0.00**	**100**

6.3.19 Sanitation and Electricity

It has been observed at the time of survey of the households that in majority of the cases people are huddled together like animals in one room tenements without any basic civic amenities like latrine, electricity, and aboveall a water proof structure to rest their heads. Dirt and dust flow all-around, filths and garbage, liquid effluents accumulate on the road and give space for the unhindered births of flies and mosquitoes. The pungent smell of un-removed garbage and filths remain unnoticed and indicate the helpless condition of the poor all-around. Even the so-called resettlement colonies look as bad as the densely populated squatters located in the study area and spread of deadly epidemic diseases like diarrhoea, malaria, jaundice, typhoid, scabies, etc. are regular phenomena of these localities. The off and on occurrence of all such diseases in the scenario of inadequate subsistence for majority of the residence compound the problem and in the absence of an effective public health delivery mechanism, the medical bills of the hapless poor sky rocketed and put the poor into the debt trap.

Table 6.32: Sanitation Facilities (Pre-Displacement)

Sl. No.	*Categories of Oustees*	*Percentage of Households Using*			
		Open Field	*Barpalli*	*Sanitary Latrine*	*Total*
1.	Lost Agriculture Land only	80.00	4.44	15.56	100
2.	Lost Homes/Homestead Land only	100.00	0.00	0.00	100
3.	Lost both Home/Homestead Land and Agriculture Land	91.89	0.00	8.11	100
	Total	**91.00**	**1.00**	**8.00**	**100**

As discussed, in pre-displacement period as Table 6.32 shows only around 9.00 per cent had access to toilet facility within the households (8.00 per cent had sanitary latrines and 1.00 per cent had barpalli latrines) and hardly 2 per cent of them had independent bathroom facility. Around 91 per cent of people used open fields for their defecation.

But after the displacement the use of open field towards defecation has changed and only 27.00 per cent households have access to open fields and rest 73.00 per cent of households have access to toilet facility within the household premise and hardly around 20 per cent of them have independent bathroom facility and it is found that almost 80.00 per cent of the sample households have access to electricity (Table 6.33). After displacement the use of open fields has been reduced and oustees faced a lot of problems towards their defecation and due to that most oustees used latrine in their premises.

Table 6.33: Sanitation Facilities (Post-Displacement)

Sl. No.	*Categories of Oustees*	*Percentage of Households Using*			
		Open Field	*Barpalli*	*Sanitary Latrine*	*Total*
1.	Lost Agriculture Land only	68.89	4.44	26.67	100
2.	Lost Homes/Homestead Land only	31.82	9.09	59.09	100
3.	Lost both Home/Homestead Land and Agriculture Land	8.11	24.32	67.57	100
Total		**27.00**	**16.50**	**56.50**	**100**

Regarding access to electricity it was found that though they resided close to the city of Berhampur, 50 per cent of the households did not have access to electricity. This improved to more than 80 per cent after displacement. Tata Steel provided free electricity for 10 years at the Rehabilitation Colony and it has been withdrawn only recently and meters have been installed so that the oustees pay for their own use. This has caused a lot of resistance among the people. At the time of survey the street lighting facility had been withdrawn by Tata Steel and not taken up by the government which caused the roads in the new colony to lie in darkness causing fear among the people to move around after dark.

6.4 Utilization of Compensation Money

A majority of the population in the project area belongs to general castes and other backward castes. Most of the people had agriculture as the main occupation in the pre-displacement period. But after the displacement they mostly depended on wage employment and providing services as required by the local village community. These backward communities, especially the Scheduled Castes and Tribals were relatively unexposed or under exposed to monetary transactions. Further, since most part of the rural economy was based on barter system, people were not well accustomed to managing cash. Hence handling huge amount of compensation amount was really difficult for them and seeing the same, the project authorities rightly deposited them in post offices and local banks after opening accounts in the name of the each individual displaced people. The most important question that arises here is that whether the PAPs were able to utilize the compensation money and rehabilitation assistance properly by acquiring productive assets or for self-employment purposes, which was expected to minimize the effect of dislocation. Quite often, the affected people being mostly illiterate and without proper guidance, they squander away compensation money. As a result, their living condition deteriorates bringing negative consequences on their future living. Therefore to understand the post-displacement living conditions of PAPs, it is necessary to study the pattern of utilization of compensation as it reveals a lot of about their attitude towards monetary transaction.

For meeting the crucial requirement to improve or at least restore the economic status of the project oustees, there was a commitment from the R&R Unit to provide a package of different rehabilitation benefits to every displaced family. As per the guidelines laid down in the rehabilitation policy such benefit includes rehabilitation assistance comprising: (a) agricultural land, (b) homestead land, (c) house construction assistance, and (d) maintenance allowance.

Table 6.34: Purpose-wise Utilization of Compensation Money

Sl. No.	Categories of Ousetees	House Construction		Purchase of Agr. Land		Purchase of Other Assets		Social Expenditure	
		No. of HHs	% of Utilised	No. of HHs	% of Utilised	No. of HHs	% of Utilised	No. of HHs	% of Utilised
1	Agr. Land only	21	28.58	2	31.50	3	8.00	37	31.22
2	Home/Homestead Land only	16	58.66	1	5.00	12	5.75	20	49.55
3	Both	89	45.36	10	9.70	18	3.28	52	39.33
	Total	**126**	**44.25**	**13**	**12.69**	**33**	**4.61**	**109**	**38.45**

Source: Field Survey 2007-08.

From the above table it can be seen that house construction was the highest component of expenditure followed by social expenditure like marriages etc. Only 12 per cent of the compensation amount was spent on purchase of agricultural land and only 4.61 per cent was spent on purchase of other assets. It can be inferred that the compensation money was mostly spent on non-income generating assets like house construction though it may have aided in improving the standard of living.

6.5 Other Impacts

6.5.1 Impact on Women

Change caused by relocation does not have equal implication for the members of both the sexes and may result in greater inconvenience to women. Due to disturbance in production system, reduction in assets like land and livestock, women have to face the challenges of running large households within limited income and resources. This, in turn, forces the women as well as their children to participate in work for supplementing the household income. In contrast to this, due to changes that takes place due to any developmental project, especially changes in environment and labour ratio, these women who at present are engaged in activities like agricultural labour, or collection and sale of forest products find themselves unemployed and dependant. This section analyzes women's role in the economy of the household, their daily routine and social positioning in terms of their say in the decision-making at the household level.

In the project under study, it has been found that the displaced community has been compelled to live with much reduced resource proximity, and what was available in relatively substantial amounts in the original villages is much more difficult to access now. And women have to spend more time now and walk greater distances for fuelwood collection, which used to be a steady income supplement previously and also not so easy to get any longer. So also, have the food supplements from the forests like fruits and tuber, declined. For collecting water, women in the new settlements have to walk 2-3 km. to fetch water as hand pumps provided by the project are either inadequate or defunct. In the summer the village ponds provided also get dry and getting water becomes difficult.

But the worst strain is on women in settlements adjacent to existing villages. Here the host community resents the increased competition for scare natural resources like fuel, and fodder. Even water resources become a cause of tension. Here the women from the displaced communities are at a constant disadvantage, as the original inhabitants claim the primary rights to the Common Property Resources (CPR).

6.5.2 Festivals and Rituals

In the new resettlement also the shrines, temples and other community facilities do not hold significance for the oustees. This pattern of interdependence between caste and tribes and the exchange of services among the kinsmen have become rare. The number of Tribal Gods and Goddesses is decreasing and seems to be losing importance. Among the oustees, the tribals are very traditional in their outlook. They value their traditions despite the hardship they face. They portray their past as glorious and feel nostalgic; the attachment they had with their tabernacles and sacred groves is emotional and cannot be returned back in the new resettlement site.

In the tribal societies prime importance is given to religious practices in every walk of life. Religion, for them, assures or explains most of the complexities of nature. Besides being the mechanism of social control various activities are smoothly organized through religions.

6.5.3 Political Life

Politically the oustees in the new resettlement site virtually have the status of non-citizens. The channels of communication and expression are very weak and poor. The members of the host community always play dominant role and have an upper hand in every aspect of life. The oustees are treated as new members or outsiders. They do not take part in decision making process in the village community. Even the oustees themselves have so many problems but they do not have motivation and interest to think about the village as a whole. They do not have a major role to play regarding the village problems or any other functions. Due to this low motivation and interest, their participation in Panchayat elections is very low. The problems of displacement and relocation issue are not issues in Panchayat and Assembly elections also.

After resettlement, particularly in the established villages, new forces of control of one group is forced upon and imposed upon the other group. This starts to disorient their relation with human, natural and spiritual domain in a cumulative manner, perhaps in an irreversible manner.

6.5.4 Community Life

After displacement, displaced people have not been resettled en-bloc in the new location site and were resettled in different clusters. As a result their family ties have been broken and their kith and kin and relatives are not staying with them. Because of this, the network of community relationship is not strong enough in the new village as it was earlier. For them network of kinship is limited and in the new village they are forced to live a marginal life. In conversation with them it was found that they seem to have developed a fear psychosis in the alien land and unfamiliar surroundings.

Cultural dissimilarity between the resettlers and the local

population is another factor, which further complicate the process of resettlement. In a multi caste village this problem ends sometimes in conflict and major confrontation. It is also observed that sometimes the way of life of the resettlers does not fit into the norms and customs of the host-community.

6.6. Risk Factor Analysis of Study Project

In the light of our above empirical analysis of the socio-economic impact of displacement in a specific context it would be worthwhile to examine a dominant model of 'impoverishment risk' caused by displacement, in order to provide deeper meanings to our several empirical findings.

Development-induced displacement has resulted in widespread traumatic psychological and socio-cultural consequences. These include dismantling of production systems, desecration of ancestral sacred zones or graves and temples, scattering of kinship groups and family systems, disorganization of informal social networks that offer mutual support, disruption of trade and market links, etc. There is also a loss of social relationships which provide avenues of representation, mediation and conflict resolution. The very cultural identity of the community, as well as the individual within it, is disrupted causing immense physiological and psychological stress. Thus, it is clear that displacement brings in its train certain adverse effects and risks which have economic, social and communal implications.

According to the World Bank guidelines, the rehabilitation policy should be such as to avoid, or minimize displacement, and in case when displacement is unavoidable, to provide to people displaced by a project with the means to improve or at least restore their former living standards, earning capacity and production levels through a process in which they participate through their own social and cultural institutions. The stress on these minimum requirements assumes importance because in almost all cases, the displaced persons face risk of impoverishment.

Similarly, the rehabilitation policies adopted by various project authorities or State Governments, have laid emphasis on improvement of the quality of life of the oustees after their displacement. It is evident that impoverishment is the key issue in development-induced population displacement and resettlement. A research study conducted by Michael M. Cernea, celebrated Anthropologist, Senior Adviser for Sociology and Social Policy of the Environment Department of World Bank, found that the worst consequences of displacement—impoverishment and violations of basic human rights—occur most frequently when national resettlement policy guidelines are absent. Consequently, equitable action strategies for socio-economic reestablishment are not pursued, and there is no independent professional monitoring and evaluation of outcomes (Cernea, 1996). The 'impoverishment risks' have been identified by Michael M. Cernea for constructing a descriptive model based on "the analysis of the vast evidence coming up from numerous displacement and resettlement process that reveals patterns of recurrent characteristics. While each of these characteristics is distinct and irreducible to the others, they have a common denominator: all are dimensions of a multifaceted process of impoverishment. These characteristics may be linked into a coherent typology or descriptive model of impoverishment risks through displacement. Such a conceptualization or descriptive model of impoverishment is a tool usable in strategy formulation and device for practical planning, because it points to the key sets of likely ill-effects that projects must purposively avoid" (Cernea, 1994). The impoverishment risks model captures not only the economic but also the social and cultural dimensions of impoverishment. It shows that during displacement the people lose: (i) natural capital, (ii) man-made (physical) capital, (iii) human capital, and (iv) social capital. The model is able to accurately predict future outcomes if the warnings are ignored. The risk model also provides a matrix directly usable for planning. It is a working tool for preparing resettlement plans and monitoring their impact. The conceptual construct of impoverishment through displacement contains in a nutshell the model for the socio-economic rehabilitation of the displaced.

The eight sub-processes that converge in impoverishment are not the only processes of economic and social deprivation, but rather the most important ones. In different locations, they occur with variable intensities. The eight dimensions of this impoverishment risks model are:

(i) Landlessness,

(ii) Marginalization,
(iii) Joblessness,
(iv) Homelessness,
(v) Food Insecurity,
(vi) Loss of Access to Common Property,
(vii) Social Disarticulation, and
(viii) Increased Morbidity and Mortality.

(i) Landlessness

"Expropriation of land removes the main foundation upon which people's productive systems, commercial activities and livelihoods are constructed. This is the principal form of de-capitalization and pauperization of displaced people, as they lose both physical and man-made capital" (Cernea, 1995).

Unless this foundation is reconstructed elsewhere, or replaced with steady income-generating employment, landlessness sets in and the affected families are impoverished. Land in India is more than a resource base and it has more than market value. It has emotional associations for those who inherit it from their ancestors; it enables to grow food for subsistence and cash crops with which to obtain money to buy essentials. It is often considered to be sacred, a status symbol that provides guarantee for easy access to loan and helps in getting better marriage alliances in the family and represents self-sufficiency an independence in a society bound by feudal norms. Besides, local religious beliefs and ritual customs are closely associated with land.

Landlessness also implies loss of access to green vegetables, religious trees, and gifts of nature. The economic value of medicinal herbs and plants with multiple usages, which are accessible to the landed people, cannot really be estimated.

Further, landlessness has very serious social and economic implications not only for the owner of the land, but also his family, children, as well as for future generations, as it provides hidden employment for every member of the family.

In all the categories covered in this study, the authorities paid compensation to those displaced people who possessed *pattas* (registered land deeds) to prevent risks of landlessness after displacement and relocation. The compensation included "the market value" of the land, and 30 per cent of that amount as solatium because of compulsory acquisition. Any delay in payment of compensation was compensated by paying interest at annual rate of 12 per cent.

As cash compensation alone is often inadequate to make up for the loss of land, as part of rehabilitation the displaced persons were sometimes provided with land and/or job. There is no option land for land in this study displaced oustees because of there is no availability of agriculture land in this area, cash equivalent of such amount of land have been provided to the displaced families in addition to the cash compensation for their land as per the rehabilitation policy. Although "land for land" option is the major principle followed in the rehabilitation policy for irrigation projects in Orissa, cash is also paid partly or sometimes fully in absence of availability of adequate land.

It is thus evident that most of the displaced persons do not have land at all. It has been observed that the compensation money was not adequate for the purchase of land of the same size as owned by the oustee in the past, due to rise in land prices in his locality in recent years. In this project the compensation money kept in the bank accounts, was not released in time or in adequate instalments when land was available for purchase. Thus, even the protective mechanism provided by the authorities often became an obstacle in the way of the oustees' attempts to buy land, thanks to the bureaucratic hurdles. But it is observed in this project that the category of lost agriculture land only increases the need for agricultural land after the post-displacement period. They utilized their compensation money towards buying agriculture land because of their main occupation is only cultivation.

Landlessness has reduced the income levels of the displaced persons in all these projects. The occupational pattern has also changed significantly, with the stress shifting from primary to secondary or tertiary activities. It has also rendered aged persons unemployed since they could not get jobs in the projects, while they could have earned something from their agricultural land had they been in possession of it. They have also lost the advantages of herbal therapy with the loss of their land and the forests where the medicinal plants used to grow and which they used for the treatment of their ailments. The loss of land has also forced them to spend more on green vegetables which they earlier grew in their own kitchen gardens.

In other words, jobs could never compensate for the land that they have lost. For them, land was a multi-purpose asset which could have been of continuous use for future generations at numerous levels. In contrast, the jobs which have been provided to the oustees by the well-meaning authorities in the projects can satisfy the immediate needs of only the present generation who are employed. These jobs can never be considered as assets that would sustain the future generations.

In view of the rise in the incidence of landlessness among the project-affected oustees, certain measures should be taken by the project authorities to overcome and counter the impoverishment risks of landlessness. The following are being suggested:

(1) 'Land for land' is considered to be the most viable option in any rehabilitation policy to pre-empt the emergence of the problem of landlessness. Hence, the Government, or the project authorities should take measures to rehabilitate the oustees on a 'land for land' basis.

(2) The land provided to the oustees should be properly reclaimed, and levelled also, so as to make it operationally productive.

(3) Land allotted to the oustees should be in one lot so that the operation on it is easy.

(4) Care must be taken to provide land to the oustees near the resettlement site.

(5) Replacement value should be paid for land so as to enable those who had lost land to purchase the same amount of land near their place of habitation.

Reasons for not overcoming the Risk Factor

There are many reasons which have landed the PDFs in the "landless" status. The main reasons are:

(i) They spend the Compensation and Rehabilitation Assistance money for unproductive purpose often spending the money for such purpose like daughter's marriage, merry making, drinking liquor and repayment of loans.

(ii) Middlemen in many cases cheat the illiterate PDPs and take away a big chunk of their entitlement.

(iii) The DPs invest the money on non-sustainable, unviable projects which have no techno-economic entitlement.

(ii) Marginalization

Marginalization occurs when families lose economic power and slide downwards. Unlike the case of those reduced to total landlessness due to displacement, middle income farm households do not become landless, but decline to the status of small land holders when displaced. Small shopkeepers and craftsmen lose their clientele, and slip below the poverty threshold after their displacement. Relative marginalization often begins long before the actual displacement. For instance, when lands are designated for future acquisition and therefore become devalued, there is no likelihood of any fresh public and private investments in infrastructural facilities, or expansion of social services, in those areas (Cernea, 1995).

But it is not only the middle farmers or the shopkeepers and artisans (who may not be landless), but also the other segments of the ousted population which get marginalized by displacement. Marginalization is caused by the deprivation of land, employment and home, and indicates that loss of land, productive assets and livelihood has resulted in a 'downward mobility' among the oustees. Resettled families, very often, cannot today fully restore the economic capacities that they possessed in their habitat prior to their displacement. For instance, if those who owned fertile land in the past are provided with unproductive and unlevelled land in new sites by the project authorities, they invariably become marginalized among the landed people. Marginalization also occurs through the loss of income from extra-agricultural sources in the locality, which again were disrupted by the acquisition of the entire area (i.e. the village, or the neighbourhood) by the project authorities.

In the project surveyed so far, the fact that marginalization has taken place can be obvious when one observes the changes in the landholding pattern of the displaced persons. For instance, in this study project, there has been increase in the number of landless among the oustees from 21.50 per cent (in the pre-displacement period) to 80.50 per cent (after displacement). But rest of all the categories of farmers of this study have decreased except large farmers which is constant, i.e. only 1 (0.50%) farmer. The number of small farmers has decreased from 62.50 per cent to 13.00 per cent, the number of marginal farmers from 8.50 per cent to 3.50 per cent and that of middle farmers from 7.00 per cent to 2.50 per cent. It seems that those who received rehabilitation cash grant diverted it to other purchasable items instead of land.

(iii) Joblessness

Landless labourers, people working in some enterprise or service, workers, artisans and small businessmen, lose their means of livelihood if they are displaced from their habitat. But creation of new jobs, or alternative sources of income for them, is difficult and requires substantial investments. The delay results in a long drawn-out period of unemployment or underemployment among the oustees after their physical displacement (Cernea, 1995).

Joblessness is a state of affairs where a person who loses his/her only source of livelihood due to displacement, does not possess any skill to learn new methods of earning his/her livelihood. In the Orissa development projects which we have studied, the overwhelming majority of the oustees were traditional cultivators who did not have skills for any other occupation. All the members of the agricultural family—men, women and children—used to contribute to the family budget by working in the fields, or supplementing the income by doing odd agriculture-related jobs. But in the monetary market that was exposed to them after their resettlement, and in which they were compelled to operate, it was the male members of the households who became the sole bread-earners, as jobs in the projects were given to them only. Their money power prevailed over the voices of the other members of the family—particularly the women who were rendered powerless—who became totally dependent on them, and ended up in frustration. In the Scheduled Caste and Scheduled Tribe families in particular, joblessness can be deciphered in terms of loss of income-earning opportunities, especially for women, who earlier used to earn by collecting and selling minor forest produce. In other words, those who were owners of the means of production before their displacement have now become daily wage earners in a situation of uncertain employment opportunities which amounts to a state of joblessness.

In the study project, oustees who had owned land were benefited by the rehabilitation policy. But artisans, share-croppers, landless labourers, those employed in services, and small businessmen, who lost their occupations and means of livelihood because of displacement, were not recognized as displaced persons eligible for rehabilitation benefits under the resettlement and rehabilitation policy of the project authorities.

(iv) Homelessness

Loss of house and shelter may be only temporary during the transition period for most of the displaced. But for some, homelessness remains a chronic problem. In a broader cultural sense, homelessness is also placelessness, loss of a group's cultural space and identity, or cultural impoverishment. And in a socio-spatial sense, placelessness is often perceived, albeit at a lower intensity, by populations subjected to compulsory villagisation schemes (Cernea, 1995). If resettlement policies do not explicitly provide improvement in housing conditions, or if compensation for demolished shelters is paid at assessed value rather than replacement value, the risk of homelessness increases.

A home facilitates the living together of the family members. It gives a sense of belonging, social and psychological security and an assurance of togetherness in times of difficulty. A home offers a psychological and a spiritual attachment with ancestors. A home provides familiar equipment for living and meeting the environmental and cultural demands. Homelessness is caused by displacement. It is also caused by the splits in the family that frequently takes place during displacement. The alternative house in the resettlement colony is given to the family, but because of the split in the family, the outgoing members become homeless. But it is observed in this study that there is only 1 (0.50%) household with only one room and the rest households have above one-bedded room house in their own, i.e.

5 (2.50%) households have two-bedded rooms, 122 (61.00%) have 3 to 5-bedded rooms and 72 (36.00%) households have more than 5-bedded rooms. It also signifies that the oustees have taken more compensation money and also diverted that money towards construction of houses after the displacement.

(v) Food Insecurity

Forced uprooting increases the risk of chronic food insecurity defined as calorie-protein intake level below the minimum necessary for normal growth and work. Sudden drops in food crops availability and/or incomes are inevitable during physical relocation and hunger or under nourishment tend to linger as long-term effects (Cernea, 1995).

In an agrarian society, crops are grown that provide food to the family for the entire year or greater part of the year. In kitchen gardens, vegetables are grown almost throughout the year. Only surplus food crops or vegetables are sold in the market. Hence, in years of good harvests, the cultivators are usually self-sufficient as far as food is concerned, and do not depend on the market. But land acquisition in the project areas has destroyed that self-sufficiency. After displacement, they now spend money to procure foodgrains and vegetables. They also have to cope with high prices of essential commodities.

In the study project the income oustees are not self-sufficient for food during the year. The displaced persons buy food items from the market with the money they earn from their jobs. As the family has to buy everything from the market, it is difficult to manage and procure adequate food, depending only on one man's salary. Besides, in many families a major chunk of the salary is diverted from food items to electronic gadgets like transistors, TV and VCR sets and motor cycles.

(vi) Loss of Access to Common Property

For poor people, particularly for the landless and otherwise assetless people, loss of access to non-individual, common property assets belonging to communities that are relocated (forest lands, water bodies, grazing land, etc.) leads to a major deterioration in their income and livelihood levels. Such lost resources are never compensated for by the government in the relocation schemes anywhere (Cernea, 1995).

The forest land or the village common land, though not owned by families, belongs customarily to the village clans or lineage group. These common property resources are used or occupied on the basis of usufruct or similar occupation-based tenure and not based on individual ownership. In such cases, as the project-affected persons did not own any *patta* to show their rights to these lands, they were held ineligible for compensation by the project authorities.

As per the procedures of Land Acquisition Act, 1994 in the sample study project, no compensation has been provided for such common properties. In the absence of any policy measure, the displaced persons could not get any replacement for the common property that they lost. No resettlement colony has been provided with common land like burial grounds or grazing land. The colonies are also located far away from the forest, as a result of which the oustees do not have any access to fuelwood and other minor forest produce which they used to collect earlier in their old habitat. In the past, many of them earned a good living by selling such produce. In the absence of these resources, the displaced people tend to encroach on reserved forests or increase the pressure on common property resources of the host population, leading to social tensions and increased environmental deterioration.

(vii) Social Disintegration

Forced displacement tears apart the social fabric and the existing patterns of social organization. Production systems are dismantled, kinship groups and family systems are often scattered, local labour markets are disrupted, and the cultural identity of the people is put at risk. Life sustaining informal social networks of mutual help among people, local voluntary associations, self-organized service arrangements, etc. are dispersed and rendered inactive. All these represent a massive loss of unquantified and uncompensated facilities. Such 'elusive' disintegration process undermine livelihood in ways uncounted by planners (Cernea, 1995). It is hard to rebuild the forms of social organization that mobilize people for actions of common interest and for meeting pressing needs, once they are dismantled (Cernea, 1996).

Household networks help people to cope with poverty through informal loans, exchanges of food, clothing and durable goods, mutual help with farming, building houses and caring for children. Social and kinship relations enable a group of people to remain a community, because they provide the bond that helps to tide over many economic and social problems. They also provide 'mutual help arrangement', labour exchange relationships, production oriented informal organization etc. All these are irreversibly affected and got lost in the process of displacement. This loss also affects the ability of the community to manage its socio-economic and even cultural affairs because of the weakening of traditional authority, leadership and social control.

Social disintegration takes place also because of lack of linkages with others and the loss of economic status. The payment of compensation and rehabilitation cash assistance granted to major sons, encouraged the latter to dominate over family affairs leading to splitting of joint families and loss of family support to the vulnerable members of the family (like old parents or grandparents or widows). Similar problems erupt when only one job is provided to one member in the family. This breeds conflicts among brothers. The old emotional bond disappears as the need for individual survival becomes greater than any other concern, and money power becomes vital.

Social disintegration has been a major impoverishment risk in all the projects studied so far. In this study, the category of lost home/homestead land only and both agriculture land and home/homestead land, the mutual help arrangement, labour exchange relationships and production oriented informal organizations etc. and other socio-economic relationships have been totally disrupted.

(viii) Increased Morbidity and Mortality

Serious diseases result form the social stress, insecurity and psychological trauma caused by displacement. Relocation-related diseases, particularly parasitic and vector-borne (malaria, schistosomiasis) break out because of unsafe water supply and poor sewerage systems in the resettlement sites, which also cause epidemics and proliferate diarrhoea, dysentery, etc. The weakest segments of the demographic spectrum—infants, children and the elderly—are the most vulnerable to these diseases (Cernea, 1995).

Displacement is associated with psychological stress that emerges out of the fear of relocation. An additional cause of stress is the fear of abandoning places of worship, which the oustees fear, may invite the wrath of gods and goddesses. The result of all this may be a rise in the incidence of mental and physical ailments, and even death. The emotional stress is aggravated by a feeling of helplessness, as no amount of argument; plea or revolt can prevent their inevitable forcible evacuation. Displacement and their subsequent resettlement, lack of food and unhygienic living and environmental conditions have adverse impact on the health of the displaced.

Thus, from the findings of our household survey and direct observation of the resettlement areas, we may now arrive at the conclusion that the general socio-economic condition of the oustee is very poor and miserable. There is existence of wide socio-economic inequalities among the oustee households due to lack of equal access to remunerative and well-paid occupations in the place of resettlement and virtual collapse of the traditional agricultural economy. Only a few of the affluent and well-to-do households among the oustees could manage to cope with the problem of involuntary displacement by migrating to urban areas on their own or by shifting their traditional occupations from agriculture to service or formal tertiary sector employment.

Due to acquisition of agricultural land, all the landed displaced families become landless. But the oustee families including landless got an opportunity to purchase a patch of agricultural land from the rehabilitation assistance. This was an opportunity for all families to become landed. In spite of getting the opportunity, all the displaced could not possess land in post-rehabilitation period as some of them squandered away the money. But in comparison to pre-displacement period, there is an increase in landless category of households and decrease in the small, marginal and medium category of households, as already seen.

After displacement, the cropping pattern has changed drastically and the pattern is almost becoming a monocrop one, with rice as the principal crop. The production of other crops like pulses, various cash crops including oil seeds and Kewra (Kewda, Ketaki and Kia) is very minimal. Not only there is a change in cropping pattern, but also considerable fall in the yields and income of different crops.

Dependence on forest was quite high during preacquisition

period. Collection of fuelwood, fodder, timber and other forest product was a regular feature. But at present, dependence on forest and forest resources has come down as most of the displaced people have resettled in plain areas. The minor forest produces which they were collecting from forest; now they are purchasing these things from the market. Not only forest, but also the dependence on trees, livestocks has reduced substantially in post-rehabilitation period.

The study of occupational pattern of the oustees shows that due to displacement and loss of agricultural land (which was not fully replaced by land for land policy) oustees have shifted to other sectors of employment. More and more households have been found engaged in agricultural labour and non-agricultural labour activities. There has been reduction in average man-days of engagement in primary and secondary occupations. Due to loss of agricultural land, decrease in dependence on forest, trees, livestock, the total household income of oustees has come down.

The family composition of the oustees shows a trend towards nuclear family. In comparison to pre-displacement period, three-fourth of the families, are found nuclear in post-rehabilitation period. The number of joint and extended families has reduced substantially. Finally ties have broken in the new sites. The network of kinship ties is limited and they are forced to live a marginal life. After several years of resettlement, still there is lack of social adjustment. In the new villages they are having the status of 'outsiders'.

6.7 Critical Areas of Concern

In this section, we make an attempt to analyze the present difficulties faced by displaced households by collecting necessary information from the selected sample households with regard to their household economy, demographic structure, social and community life, common property resources, ecological set-up of the original villages, land holding pattern, class-caste relationship, non-farm economic activities of the landless families and the like. It may be mentioned that development related displacement and resettlement of human population in a new locality generate different types of effects, such as economic, sociological, cultural, psychological, ecological and aboveall spread and backwash effects in the centre and periphery. Of course, such effects represented in assessment studies rarely find proper place in the traditional cost-benefit analysis of the development projects done by the economists and technocrats.

6.7.1 Lack of Basic Amenities

It is well recognized that access to basic amenities must be an integral part of the strategy not only for alleviating poverty but also for improving the quality of life of the people of the study area. The socio-economic development condition attracts or includes development whereas the availability of basic amenities facilitates the process of growth. Since the beginning of the planning of R & R policy, various steps have been initiated to provide minimum basic amenities to the people which include:

- (i) Provisions of covering safe drinking water in rural and urban areas.
- (ii) Efficient primary health care for every resettlement colony.
- (iii) Adequate arrangement for universalization as well as compulsory education.
- (iv) Connectivity to all colonies by providing an all-weather roads.
- (v) Streamlining the public distribution system with special focus on the poorest people.

As the provision of providing safe drinking water is limited, the resettlement colonies face acute problem of drinking water. At the time of summer season the open wells become dry and for drinking purposes many people depend upon nearby village which is at a distance of nearly 1 to 2 kilometres.

In resettlement colonies most oustees faced lack of availability of wage work. Due to this, most oustees have migrated to outside of the district and state. A number of the oustees in this study households have migrated to Surat, in the State of Gujarat for working in spinning mills and Mumbai for non-agricultural works. They are working there for 12 hours per day and also face more difficulties towards paying house rent and other day-to-day activities.

Due to the destruction of vast forests and loss of access to other forests, the oustees can no longer obtain medicinal herbs which they could collect earlier. As a result, the oustee families today have to spend a lot on buying medicines, which in the past the forests provided them gratis.

Women play a vital role in the family, community and society. Earlier, among many oustee families, due to her ability to earn independently (either as a farm labourer, or as a peddler of goods, or as a livestock-keeper), she could assert herself in any decision-making process in the family. But now after displacement, her income has either declined, or has been disrupted, and her total dependence on her husband/son for household expenditure has reduced her powers and changed her role in the family. She is no longer involved in decision-making.

Relationships among the family members were normally cordial and intimate before land acquisition and displacement. The loss of agricultural land in the projects, disruption in the sources of earning, decrease in family income and increase in the number of family members have created conflicts and bitterness among them. Sometimes they take violent forms.

The mode of paying compensation through cash has made ready money easily available to the male oustees. This makes if difficult for the women in the projects to control their spendthrift husbands. The men spend a large amount of the compensation money and their wages on consumer durables and liquor. Whenever the women try to control them, they are battered by their husbands. The women are also in constant fear of their husbands and sons, as their drunkenness quite often leads to accidents or violent conflicts. The women do not dare to report such matters to the police for fear of physical abuse or corporal punishment of their men-folk by the police. Some women complained about the negative effects of alcoholism and domestic conflicts on the children in the family. Increased alcoholism has led to a rise in crimes like rape, molestation, child abuse, etc. in these areas.

The women oustees face greater difficulties in getting married because of the demand for more dowry and the loss of their traditional sources of earning in the family (e.g. from forest resources, cottage industries, crafts, etc.). The cash compensation which the oustee family received for the acquisition of their land, house and other assets, ironically enough often turned into a centre of attraction for bridegrooms and their parents looking for a hefty dowry. As a result, a daughter's marriage in an outsee family often led to the wastage of the compensation money on dowry and other wedding expenses, leaving the family totally pauperized.

VII

Summary and Conclusions

This chapter brings together the summary, conclusions and recommendations of the entire study. It is divided into three sections. The first section describes the unique nature of the project and creates the basis for the conclusions which are presented in section 2. The summary of findings and conclusions are based on three aspects—social, economic and politico-cultural. Recommendations flowing from the conclusions are presented in the last section.

7.1 Unique Issues of the Project

The Tata Steel Gopalpur project is a unique case in point because in spite of a delay of 12 years, the project could not come up. Now there are talks with the Government of Orissa to set up a SEZ on the land acquired for the Steel Project. The SEZ would have some units set up by Tatas but primarily leased out to other industries. Till date there is no sign of the infrastructure promised by the Government for the Steel Plant and which is necessary for the SEZ. As per various Land Acquisition Acts and directives of Supreme Court, usually the land acquired for a project if not utilized for the project for a period of 5 to 6 years, should be returned back to the people. This has become a contention among the affected people and there is simmering discontent among the people on this issue. The main issues are the lack of jobs and training promised by the project as also the feeling of victimization caused due to land acquisition and loss of source of livelihoods. The question also arises whether the affected people would benefit from the SEZ which is proposed to be set up and what control Tata Steel can have over the other industries in ensuring jobs with their units in the SEZ as it is intended to be a purely commercial nature.

As the project could not come up, till now only 306 affected persons were given training and 95 persons given employment in Tata run units in other areas. In the absence of land for land based rehabilitation, employment in the industry, ancillaries, construction work and all other activities and micro enterprises stemming from the project could have been the only measures to rehabilitate the people. With full-fledged rehabilitation efforts also it is seen that displacement leads to impoverishment. In the absence of the crucial rehabilitation efforts it becomes interesting to know how deeply the affected people have been impacted and what could be the suggestions for changing their future. It is in the context of this unique nature of the project that the conclusions have been drawn up and the impoverishment effects analyzed.

7.2 Conclusions

7.2.1 Social

1. Castes

General castes account for only 33 per cent of the population, whereas Scheduled Castes account for 19 per cent and other Backward Castes account for 48 per cent. The high percentage of Backward and Scheduled Castes signify that most of the people belong to the disadvantaged or vulnerable section of society for which special efforts should have been made for skill upgradation.

2. Change in the Family Structure

There has been a shift from joint families to nuclear families. Before displacement 64.5 per cent of the families were joint and only 35.50 per cent were nuclear. After displacement the percentage of nuclear families increased to 73 per cent and only 26.50 per cent remained as joint families.

3. Marital Status

Around 7 per cent were either widows, widowers or separated persons needing special attention for restoration of livelihoods.

4. Sex Ratio

Unfavourable sex ratio was observed across the sample. Sample population sex ratio across all age groups was 912 as compared to 972 per thousand males according to 2001 Census for India. For the age group of 45 years and above it was more than 1000 and as high as 1173. In the 0-6 age group it was low at 733 and also 787 for the 6 to 14 age group indicating that female mortality rate is relatively higher in these age groups. Female child may not be getting adequate attention as compared to the male child. The high sex ratio in the age group of 45 and above could indicate that due to higher numbers the women may have a stronger role in the decision making process within the household which is a feature of the culture of south Orissa where the project is located.

5. Dependency Load

The dependency load of working population is effective as 62.93 per cent belong to the 14 to 60 year group and more than 50 per cent, i.e. 55.08 per cent lie in the 18 to 60 year group.

6. Education and Literacy

Literacy levels decreased from 27.54 per cent in the pre-displacement period to 26.68 per cent in the post-displacement period, which is an insignificant change, but then the already low literacy rate in the pre-displacement period has not improved.

Similarly, no significant change was observed at other levels of education. In the post-displacement period only 5.70 per cent were matriculates and only 2.05 per cent were graduates.

It indicates that the people had very low potential to be absorbed in skilled professions had the project come up or even in the areas in which Tata Steel was helping them in getting employment and training as of now. The percentage of people who received technical education was only 0.41 per cent in the pre-displacement period and it increased to 2.18 per cent in the post-displacement period. It is but natural that technical education cannot be imparted unless the candidate has minimum qualifications which were lacking in this area.

7.2.2 Economic

1. Occupational Shift-Main Workers

Due to loss of agricultural land the occupational pattern of the oustees has shifted from agriculture to other sources of employment especially in the informal sector. In the context of the Steel Plant project not being set up, they could not avail of any occupation which would have stemmed from construction and any other technical activities relating to the plant.

In the pre-displacement period nearly half of the main workers, i.e. 54.96 per cent reported cultivation as their main source of livelihood whereas this got reduced to 12.97 per cent in the post-displacement period. Another 24.12 per cent were engaged as agricultural labourers bringing the total percentage of people engaged in agricultural activities to 79.08 per cent. In the post-displacement period only 18.65 per cent were engaged as agricultural labourers and the total percentage of people engaged in agriculture was 31.62 per cent. There was almost a hundred per cent reduction in the number of persons engaged in agriculture.

Only the people who could purchase lands or who lost part of their agricultural land could continue to cultivate their lands. Because of the rise in land prices and unavailability of good cultivable land, people had to shift to other occupations. It was also not that easy to get work as agricultural labourers in the new areas where they shifted because of the competition and hostility faced from the host villages.

This can be observed from the fact that percentage of persons engaged in the skilled and semi-skilled category has gone up from 11.37 per cent to 37.57 per cent in the post-displacement period. They comprised masons, carpenters, mining and quarry workers, transport workers etc. which is basically non-agricultural work.

People also went for trend towards self-employment in small and petty business in informal sector activities like grocery and stationary shops, vegetable vending, tea stalls, sweetmeat shops, *jhompri* hotels, and eateries, betel shops and the like. In the pre-displacement period only 3.76 per cent of households had taken up such activities which increased to 19.73 per cent in the post-displacement period. This group also comprised people engaged in contractual or piecemeal work like plumbers, electricians, painters, laundry man, barbers and other service providers.

The occupational pattern of the main workers clearly shows that earners are low skilled with high risk of employment insecurity and have little potential to earn enough to cross the poverty barriers. The average days of employment of a wage worker varies between 20 to 22 days in a month and comes down to a low of 15 days in a month during the rainy season. They also have to travel long distances to the nearby town of Berhampur and other towns to find employment.

2. *Subsidiary Occupation*

Of the 200 households surveyed, 57.5 per cent had a subsidiary occupation before displacement and this got reduced to 19 per cent in the post-displacement period indicating that after displacement people got less scope to undertake subsidiary activities. This is an indicator of the narrowing down of income earning opportunities.

In the pre-displacement period, 13.91 per cent were engaged in agriculture, 55.65 were agricultural labourers, 18.26 were non-agricultural labourers and 12.17 were engaged in petty business as subsidiary occupations while in the post-displacement period the respective percentages were 18.42, 50.00, 23.68 and 5.26. This shows that agricultural labour was the most common subsidiary occupation, followed by non-agricultural labour, agriculture and petty business. There has not been any significant change in the pattern of subsidiary occupation after displacement.

No new source of subsidiary occupation has emerged in the post-displacement period, because of lack of avenues. The families who had earlier taken up minor forest collection were compelled to take up other avenues or remain idle as no forests are found near the new colony. Similarly the people engaged in Kewra collection also had to give up their activities and forego losses.

3. Composition of Main and Marginal Workers

Main workers comprised 76.43 per cent of the total workers in the pre-displacement period which increased to 90.69 per cent after displacement. In comparison the percentage of marginal workers reduced from 22.60 per cent to 9.31 per cent after displacement. This signifies that post-resettlement a higher percentage of people had employment for a longer duration of time than prior to displacement perhaps due to reduced dependence on agriculture which could have a positive bearing on their income earning capacity.

4. Child Labour

The component of child labour has come down from 7 per cent of households to 2 per cent after displacement. It is to be noted that 5.03 per cent of children in the age group of 6 to 14 do not attend any school. It is quite possible that such children are either working as child labour or doing domestic chores at home. However, the existence of child labour is indicative of unfavourable quality of life. Acute poverty and insufficient earnings was cited as the main reason for child labour.

5. Land Holding Pattern, Income from Land and Cropping Pattern

Due to acquisition of agricultural land all the land owning families became landless and of these only few could buy land using compensation money. The percentage of landless people and small and marginal farmers has increased after resettlement while the percentage of large and medium farmers has reduced drastically. The average land holding size of households has reduced from 1.36 acres to 0.54 acre. The shift towards landlessness and marginal farmers as well as reduction in the size of land holdings indicates that land is no longer available in an economically viable size for cultivation. The annual income from land which was Rs. 9,729 per household also declined to Rs. 2,470 after resettlement.

Before displacement, a variety of crops such as paddy, pulses, ragi, millet, maize, various types of oilseeds, vegetables and tobacco were grown. Kewda, a shrub plant whose flowers are used for extraction of perfume was grown on public land in the area and along the boundaries of the agricultural fields. After resettlement the cropping pattern became almost monocrop with paddy as the principal crop. Kewda cultivation which was highly lucrative had to be given up as suitable land was acquired by the project.

6. Household Income, Expenditure and Savings

The changes in household income have been analyzed after converting nominal GSDP to real GSDP by using appropriate deflators and the real income has thus been calculated. Average annual household income has reduced from Rs. 37,692 to Rs. 21,528 after displacement, which is a decrease by 42.88 per cent and is stark in nature. Similarly the current average monthly income also declined from Rs. 3,141 to Rs. 1,794. While there has been perceptible decline in household income following displacement, it should however be noted that in terms of certain household amenities like housing, sanitation, electricity, there has been a fair degree of improvement following displacement. What this perhaps means is that the cash compensation has made such improvements possible whereas the livelihood base of the oustees has not been strengthened after displacement.

Average annual household expenditure was less than that of income indicating that people had the capacity to make some savings. The expenditure was Rs. 30,754 before displacement and Rs. 19,545 in the post-displacement period compared to income figures of Rs. 37,692 and Rs. 21,528 respectively, implying a decline in the level and rate of savings. Though on the average there is a gap between income and expenditure accounting for a saving of Rs. 6,938 per household in the pre-displaced period, it got reduced to Rs. 1,983 in the post-displaced period, i.e. a decline by 71.41 per cent. It can be interpreted that the capacity for savings has gone down after resettlement or the income has not increased proportionately to the increase in expenditure. This also is a sign of impoverishment of the oustee population.

There has been no change in the pattern of consumption of the households. The average consumption expenditure of the sample households on food and non-food related items are 57.45 per cent and 42.52 per cent respectively, in the pre-displacement period and

55.48 per cent and 44.52 per cent respectively in the post-displacement period. Usually with the improvement in the standard of living the percentage of expenditure on non-food items goes up and the component of food expenditure reduces. Since this has not happened it can be concluded that the standard of living has not improved.

Only 10 per cent of families save money regularly, either on a monthly or yearly basis. Around 72 per cent of the sample households are undertaking monthly savings and 25.50 per cent have been covered under life insurance schemes. Majority of the households comprising 56.94 per cent and 20.14 per cent save up to Rs. 100 and Rs. 100-150 per month respectively. Annually it ranges from Rs. 1800 to Rs.1200 which is insufficient for assuring them of any security or for starting any micro-enterprise. It is only with the initiation of micro savings through SHGs, government agencies and NGOs that people have adopted the saving habit and understood its importance.

7. Poverty Status: Post-Displacement

The official poverty line estimated for Orissa during 2004-05 and based on MPCE (Monthly Per Capita Consumption Expenditure) was Rs. 325.79 for rural areas and Rs. 528.49 for urban areas (Mahendra Dev and C. Ravi, 2008). After including per capita expenditure on health and education, the revised estimates are Rs. 348.68 for rural Orissa and Rs. 585.39 for urban Orissa (*ibid.*). As the oustees under the study inhabit rural Orissa, the figure of Rs. 348.68 has been used to calculate the poverty line of the households. The average size of family for the sample households was 5.22. Therefore, the poverty line works out to Rs. 21,841 (Rs. 348.68*5.22*12) per household per annum.

Applying this estimate and rounding off the BPL (Below Poverty Line) income to Rs. 21,000 per annum it can be found from Table 6.18, that almost half, i.e. 44 per cent of the oustees presently live below the poverty line. However, this would be an underestimate of the extent of poverty since it is based on poverty line income of 2004-05 and not on that of 2007-08 and also poverty line income has been rounded off downwards. As against this, it is found that according to NSS, 2004-05 (Mahendra Dev and C. Ravi, 2007) 47.76 per cent of the people in rural Orissa live below the poverty line based on a uniform recall period. As compared to the incidence of poverty in rural India at 29.18 per cent, that of Orissa at 47.76 per cent is very high and indeed the highest in India. The condition of oustees is almost at par with that of Orissa and indicates the acute nature of poverty.

As per the standard norms, ultra poor households are identified by those falling below 75 per cent of the BPL level of income, which in this case works out to Rs. 16,381 and is rounded off to Rs. 16,500. It is found from Table 6.18 that 29 per cent of the total oustees or around 65.9 per cent of the BPL households are categorized as ultra poor households. These figures are higher than the state estimates of ultra poor at 25.16 per cent and 52.68 per cent of the population and all poor (Mahendra Dev and C. Ravi, 2007). This clearly reflects the deteriorated living condition of the oustee families at present compared to the state as a whole after displacement.

8. Indebtedness

To encourage the households to take up new livelihoods the government has advanced loans through commercial banks at low rates of interest. Oustees have also borrowed from the informal sector at high rates for immediate consumption needs like marriages, birth and death rituals, illness of family members and the like. Around 60 per cent of the households surveyed were found to be indebted, with average amount of debt at Rs. 11,644 per household. This is again a sign of impoverishment of the households after displacement.

9. Asset Structure

The average value of assets owned by households is worth Rs. 32,280 only. This includes all consumer durables, including gold and silver ornaments in majority of households. Almost one-fifth of households possess less than Rs. 10,000 worth of assets while almost one-fourth possess assets valued at more than Rs. 50,000.

A comparison between the pre- and post-displacement years shows that the average quantity of agricultural land per household has reduced by 60.29 per cent, i.e. from 1.36 acres to 0.54 acres. Homestead land has declined by 83.78 per cent per household, i.e. from 1.11 acres to 0.18 acre. Average value of livestock has also declined from Rs. 3,411 in pre-displacement period to Rs. 961 per family in the post- displacement period which is a 71.82 per cent reduction. Even the quantity of assets like farm equipments like sickles, axes, spades and wooden ploughs has come down as households have limited access to agricultural land after displacement.

In contrast, the financial assets of household have increased as the families got cash compensation in lump sum and some of them deposited money in financial institutions. Due to the same reason the average value of consumer durables increased from Rs. 1,332 per household to Rs. 2,643 in the post-rehabilitation period, recording an increase of 98.42 per cent. The value of other assets like gold, silver, watches, bicycle, radios which was Rs. 799 per family in the pre- displacement period became Rs. 3427 per family after post-displacement period and such an increase in the average value of assets as already mentioned, is due to the fact that displaced people received cash compensation in lump sum and purchased various household assets. However, all the non-land physical assets acquired by the oustee households are unproductive and do not contribute anything to the current income stream.

10. Housing

In the pre-displacement phase, out of 200 sample households, 52 per cent were staying in kutcha houses, 32.50 per cent resided in semi-pucca (tile/asbestos) houses and only 18.50 per cent stayed in pucca houses. In the post-displacement period, only 5.5 per cent stayed in kutcha houses, 8.5 per cent occupied semi-pucca (tile/asbestos) houses and 86 per cent resided in pucca houses.

The situation has improved drastically in the post-displacement period as more than 80 per cent of the people resided in pucca houses and only 5.50 per cent stayed in kutcha houses. The two main reasons which have been identified are; the provision of pucca houses by the Tata Steel in the Rehabilitation Colony and also expenditure incurred by the oustees on house construction from the compensation amount.

Though the project authorities had provided a single room house it was extended up to a maximum of 7 to 8 rooms by the oustees. The families who were only project affected and not physically displaced also converted their houses into pucca or semi-pucca and added more number of rooms.

During the pre-displacement period, 2 per cent of households stayed in single room houses, 23 per cent in double room houses and 59 per cent in three to five room houses. In the post-rehabilitation period this changed to 0.5 per cent of households in single room houses, 2.5 per cent households in double roomed houses, 61 per cent in three to five roomed houses and 36 per cent in more than five roomed houses. Around 97 per cent of the household resided in houses with more than three rooms. It was rarely found that one of the rooms was utilized as a shop or rented out which could fetch a steady source of income.

The fact that around 97 per cent of the households resided in more than three rooms could also be a sign of wasteful expenditure as compensation money could have been used for other income generating assets. House construction comprises the highest component of utilization of compensation money.

Though off hand it can be said that living conditions have improved, it cannot be explicitly concluded if compared with the gain of income which could have accrued had the money been used for commercial construction or invested in some profitable ventures or even in financial assets like fixed deposits. Also the condition of the houses constructed is not up to standard and some of the houses provided by the project are not in a livable condition anymore and have a chance of collapsing at any moment though they are classified as pucca houses.

Analysis of the condition of the houses constructed shows that only 65 per cent of the houses were in good condition, 10.50 per cent in moderate condition and 24.5 per cent are in bad condition. It is alleged that the houses provided by the Tata Steel at the Rehabilitation Colony is of very poor quality and the same was observed during the survey. Even the houses constructed by the oustees or extensions made were hurriedly done without much care for quality.

11. Sources of Fuel for Cooking Purposes

During the pre-displacement period it is seen that 94 per cent of households used wood for cooking purposes, 1 per cent used LPG and 5 per cent used other sources. In the post-displacement period the households besides adopting modern methods, also used multiple sources of fuel. Around 94 per cent continued using firewood, 23 per cent used LPG and 33 per cent used other sources like cow dung, straw etc. This implies a marginal change in living standards.

12. Sources of Drinking Water

Prior to displacement, about 66 per cent of families depended on open wells, 2 per cent on hand pumps, 31 per cent on tube wells and 1 per cent on rivers for drinking water purposes. After displacement 59 per cent of households depended upon open wells, 4 per cent on hand pumps and rest 37 per cent on tube wells. There is hardly any improvement in the status. Besides, the oustees complain that the water level of tube wells and open wells goes down considerably during summer and they face great deal of difficulty in fetching water. Some hand pumps and tube wells are defunct and not being repaired regularly. The quality of water from tube wells in the colony is not of good standard and in some cases completely unfit for drinking and the oustees have to walk a long distance to fetch water.

13. Sanitation and Access to Electricity

In the pre-displacement period only around 9 per cent had access to toilet facility within their households (8% had sanitary latrines and 1% had barapalli) and hardly 2 per cent had independent bathroom facility. Rest of 91 per cent of the people used open fields for defecation.

But after displacement, the use of open fields for defecation has changed and only 27 per cent households have access to open fields and rest 73 per have access to toilet facility within the household and hardly 20 per cent have independent bathroom facility. One of the major reasons for increased use of sanitary latrines was the fact that in the displacement colony the Tata Steel provided houses with latrines. Also in the affected areas people got a lump sum as compensation which they used for construction of houses and latrines and also open wells or bore wells for personal use.

Access to water sources encouraged better sanitation practices. At the same time it is alleged that the sanitary latrines provided by the project were of low quality and did not last so the oustees had to construct them again on their own.

Regarding access to electricity it was found that though they resided close to the city of Berhampur, 50 per cent of the households did not have access to electricity. This improved to more than 80 per cent after displacement. Tata Steel provided free electricity for 10 years at the Rehabilitation Colony and it has been withdrawn only recently and meters have been installed so that the oustees pay for their own use. This has led to a lot of resistance among the people. At the time of survey the street lighting facility had been withdrawn by Tata Steel and not taken up by the government which caused the roads in the new colony to lie in darkness causing fear among the people to move around after dark. People reported that thefts had also become more common and especially the womenfolk and girls felt scared.

7.2.3 Cultural and Political

1. Impact on Women

Women are the worst affected compared to the menfolk as they have to manage large households with limited resources due to limited access to land and livestock. Also women who were engaged in agricultural activities and collection of minor forest produce had to shift to other occupations or spend time in the house. It was difficult to find sources of labour in the new areas and get acceptance by the host community. Most women had to travel long distances to the nearby towns to get employment as non-agricultural labourers. The rehabilitation colony is built more like an urban colony with the houses at a distance from each other and there the common facilities like tube wells etc. are at a distance from the houses. So women had to walk a distance of 2-3 kms to fetch water. They also lost the sense of security which they had in their erstwhile villages where the community was closer knit and houses located next to each other. Even in the villages where the people did not lose lands, disparity was created among the families because of differences in the compensation money received which disturbed the established socio-cultural milleu.

2. Festivals and Rituals

Though the temples and shrines have been shifted to the new colony, festivals and rituals do not hold the same significance as they used to in the erstwhile villages. Cohesiveness of the society has been lost. They portray their past as glorious and feel nostalgic about the cultural traditions prevailing earlier. Social traditions were smoothly maintained through religious medium and lapses in the religious traditions could ultimately impact the social dynamics.

3. Political Life

It was found that the host community played a dominant role in every aspect of life and this extended to politics. The oustees are almost treated as non-citizens and do not have scope for expression or communication. They have such problems of their own that they do not have the motivation or interest to think about the village as a whole. The colony was strife ridden with the influence of various political parties and bordered on conflicts among the oustees. Only under the banner of agitating against the project they come together to express themselves as one unit.

4. Community Life

Breakdown of the joint family system and resettlement in clusters has led to weakening of family ties and social strength. Network of kinship is limited and they are forced to lead a marginal life. Cultural dissimilarity between the resettlers and the local population is another factor which complicates the process of rehabilitation. In conversation with them it was found out that they seem to have developed a fear psychosis in the alien land and unfamiliar surroundings.

7.3 Recommendations

Most of the recommendations made earlier have been included in the draft national rehabilitation policy of 2007 and the latest Orissa Government Policy of 2006. They have been discussed in the two chapters on policy analysis. The recommendations made in this section go beyond it and are specific to this project where a SEZ is proposed to be set up in lieu of a steel plant after a period of 12 years. The opportunity cost of the people in terms of losing their sources of employment in the absence of the Steel Plant have been taken into account while making these recommendations. As mentioned at the outset, a SEZ will be a purely commercial venture between Tata Steel and the other industries and the Tatas may set up a few units of their own. The question now arises as to how much control Tata Steel or the Government of Orissa can exercise over the other units in ensuring that the oustees get employment and other opportunities. Will the role of Tata Steel become that of a middleman or intermediary for land acquisition or can it play an important role in assuring the oustees of restoring their livelihoods. Should the land which had been initially acquired for a Steel Plant, be converted for a SEZ?

As of now, the MOU between the Government of Orissa and Tata Steel for a Steel Plant remains to be renewed for the last 7 years. There is no written agreement between the two parties regarding the SEZ and talks are merely going on. Oustees are most insecure about this state of affairs and feel suspicious about the intention of Tata Steel. Against this background the oustees are agitating and are going to file a PIL for regaining their lands. Since the purpose for which land was acquired has not been achieved they are claiming that land should be returned to them as per the directive of the Supreme Court which says that if the land is not used for a period of 5 years, it should be returned to the people. It is alleged by the people that they have not been able to shift to non-agricultural sources of occupation in a viable manner and their loss of livelihood has not been compensated by jobs as promised, they have been forced into worse conditions of poverty. Even setting up a SEZ, according to them, violates the agreement that Tata Steel had made with the government and people.

That delay in projects has of this kind adverse effect has also been observed in the case of Utkal Alumina in Kasipur where the project has not been started in spite of a lapse of 8 years after land acquisition. This is not the only case. There are many projects which are held up due to lack of infrastructure promised by the government and land acquisition has been made and the oustees are subject to victimization in the face of government and corporate inertia.

The recommendations in the background of this unique situation and based on the findings are given as follows. For all purposes, in the following section the project refers to the proposed SEZ to be set up by Tatas. It has been observed from the findings that displacement has led to impoverishment of the oustees. The purpose of the recommendations is to ensure that the oustees not only regain their previous economic condition, but go beyond it and improve both economically and socially. The suggestions given as follows are also meant for all projects where the aim is to improve the condition of oustees after displacement.

1. Certain number of shares of the project should be offered to the oustees on the basis of their annual earning from their land/assets or CPRs (Common Property Resources). There should be a lock-in period of 20 years so that the oustees cannot just sell off or transfer the shares. Considering the low levels of education, the project can appoint an NGO to manage the affairs of the people in this regard. In case of Tatas it can entrust this work to its own NGO, TSRDS (Tata Steel Rural Development Society) so that credibility and transparency are ensured. Through such a measure, the project affected/displaced people can be made primary stakeholders in the corporate body.
2. A certain percentage of the total net profit earned by the project every year can be earmarked for developing the social and economic infrastructure of the residential area of the affected persons. This will ensure that the people have better access to common infrastructure like education, health, water and sanitation and enjoy a better standard of living.
3. Instead of acquiring land or buying the land, the project can take land on lease from the people for a period of 20 years with annual lease value equal to the earning from land, with the option to the land owner to sell if he likes at any time. Through this the people will get a chance to restore their livelihoods and income, caused by loss of land. They will not have the problem of receiving huge amounts of compensation money at one time and spending on wasteful and non-income generating sources.
4. It has been observed that the oustees' education and skill levels are very low and even with training and skill upgradation only a few, a very limited number can be absorbed in technical positions in the project. Majority of them can be utilized in low skilled jobs. Preference has to be

given to the oustees at the construction stage of the project.

5. Potential shops/establishments near the factories/residential area may be constructed by the project authorities and given on lease/outright grant to the oustees for their business enterprises.
6. All contractual jobs like transport, supply of services, security, plumbing, electrical repairs etc. should be entrusted to the oustees.
7. Exclusive preference should be given to the oustees for setting up ancillary and downstream industries. In this case there are few people who would have the capacity to invest or the technical know how to manage such units. The project authorities should help them in all ways to set up these units, failing which preferential employment in these units should be ensured.
8. Tata Steel, while entering into agreements with the units of SEZ can ensure that preferential treatment is given for direct employment with the units. The industries should also be made responsible for technical training which will lead to employment. The oustees can at least get absorbed in jobs which require a minimum qualification of matriculation. The oustees who have already received technical training by Tata sponsored agencies and government can also be suitably employed.
9. Services like health, education, electricity etc. which are given to the employees of the project should be offered at the same standard to the oustees.
10. The site of the project should be chosen where the number of displaced would be minimum. Instead of Gopalpur, Thumri-Tampara would have been a better choice in terms of minimizing displacement.
11. Usually it is seen that the project acquires almost twice or more of the quantity of land which is actually required for the project. For example, in Taiwan a 80 lakh tonne capacity steel plant requires 1500 acres, in South Korea 110 lakh tonne capacity is set up on 3700 acres of land whereas for a 25 lakh tonne capacity steel plant,7346 acres were required. The land actually acquired by Tata Steel is around 4000 acres

which is also high compared to the fact that it planned for a Steel Plant operating at the highest international standards. Therefore, the land requirements of the projects and their location options have to be seriously examined in the light of minimizing displacement of people.

12. Though Cost Benefit Analysis (CBA) in such displacement projects is a difficult issue, attempts may be made to undertake a CBA incorporating all quantifiable social costs so that even before displacement takes place, the consequences can be studied and apt decisions can be taken.

Bibliography

Agnihotri, Anita, (1998). '*Poverty Alleviation Concerns in the Orissa State Policy on Resettlement*', in Harimohan Mathur and David Marsden (eds.), Development Projects and Impoverishment Risks-Resettling Project Affected People in India, Oxford University Press, New Delhi.

Agnihotri, A. and A.B. Ota (eds.) (1996) *Involuntary Displacement in Dam Projects*. New Delhi: Prachi Prakashan.

Areeparampil, Mathew, (1989). 'Industries, Mines and Dispossession of Indigenous People: The Case of Chhotnagpur', in Walter Fernandes and E.G. Thukral (eds.), *Development Displacement and Rehabilitation*, Indian Social Institute, New Delhi.

Baboo, Balgobinda, (1992). *Technology and Social Transformation: The Case of the Hirakud Multi-purpose Dam Project in Orissa*, Concept Publishing Company, New Delhi.

Behura, N.K. and P.K. Nayak, (1993). 'Involuntary Displacement and Changing Frontiers of Kinship: A Study of Resettlement in Orissa' in Michael M. Cernea and S.E. Guggenhein (eds.), *Anthropological Approaches to Resettlement: Policy Practice and Theory*, Westview Press, Boulder Colorado.

Bhaduri, Amit (2008) 'Predatory Growth', *Economic and Political Weekly*, 43(16): 0-14.

——, (2007) 'Alternatives in Industrialisation', *Economic and Political Weekly*, 42(18): 1597-1600.

Cernea, Michael, M., (1988). 'Involuntary Resettlement in Development Projects, Policy Guidelines in World Bank Financed Projects', *World Bank, Technical Paper No. 80*, Washington D. C.

——, (1991) 'Involuntary Resettlement: Social Research, Policy and Planning', in Michael M. Cernea (ed.) *Putting People First: Sociological Variables in Rural Development*. Second Edition. New York: Oxford University Press.

——, (1990). 'Poverty Risks from population Displacement in Water Resources Development', *Development Discussion Paper, No. 355*, Harvard Institute of Internal Development, Harvard University.

——, (1993). 'Anthropological and Sociological Research for Policy Development on Population Resettlement' in Michael M. Cernea and S.E. Guggenheim (eds.), *Anthropological Approaches in Resettlement Policy Practice and Theory*, Westview Press, Boulder Colorado.

——, (1994). '*Impoverishment Risks from Population Displacement Policy and Operational Issues*', World Bank, Reprint Series, No. 476, UNCRD.

——, (1995) 'Understanding and Preventing Impoverishment from Displacement: Reflections on the State of Knowledge', *Journal of Refugee Studies* 8(3): 245-64.

——, (1996a) *Eight Main Risks: Impoverishment and Social Justice in Resettlement*. Washington DC: The World Bank, Environment Department.

——, (1996b) 'Understanding and Preventing Impoverishment from Displacement', in Christopher McDowel (ed.) *Understanding Impoverishment: The Consequences of Development-Induced Displacement*. Oxford: Berghahn Books.

——, (1996c) 'Public Policy Responses to Development-Induced Population Displacement', *Economic and Political Weekly*, June 15.

——, (1998). 'Impoverishment or Social Justice? A model for Planning Resettlement' in Hari Mohan Mathur and David Marsden (eds.), *Development Projects and Impoverishment Risks Resettling Affected People in India*, Oxford University Press, New Delhi.

——, (1999). 'Why Economic Analysis is Essential to Resettlement—A Sociologists View', *Economic and Political Weekly*, Vol. XXXIV, No. 31. July 31-August 6.

——, (2008). 'Can Compensation Prevent Impoverishment—*Reforming Resettlement through Investments*' in Hari Mohan Mathur (eds.), Oxford University Press.

Chakravarty, Manab (1987), 'Settlement of Large Dam Oustees in

India', People and Dams, *Participatory Research in Asia* (PRIA), New Delhi.

Cobden Ramsay, L.E.B.,(1982). *Feudatory States of Orissa*, Firma KLM Private Ltd., Calcutta.

CSE (Centre for Science and Environment), (1982), '*The State of India's Environment*: *The First Citizen Report*', CSE, New Delhi.

——, (1985) *The State of India's Environment 1984-85*: *The Second Citizens' Report*. New Delhi: Centre for Science and Environment.

Dalwai, A. K., (1991). *Irrigation in Orissa, Water and Land Management Institute* (WALMI), Pratapnagari, Cuttack.

——, (1993) '*Environmental Impact of Large Reservoir Project on Human Settlement in Orissa*, Ashish Publishing House, New Delhi.

——, (1998). 'Resistance to Resettlement and Rehabilitation and Empowerment' in P. Mohapatra *et al*. (eds.), *Development Induced Displacement and Rehabilitation*, Prachi Prakashan, New Delhi.

——, (1998), 'Integrating Ongoing Development Programmes of the Government with R & R Package in Pyarimohan Mohapatra, A.B. Ota and R.N. Mohanty (eds.) *Development Induced Displacement and Rehabilitation*, Prachi Prakashan, New Delhi.

De, Subrata (2000) '*The Impact of Industrial Development on the Local Economy of Korba*', The Eastern Anthropologist, 55(1 and 2): 95-119.

Dutta, Ashirbani, (2007). *Development Induced Displacement and Human Rights*, Deep and Deep Publication Pvt. Ltd., New Delhi.

Fernandes, Walter (2008) 'India's Forced Displacement Policy and Practice: Is Compensation up to Its Functions?', in Michael M. Cernea and H.M. Mathur (eds.) *Can Compensation Prevent Impoverishment? Reforming Resettlement through Investments and Benefit-Sharing*, pp. 180-207. New Delhi: Oxford University Press.

Fernandes, W., (1994). *Development Induced Displacement in the Tribal Areas of Eastern India (Mimeo)*, Indian Social Institute, New Delhi.

Fernandes, Walter (1985). 'The National Draft Policy for Rehabilitation: Principles of the NGO Alternative' in Hari Mohan Mathur and David Marsden (eds.) *Development Projects and Impoverishment Risks-Resettling Project Affected People in India*, Oxford University Press, New Delhi.

Fernandes, Walter and E.G. Thukral, (1989). *Development,*

Displacement and Rehabilitation, Indian Social Institute, New Delhi.

Fernandes, Walter and S. Anthony Raj (1992) *Development, Displacement and Rehabilitation in the Tribal Areas of Orissa.* Indian Social Institute, New Delhi.

Fernandes, W. and S.R. Anthony, (1992). *Development, Displacement and Rehabilitation in Tribal Areas of Orissa,* Indian Social Institute, New Delhi.

Fernandes, W., J.C.: Das and S. Rao (1989) 'Displacement and Rehabilitation: An Estimate of Extent and Prospects', in Walter Fernandes and E. Ganguly Thukral (eds.) *Development, Displacement and Rehabilitation.* Indian Social Institute. New Delhi:

Government of India, MoRD (Ministry of Rural Development) (2007) 'The National Rehabilitation and Resettlement Policy, 2007', *Gazette of India, Extraordinary, Part I, Section I,* 31st October, 2007, pp. 33-60.

——, MoRD (Ministry of Rural Development) (2004) 'National Policy on Resettlement and Rehabilitation for Project Affected Families-2003', *Gazette of India, Extraordinary, Part I, Section I.*

——, (2008) *Economic Survey 2007-08.* New Delhi: Ministry of Finance.

——, (2002) *Tenth Five Year Plan (2002-2007),* Vol. II, Sectoral Policies and Programmes. Planning Commission. New Delhi.

——, (2007) *Eleventh Five Year Plan (2007-2012).* Planning Commission. New Delhi.

——, (1985) *Report of the Committee on Rehabilitation of Displaced Tribals due to Development Projects.* Ministry of Home Affairs. New Delhi.

Government of Orissa (1968) Report on the Benefits of Hirakud Irrigation: A Socio-Economic Study. *Bureau of Statistics and Economics.* Cuttack.

——, (1990) R and R Plan of Ichha Reservoir (Orissa Portion), *Subarnarekha Multi-purpose Project*, Chief Engineer, Subarnarekha Irrigation Project, Baripada.

——, (1993) *Status Report of Upper Indravati Project*, Department of Irrigation, Bhubaneswar.

Goyal, Sangita (1996) 'Economic Perspectives on Resettlement and Rehabilitation', *Economic and Political Weekly*, 31(24): 1461-7.

Hansda, Subotu, (1983), 'Agricultural Development in Tribal Areas' in S.N. Mishra and Bhupinder Singh (eds.) *Tribal Area Development, Society for the Study of Regional Disparities*, New Delhi.

Iyer, K. Gopal (ed.) (2007) *Sustainable Development: Ecological and Socio-Cultural Dimensions*. New Delhi: Vikas Publishing House.

Jena, Pradeep (1998), Institutional Arrangements in Resettlement and Rehabilitation' in Pyarimohan Mohapatra, A.B. Ota and R.N. Mohanty (eds.) *Development Induced Displacement and Rehabilitation*, Prachi Prakashan, New Delhi.

——, (1998), 'The Role of Resettlement and Rehabilitation Unit in Dam Displacement Project: With Reference to Upper Indravati Project, in Pyarimohan Mohapatra, A.B. Ota and R.N. Mohanty (eds.) *Development Induced Displacement and Rehabilitation*, Prachi Prakashan, New Delhi.

Kanbur, Ravi and Cernia M., (2002) 'Development Economics and Compensation Principle' *International Social Science Journal*, 55(175).

Kar, N. C., (1991). *Socio-Economic and Cultural Impact of NALCO on Local Tribals in Damonjodi Project Area*, Nabakrushna Choudhury Centre for Development Studies, Bhubaneswar, (Mimeo).

Mahapatra, L.K. (1960). *A Hill Bhuyan Village: An Empirical Socio-Economic Study*, Humberg University, (Mimeo)

——, (2004) 'Displacement, Impoverishment and Redevelopment of the Deprived Oustees in India: A Country Synthesis', *Occasional Paper 2004*. Anthropology Department, Bhubaneswar: Utkal University.

——, (2000) 'Resettlement with Participation: The Indian Experience', *the Eastern Anthropologist*, 55 (1 and 2): 121-38.

——, (1999a) *Resettlement, Impoverishment and Reconstruction in India*. New Delhi: Vikas Publishing House.

——, (1999b) 'Testing the Risks and Reconstruction Model on India's Resettlement Experiences', in Michael M. Cernea (ed.) *The Economics of Involuntary Resettlement: Questions and Challenges*. Washington, DC: The World Bank.

——, (1994) *Tribal Development in India: Myth and Reality*. New Delhi: Vikash Publishing House.

——, (1991) 'Development for Whom? Depriving the Dispossessed Tribals', *Social Action,* 41(3): 271-87.

——, (1990) 'Development of Tribals Affected by Major Dams and Other Projects in Orissa' in A.P. Fernandes (ed.), *A Report of the Workshop on Rehabilitation of Persons Displaced* by Development Projects, Institute for Social and Economic, MYRAD, Bangalore.

Mohapatra, P., A.B. Ota and R.N. Mohanty (eds.), (1998). *Development Induced Displacement and Rehabilitation*, Prachi Prakashan, New Delhi.

Mahendra Dev, S. and C. Ravi, (2007), 'Poverty and Inequality: All-India and States, 1983-2005' in *Economic and Political Weekly*, 10-16 February, Vol. XLII No. 6, 2007.

——, (2008) 'Revising Estimates of Poverty', *Economic and Political Weekly*, 8-10 March, Vol. XLIII, 2008.

Mankodi, Kashyap, (1989), 'Displacement and Relocation: Problems and Prospects' in Walter Fernandes and E.G. Thukral (eds.), *Development, Displacement and Rehabilitation,* Indian Social Institute, New Delhi.

Mathur, H.M. (2006) 'Urban Development and Involuntary Resettlement', in H.M. Mathur (ed.) *Managing Resettlement in India: Approaches, Issues and Experiences*, pp. 195-213. New Delhi: Oxford University Press.

——, (2008) 'A New Deal for Displaced People: Orissa's Involuntary Resettlement Policy', *Social Change*—December, Vol. 38 No. 4.

Meher, Rajkishor (2004) *Stealing the Environment: Social and Ecological Effects of Industrialization in Rourkela.* New Delhi: Manohar.

——, (2003) '*The Social and Ecological Effects of Industrialization in a Tribal Region: The Case of the Rourkela Steel Plant*', Contributions to Indian Sociology (n.s.) 37(3): 429-57.

——, (2002) 'Development Scenario of the Village', in *Orissa State Development Report 2002.* New Delhi: Planning Commission.

——, (1999a) 'Interstate Disparities in Levels of Development and the Implications of Economic Liberalization on Regional Economies of India', *Review of Development and Change*, 4(2): 198-224.

——, (1999b) *Development Disparities in a Backward Region: A District Level Analysis.* New Delhi: APH Publishing Corporation.

Ota, A.B. (2006) 'Critical R&R Issues of Displaced Tribals in Mining Projects', *Adivasi*, 46(2): 99-108.

——, (1999) 'Resettlement and Rehabilitation Policies of Different Sectors for the Affected People in the State of Orissa'. Bhubaneswar: Department of Water Resources, Government of Orissa (Mimeo).

——, (1998) 'Countering Impoverishment Risks: The Case of Rengali Dam Project', in H.M. Mathur and David Marsden (eds.) *Development Project and Impoverishment Risks: Resettling Project-Affected People in India*, pp. 125-33. New Delhi: Oxford University Press.

Pandey, Balaji, (1998), 'Depriving the Underprivileged', *Institute for Socio-Economic Development*, Bhubaneswar, Orissa.

Patnaik, S.M. (2000) 'Understanding Involuntary Resettlement: An Anthropological Perspective', *The Eastern Anthropologist*, 53(1 and 2):141-59.

Pattnaik, S. K., B. Das and A. Mishra (1987), 'Hirakud Dam Project: Expectations and Realities', *People and Dams*, PRIA, New Delhi.

Ravindran, Latha (1998), 'Resettlement and Rehabilitation: From Policy Guidelines to Practice', in Pyarimohan Mohapatra, A.B. Ota and R.N. Mohanty (eds.) *Development Induced Displacement and Rehabilitation*, Prachi Prakashan, New Delhi.

Reddy, I.U.B. (1992) *Displacement and Rehabilitation*, Mittal Publications, New Delhi.

——, (1993). '*Displacement and Rehabilitation*', Mittal Publication, New Delhi.

——, (1998) 'Marginalization of Project Affected People: A Comparative Analysis of Singrauli and Rihand Power Projects', in H.M. Mathur and David Marsden (eds.) *Development Projects and Impoverishment Risks: Resettling Project Affected People in India*. New Delhi: Oxford University Press.

Robinson, W. Courtland (2003), 'The Causes, Consequences and Challenges of Development-Induced Displacement', *The Brookings Institute-SAIS, Project on Internal Displacement*.

Rout, Kulamani, (1991). 'Rehabilitation and Resettlement of Project Affected Persons in Angul District' in 31st *Annual Conference of Orissa Economic Association*, 13-14 February, Talcher College, Talcher Orissa.

Sahu, Bholeswar (2000) '*Development and Displacement: A Case Study of Rengali Dam Project in Orissa*'. Ph.D. Dissertation, Utkal University, Bhubaneswar.

Samal, K.C., (1995). *Socio-Economic Impact of NALCO Angul Sector-Involuntary Displacement and Adjustment*, Nabakrushna Choudhury Centre for Development Studies, Bhubaneswar, Orissa, (Mimeo).

——, (1997), 'Informal Sector in an Emerging Urban Industrial Urban Centre and its Policy Implication—Case Study of NALCO Nagar', *Ngarlok*, Vol. XXIX, July-September, No. 3.

——, (1998). 'The Socio-Economic Impact of NALCO Angul Sector', *Social Action*, 48(1).

——, (2009). '*Mega Projects—Protests, Displacements and Resettlement*', Unpublished.

Saxena, N.C. (2006) 'The Resettlement and Rehabilitation Policy of India', in H.M. Mathur (ed.) *Managing Resettlement in India: Approaches, Issues, Experiences*. New Delhi: Oxford University Press.

Sen, Jai, (1995). 'National Rehabilitation Policy: A Critique', *Economic and Political Weekly*, 4, February.

Sengupta, A. (1995), 'Displacement or Development?', *The Economic Times*, March, Calcutta.

Sengupta, N. (1983) Contract Labour in the Steel Region, Rourkela. Rourkela: *Asian Workers' Development Institute (Mimeo)*.

Sharma, R.N. (2003) 'Involuntary Displacement: A Few Encounters', *Economic and Political Weekly*, 38(9): 907-12.

Somayaji, Sakarama (2008), 'Man Made Disasters, Displacement, Resettlement and Rehabilitation in Orissa—Reflections from the Field,' *Social Change*, Dec. 2008, Vol. 38, No. 4.

World Bank (1982), *Staff Appraisal Report, India. Subarnarekha Irrigation Project*, Washington, D.C.

World Bank (1994a) *Resettlement and Development: The Bank-wide Review of Projects Involving Involuntary Resettlement 1986-93*. Washington DC: World Bank, Environment Department.

World Bank (1994b) *Resettlement and Rehabilitation in India: A Status Update of Projects Involving Involuntary Resettlement, Volume I: The Review*. Washington DC: The World Bank.

Index